D1095272

PSYCHOANALYSIS AND
PERSONALITY

PSYCHOANALYSIS AND

PERSONALITY A DYNAMIC

THEORY OF NORMAL PERSONALITY

42460

BY JOSEPH NUTTIN

Professor at the University of Louvain

TRANSLATED BY GEORGE LAMB

1953 · NEW YORK · SHEED AND WARD

At the present time, psychoanalysis is going through an important phase of development. As an isolated dogmatic system Freudism is out of date, but as a source of new ideas about man's psychic life it was never more active or more fruitful.

To adopt a satisfactory *positive* attitude towards contemporary psychoanalysis, Freudism must be studied *as an ordinary scientific system*. This means disentangling the controversies and theories which have a definite value from the hasty generalizations lying behind some of the theories (Chapter I).

As a therapeutic method psychoanalysis must be seen in the light of many more recent trends which have developed either as a continuation of Freudian teaching or in opposition to it (Chapter II).

In the third chapter, psychoanalysis is considered as depth-psychology or the psychology of the unconscious, whose conceptions have changed the idea of man in the culture of today. The author compares the psychoanalytical conception of unconscious motivation with the traditional conception of freedom in the behaviour of normal man. He shows in detail the *complexity* of the motivation of human behaviour. In connection with the problem of freedom of behaviour he discusses certain problems of psychotherapy from the point of view of morality.

Thus the first part of the book attempts to "place" psychoanalysis in the framework of (1) the science of psychology, (2) contemporary psychotherapy, and (3) the general conception of man as found in our Western culture. The three chapters composing this first part of the book are preceded by an Introduction which gives a critical sketch of psychoanalysis as a whole for the benefit of the non-specialist reader.

Our most important task, however, will be to develop a conception of the dynamic structure of personality *from the point of view of general psychology*, in order to complete, *positively*, *the one-sidedly pathological view* which has been maintained by psychoanalysis. This is the chief aim of the present work, and to it the whole of the second part of the book is devoted.

This second part, entitled *A Dynamic Theory of Normal Personality*, has been inspired by the insights of depth-psychology and the facts of general psychology. Instead of basing our dynamic theory of personality on *psychopathological* mechanisms, we have tried to ascertain first of all the *normal* functioning of psychic dynamics. Further, we are convinced that the general laws of the development of the *personality* cannot be different from the laws covering the development of *behaviour* studied by general and experimental psychology. It is for this reason that we have endeavoured to sketch a theory of personality according to the laws governing the development of human behaviour, and, more particularly, according to the law of *effect*. Such a *rapprochement* between the study of personality and the general psychology of behaviour seems to us an urgent need at this stage of the science of psychology. We have also tried to stress the importance of cognitive and "rational" (or "spiritual") functions in the development of human dynamics and motivation. We agree with Percival M. Symonds when he says that "insufficient attention had been given to the rational and self-determining side of man."[1]

We should, however, like to stress the fact that the dynamic personality theory we propose in this book is only sketched on very general lines. Our purpose has been to develop the theoretical perspective in which more detailed data can be viewed and interpreted without distorting the normal personality as a whole.

[1] *The Ego and the Self* (1951), p. vii.

When they are studied in this context of the general psychology of the *normal* human being, the psychic realities corresponding to the ideas of *repression, sublimation,* the *unconscious,* etc., take on a somewhat different significance. The very forces or "instincts" which, according to psychoanalysis, lie at the root of psychic life have to be looked at again, and then take their place in the wider perspective of the *total dynamism* of the personality.

Thus the present book aims, in the first place, *at integrating psychoanalysis with the whole science of psychology,* and at making a positive contribution to the study of *normal personality dynamics* from the point of view of *general* psychology. This point of view, we hope, will allow us to complete certain partial views advanced by depth-psychology. This should make clear the bond uniting the two points of view from which we have endeavoured to study psychoanalysis—the point of view of *general* psychology, and that of a psychology which emphasizes the *specifically human* elements in man's activity. We are convinced that some more general ideas on human nature are more or less implicitly involved in all theories on personality dynamics. In our opinion human activity and human drives are not to be simply *reduced* to "tissue needs" and to the lower levels of animal drives. The traditional doctrine about the so-called "spiritual," i.e. *specifically human,* components in man's motivation and behaviour seems to us to be true.

In this book we refer throughout to the original text of the *Gesammelte Werke,* the new German edition of Freud's works. This edition, edited by Anna Freud and various collaborators, was published in London by the Imago Publishing Company, under the title *Gesammelte Werke chronologisch geordnet.*

For a proper understanding of this book some acquaintance with Adler's *Individual Psychology* is also necessary, and for this reason a brief sketch of this is given in the Appendix.

Finally, the reader will find in the Suggestions for Bibliography, references to books which we consider important in the various branches of psychology discussed in the text.

The specialist can limit himself to the second part of the book;

this contains the book's positive contribution to the dynamic theory of personality and is independent of the first part.

Finally, I should like to thank all those who have collaborated in the production of this book.

J.N.

Louvain, July 1st, 1952

CONTENTS

Chapter III. Psychoanalysis as the Psychology of the Unconscious (Depth-psychology) 114

PART TWO

A DYNAMIC THEORY OF NORMAL PERSONALITY

APPENDIX

Adler's Individual Psychology

PSYCHOANALYSIS AND

PERSONALITY

FREUDIAN PSYCHOANALYSIS:
A PRELIMINARY SURVEY

The best way to understand psychoanalysis as a *psychological* system and a *therapeutic method* is genetically, by considering it as it was gradually developed by its founder, Sigmund Freud.[1] In this introduction we shall be chiefly concerned, first, to define the methods used by psychoanalysis in acquiring its data and elaborating its theories, and then to estimate their value.

The *starting-points* of Freud's doctrine are to be found in the work of the French psychiatrists Charcot and Bernheim on hyp-

[1] Sigmund Freud was born of Jewish parents on May 6th, 1856, at Freiberg, a small town in Moravia. At the age of four he went to Vienna, and he received the whole of his education there. For six years he attended the Gymnasium, where he was an outstanding pupil. Although his parents were in poor circumstances, young Freud began to attend lectures at the University in 1873, studying medicine, about which he says: "Neither in my youth nor later did I have any predilection for medicine. I was impelled rather by a 'desire for knowledge,' but a desire that tended towards human relationships rather than the things of nature." (Cf. *"Selbstdarstellung,"* *Gesammelte Werke*, XIV, p. 34.)

Being a Jew, he felt that he was considered to belong to an inferior race and *"nicht volkszugehörig."* He has told us himself that in his student days he reacted violently against this situation. When the Nazis began their persecution of the Jews, Freud took refuge in England. He died there in 1939. He is the author of a number of important works, amounting, in the new *Gesamtausgabe*, to seventeen volumes

nosis and also in the discoveries made by the Viennese doctor Breuer, with whom Freud collaborated for some time.

Hypnosis and Catharsis

The original aim of psychoanalysis was to discover a new explanation and effective treatment of what is called neurosis, particularly hysteria.

When Freud was studying medicine and psychiatry in Vienna it was still generally considered that the cause of neurosis was to be found in lesions of the nervous system. It was to be observed, for example, that besides cases of organic paralysis there were other cases of paralysis for which no organic cause could be found. Such cases, known as "hysterical paralysis," were thought to belong to the same kind of disturbances in the brain centres as caused organic paralysis, but to disturbances less profound and hence more difficult to trace.

In 1885 Freud went as a travelling student to France, and it was from the knowledge gained during this journey of the effects of hypnosis as practised by Charcot in Paris that for the first time he got some idea of the *psychic* nature of hysteria. By means of suggestions made during hypnotic trance Charcot was able to excite a great variety of symptoms in his patients. One of these was hysterical paralysis. It was such phenomena that drew Freud's attention to one first essential fact—the *psychic*, as distinct from the organic, character of hysterical phenomena.

Later, Freud visited Bernheim at Nancy, where he studied the phenomenon of *post-hypnotic suggestion*. Here his attention was drawn to a second important fact: he realized that conduct could be influenced, not only by conscious, but quite as powerfully by *unconscious* psychic contents.[1]

The psychic nature of neuroses and the possibility that the unconscious may influence human conduct are two essential features resulting from this study of hypnosis. They became the starting-point of Freud's doctrine and constitute a permanent enrichment of our ideas about man's psychic life.

For his second series of discoveries, Freud was indebted to

[1] For post-hypnotic suggestion, see page 123.

Joseph Breuer, a Viennese doctor. Breuer, even before his collaboration with Freud—between 1880 and 1882, in fact—had treated a patient for hysteria in a way that was to play an important part in the development of psychoanalysis, but he had not immediately made public the discoveries to which his treatment had led, and it was as a result of his contact with Freud, that he published them.[1]

The patient in question, who had become ill while looking after her sick father, manifested serious symptoms such as paralysis, speech-defects, phobias, etc. From time to time she would mutter to herself incoherently, and Breuer took good care not to miss what she said. On the patient's own request—she was a highly intelligent girl of twenty-one—Breuer hypnotized her. During the trance he repeated some of the words he had overheard and asked her to disclose what the words meant to her. In this way he managed to obtain long accounts, highly charged with emotion, which usually had as their starting-point a scene in which a girl was present at her father's bedside.

To his great surprise Breuer discovered that after these seances an improvement could be observed in the patient's condition, and that for a few hours at least she seemed completely cured. The girl herself, who at this stage of the treatment could speak and understand only English, called this new treatment a "talking-cure" or "chimney-sweeping."

These conditions led Breuer to conceive the idea that some connection existed between the symptoms of the illness and the girl's emotional outpourings. He assumed that it might be possible for the girl to gain more than a temporary improvement by means of such an emotional release if, during hypnosis, she could tell the whole story behind the event that caused her such emotion.

This assumption was borne out by experience, and Breuer made discoveries of the greatest interest in the development of psychotherapy and, in particular, of psychoanalysis.

To give a clearer idea of the exact significance of these discoveries, we shall now give, in Breuer's own words, his own first-hand account of this case, thanks to which, in the course of treating this hysterical patient, he arrived at his new idea.

[1] Cf. *Studien über Hysterie* (Leipzig and Vienna, Deuticke, 1895).

During this summer there was a period of very great heat, during which the patient was tormented by thirst. Suddenly, for no apparent cause, she found herself unable to drink. She would take hold of a glass of water, then, as soon as it touched her lips, put it down again, as though she were suffering from hydrophobia. . . . This went on for about six weeks until one day, under hypnosis, she mentioned her lady-companion, an English-woman whom she disliked. She went on to relate, with many signs of repugnance, how she had once gone into this woman's room and seen her dog (which the girl disliked intensely) drinking from a glass. Out of politeness the patient had said nothing. Now, having given vent under hypnosis to her suppressed annoyance, she asked for a drink, swallowed a large quantity of water without the slightest difficulty, and woke up out of her trance with the glass at her lips. It was under these conditions that the symptoms of hydrophobia disappeared for good.[1]

During the lecture which Freud gave in America in 1909 on the origin of psychoanalysis, he added this:

No one had ever cured an hysterical symptom by such means before, nor had anyone come so near to understanding the cause. It would be a remarkable discovery if there could be any hope of the other symptoms—perhaps most of them—arising in the same way and being eliminated by the same method. Breuer subjected his patient to a systematic investigation in his search for the pathogenesis of the other, more serious symptoms—such as, for example, paralysis of the left arm. This proved to be the case: nearly all the symptoms came into being in exactly the same way, as the residue—a sort of deposit—of highly charged emotional experiences which, for that very reason, we have since called "psychic traumatisms." *The nature of the symptoms became clear through their connection with the event that had caused them.*[2]

The important theoretical results arrived at by Breuer in this field may be summed up as follows:

1. The nature of the symptoms was made clear: symptoms of hysteria seemed to be *significant,* and their significance lay in *their connection with an emotional occurrence in the past (psychic traumatism).* Symptoms are, so to speak, the remains and "mnemonic symbols" of these traumatic experiences.

2. In these traumatic events, the patient must have had habitually to repress a strong emotion—i.e., the emotion had not been

[1] Cf. Freud, "*Über Psychoanalyse," Gesammelte Werke,* VIII, p. 8; and Breuer and Freud, *Studien über Hysterie,* 4th ed., p. 26.
[2] Cf. Freud, "The Origin and Development of Psychoanalysis," p. 185; *The American Journal of Psychology,* 1910, XXI, pp. 181–218.

able to find free expression in words or action (as, for instance, in the scene between the companion and her dog).

3. Breuer established the fact that there was no sign of any weakening of the symptoms when the traumatic event was described without any emotional release.

On the basis of these assertions it could be assumed that a person becomes hysterical when the emotion which develops in the pathogenic situation cannot express itself normally, and that the essence of the illness lies in the fact that these imprisoned (*eingeklemmt*) emotions *undergo* a series of *abnormal changes*. They then cause unusual innervations and inhibitions which appear as symptoms of that particular case (hysterical conversion).

4. These traumatic events were forgotten in daily life—or at least the patient seemed to have forgotten them. It was only under hypnosis that they could be brought back to mind. This evocation of the original happening, like the emotional release, had a "purifying" and curative effect: this constitutes the *cathartic method*.

It is easy to see the importance of the facts and interpretations which Breuer thus reached. However, it is possible that without Freud's intervention these discoveries might never have been brought to light.

Freud's New Method and Ideas

Many different circumstances led Freud, from 1895 onwards, to draw further and further away from Breuer and to follow his own course. It is here that we discover the true starting-point of Freud's own doctrine and method. On the one hand, he gives up hypnosis and succeeds in elaborating a *personal technique*. On the other hand, he develops a *new theory* of the ultimate cause of neurotic complaints: he comes to believe that their origin is to be found in *sexual desires and conflicts*.

I. THE SEXUAL INTERPRETATION

It is a fact that traumatic events and repressed emotions do not in all cases lie behind pathological symptoms.

Breuer explained the fact that only a certain number of traumatic events become pathogenic by his theory of a split consciousness, a theory which was *based on physiological foundations*.[1] Freud, as he himself said ironically, was to conceive things "less and less scientifically."[2]

In his treatment of cases of hysteria he was struck by the fact that the trouble was usually bound up with sexual difficulties either present or past. He was reminded that Charcot, Breuer and Chrobak had earlier drawn his attention to the fact that sexual problems were always to be found at the root of hysterical cases.[3] He was struck by the further fact that during the course of treatment there usually developed a transference of affection from patient to therapist which had a very marked sexual tinge.[4]

On the basis of these discoveries Freud arrived quite early at the conclusion that the origin of hysterical troubles was generally to be found in sexual tendencies. From 1896 onwards he attached more and more importance to the part played by sexuality in the aetiology of neuroses. And in 1906 he wrote: "By a rule that I have found confirmed over and over again, but which I had not had the courage to formulate into a general law, a symptom signifies the realization of a phantasy with a sexual content, hence a sexual situation."[5]

Thus Freud abandoned the restricted domain of hysteria and began to study the sexual life of patients suffering from many different kinds of neuroses besides that of hysteria. It was from this study that his new theory of sexuality was soon to be born.

2. FREE ASSOCIATION AND REPRESSION

At the same time Freud was to introduce modifications into the technique of therapeutic treatment. He had observed that cures obtained by hypnosis were not permanent: the illness recurred when the bond was broken between patient and therapist. More-

---

[1] Hypnoid states. Compare with Janet's theory, *infra*, p. 117.

[2] Cf. Freud, *"Zur Geschichte der psychoanalystischen Bewegung,"* *Gesammelte Werke*, X, p. 48.

[3] Breuer and Chrobak later denied this. Chrobak was a gynaecologist at Vienna University.

[4] For the demonstrative value of this fact, see page 29.

[5] Cf. Freud, *"Bruchstück einer Hysterie-Analyse,"* *Monatschrift für Psychiatrie und Neurologie*, 1906, XVIII, p. 413.

over, Freud did not always manage to hypnotize his patients satisfactorily, and it was for this reason that he began to seek another method which would allow the patient to remember his forgotten traumatic experiences whilst remaining under *perfectly normal conditions*.

Freud remembered what Bernheim had taught him in this connection.[1] It is well known that patients, on coming out of a trance, have usually forgotten all about what went on while they were in it; but Bernheim had proved that later on they were able to remember all kinds of things that had happened while they were in the trance. If the psychiatrist insisted sufficiently on the patient's answering his questions, and assured him that he could remember perfectly well what had happened, it was possible to obtain all sorts of data which the patient had at first claimed, in all good faith, to have forgotten.

Freud relates that, working on these facts, he gave patients who had not been hypnotized a "leading-word" and then asked them to make whatever associations such a word aroused in them, and express the associations quite freely. He did this in the hope of finding the way back, by way of these associations, to what had been forgotten. At first he started from some word or other which seemed to be connected with the symptoms, but later he stated that it was not necessary to insist on this, because "Almost always the patient has a number of ideas (*'Einfälle'*) that come to the surface, despite all the pretexts he may raise as obstacles to the communication of these ideas, or even to their entering into his consciousness."[2]

This reaction by the subject, consisting of an evocation of ideas rising from some leading-word or other, became Freud's new method of treatment. *Its objective was to discover the connections between symptoms and the lived experiences which gave them their meaning, and to discover their cause.* It is the *method of free association.* The fundamental assumption of this technique is that these ideas, *which appear to be purely fortuitous, are not fortuitous at all.* Whatever is *evoked* in a patient by the leading-word through the method of association is supposed to be "in-

[1] Cf. Freud, *"Psychoanalyse," Gesammelte Werke*, XIII, p. 214.
[2] *Ibid.*

wardly related" to this word, and the course of the association therefore psychologically *determined*.[1]

This new technique supplied Freud with the basis of facts which became the starting-point of his new theoretical conceptions, especially about *repression*. Under hypnosis, Freud said, the play of forces which is to be found at the root of the neurosis had remained hidden. This conflict became evident for the first time in free association—which in fact showed that there was a *resistance* to the communication of certain ideas. The patient would suddenly discover all kinds of good reasons for not communicating certain associations, saying that they were far too unimportant or that they obviously had nothing to do with the question, etc. Freud discovered later that these were the very associations which turned out to be important in the search for the "forgotten."[2]

Freud thought he saw an important clue in this resistance. He had already understood intuitively that the cause of neurosis was intimately bound up with tendencies and conflicts. He now saw in this resistance proof that *an obstacle* existed which prevented the "forgotten" from being fully recalled to consciousness. *The power that prevented these dynamic contents from rising to the surface was likely to be the very power which had in the first place forced or "repressed" them out of consciousness.* Since in Freud's opinion sexual difficulties lay at the root of neurosis, his conclusion was bound to be that certain *sexual* tendencies had not been accepted by the conscious mind, but had been "censored" and repressed.

Freud originally thought that this censorship and repression were exerted by the conscious *ego* (*Ich*). Later he came to consider repression as largely an *unconscious* process arising from the *super-ego* (*Über-Ich*) (or *ego-ideal*) rather than from the ego itself.

But the things that have been repressed out of consciousness do not on that account lose their dynamic force. Freud compares them to people who get uproarious at a meeting and are ejected

[1] "Behind the use of the technique which was to take the place of hypnosis there lay undoubtedly an absolute confidence in the strict determinism of psychic phenomena." *Ibid.*, p. 214.

[2] From 1895 onwards Freud had made similar use of the idea of psychic *resistance*.

by the chairman for their disturbing behaviour. But that does not make them any calmer. Outside, they make more din than ever, banging at the doors and windows and making it quite impossible for the meeting to continue on its normal course.

Such is the case with repressed sexual desires. From their home in the unconscious they can upset the whole psychic life and thus cause psychic disturbances and neurosis. Part of the repressed energy can, however, be "sublimated" into effort and activity that is socially acceptable.

3. PSYCHOANALYSIS AS AN ART OF INTERPRETATION (DEUTUNGS-KUNST)—FUNDAMENTAL LACUNAE

The technical method of free association, which gave Freud some idea of the play of forces at work in the psyche, made it possible for him to elaborate his cardinal theory of psychic resistance and repression. This is why Freud considered this new method *the* great step forward taken by psychoanalysis. And yet it is possible that Freud did not sufficiently expose the deficiencies and the dangers of this technique.

Free association is supposed to put the psychoanalyst on the track of repressed experiences, as, previously, hypnosis had done. But whereas during a trance the therapeutist obtained an account of the traumatic experience itself, by the method of free association he only gathers "a rich body of ideas which can *put the analyst on the track* of what the patient has forgotten." "These facts, it is true," Freud goes on, "do not make clear what has actually been forgotten, but they give the individual *such clear abundant signs,* that from them, and *with the help of certain additions ('Ergänzungen')* and interpretations *('Deutungen'),* the doctor can *conjecture or reconstruct ('erraten,' 'rekonstruieren')* what has been forgotten."[1]

---

[1] Cf. Freud, "*Kurzer Abriss der Psychoanalyse*," *Gesammelte Werke,* XIII, p. 411 (our italics). When Freud had substituted free association for Breuer's cathartic method, he "chose the name psychoanalysis for *his method of treatment.*" Freud adds: "Psychoanalysis was now, in the first place, an *art of interpretation* ('Kunst der Deutung')." Cf. *Gesammelte Werke,* XIII, p. 215.

It is worthwhile noting that hypnotic methods are having a new vogue, being recognized as more effective than Freudian analysis for the discovery of traumatic experiences. Hypnotherapy and hypnoanalysis today frequently use drugs to produce the state of hypnosis.

No doubt Freud is right in emphasizing the "clear abundant signs" contained in the "ideas" which surge up into the patient's imagination, but this does not contradict the fact that the technique which was to make possible the elaboration of psychoanalytical doctrine was essentially, in Freud's own words, an *interpretative art* (*"Deutungskunst"*). So long as this interpretative art remains simply a method whose objective is limited to dealing with clinical cases, no serious difficulties arise, for then it is simply a case of getting the patient better. But when, as we shall see later on, psychoanalysis, using the material it thus "interprets" (*"deutet"*), claims to have elaborated a complete system of human psychology and a philosophy of culture, this method becomes a more hazardous proceeding. Anyone who is looking for a psychological system with a firm scientific basis, and who knows very well what people can "conjecture" and "reconstruct" upon a stream of "ideas," will not on that account reject the Freudian method *a priori;* but he will feel obliged to maintain a critical spirit and to inquire very closely into the value of the data which such a method supplies. It is true that the psychoanalytical method has led to the discovery of important things in psychic life, things which from a whole host of converging facts and confirmations have acquired a likelihood not easily to be discounted in the study of man's inner life. But it is equally true that psychoanalysis has allowed itself to be carried to excessive lengths by this "interpretative art."

The description which Freud gives us of his method of working makes it even clearer that it has many important deficiencies as a *scientific* instrument, even when it reveals itself as an excellent *clinical* technique.

It was now (he says) a question of realizing that the material supplied by the patient's ideas has a hidden meaning, and of conjecturing this meaning from the given material. Experience soon showed that the most effective attitude for the analyst to adopt was to abandon himself to his own unconscious mental activity in a state of uniform "global" attention (*"gleichschwebender Aufmerksamkeit"*). It was best for him to avoid as far as possible all reflection and conscious expectancy, and aim to remember as little as possible of what he heard. In this way he received the patient's unconscious into his own. When the relationship was fairly favourable, the patient's ideas were found to accumulate like allusions to a definite theme; and the doctor had only to risk going one step in advance in order to conjecture what lay hidden and communicate it to the patient. Obviously this method of interpretation cannot be made into a fixed routine, and it leaves plenty of scope for the doctor's own tact and skill—it was only when impartiality was combined with practice that absolutely certain results were obtained—i.e., results that were confirmed by repetition in similar cases . . . Analysis is still being conducted in the same way, moreover, despite the fact that at present there is a stronger conviction of the value of analysis and a better idea of its limits.[1]

It is interesting to observe that Freud himself occasionally came to the conclusion that he had make mistakes in "interpretation." Thus he thought originally that he could assume, from the thought associations of neurotics, that *seduction* often played an important part in their past sexual development; but eventually he had to confess that he had allowed himself to be misled on this point by the neurotics themselves, through not having taken sufficiently into account the liveliness of their imaginations. This was a bitter pill for Freud to swallow, as he confesses in the following passage:

My confidence in both my technique and its results suffered a severe blow; it could not be disputed that I had arrived at these scenes by a technical method which I considered correct, and their subject-matter was unquestionably related to the symptoms from which my investigation had started. When I had pulled myself together, I was able to draw the right conclusions from my discovery: namely, that the neurotic symptoms were not related directly to actual events but to phantasies embodying wishes, and that as far as the neurosis was concerned, psychic reality was of more importance than material reality. I do not believe even now that I forced the seduction-phantasies upon my patients, that I "suggested" them. I had in fact, for the first time, stumbled upon the *Oedipus complex*, which was later to assume such an overwhelming importance, but which I did not recognize as yet, because it was disguised in phantasy.[2]

With his new method of treatment, and his new idea of the part played in neurosis by sexuality, Freud had broken with Breuer and developed his own therapeutic: this was psycho-analysis.[3] He was now to develop his theory and his method still further. His method was to be considerably enlarged by his

[1] Cf. Freud, *"Psychoanalyse,"* *Gesammelte Werke*, XIII, p. 215.
[2] Cf. *"Selbstdarstellung,"* *Gesammelte Werke*, XIV, p. 60.
[3] Freud used this expression for the first time in 1898, when in an article in the *Monatschrift für Psychiatrie und Neurologie*, Vol. IV, he spoke of a "psychoanalystische Kur" (p. 441).

interpretation of dreams (1900) and later by his explanation of trivial errors in daily life, such as slips of the tongue, misreading, forgetting, etc.; whilst *an entirely new theory of sexuality*, and of the stages in its development, was soon to take shape (1905).

The Development of the Theory

I. INFANTILE SEXUALITY

The traumatic expressions and experiences which were revealed by the method of association led Freud to the discovery of memories and conflicts which were all more or less sexual in nature and which went further and further back into the subject's past life. Neurosis went back to the sexual conflicts *of infancy;* such was the solution which imposed itself more and more forcibly on Freud's mind in answer to the question of the origin of neurosis. Symptoms of illness were *substitutes* for the satisfaction of sexual desires which had been repressed.

No doubt a superficial examination of the patient did not *usually* show the origin of the symptoms to lie in traumatic events of a sexual nature. Think, for example, of the scene between the lady companion and the little dog, or the girl at her father's bedside in Breuer's first case. *But as Freud saw it, such non-sexual traumas only became pathological to the extent that they were bound up with sexual experiences of the first years of infancy.* The scenes with the girl at her father's bedside became pathogenic as a result of the girl's emotional attitudes towards her father, emotional attitudes which had been repressed and which were sexual in nature (Oedipus complex).

These ideas brought Freud into conflict with the view of his contemporaries, according to which sexuality was determined primarily by the reproductive process and the genital organs and did not show itself in man until puberty. The opposition he received led him to a reconsideration of the whole problem of sexuality,[1] as a result of which he was to enlarge the ideas held on the subject. Was it quite certain, he asked, that sexuality was

---

[1] Cf. especially Freud, "*Drei Abhandlungen zur Sexualtheorie*," which appeared for the first time in 1905. *Gesammelte Werke*, V.

essentially dependent on reproduction and the genital organs, and that it only manifested itself at puberty?⌋

⌊On the basis of phenomena observed in *abnormal* sexual life Freud built up a new and broader theory. As his starting-point he made use of three kinds of pathological phenomena. First, in certain persons sexuality is directed exclusively towards people of the same sex and thus can have no connection with reproduction. Again, there are people who seek sexual satisfaction, and find it, without any assistance from the genital organs or their normal functioning (as, for instance, in sexual fetishism). Finally, a number of children—and a much greater number than one would imagine at first sight—seem to show an interest at an early age in sexual matters and to find pleasure in them. Therefore sexuality does not begin with puberty.⌋

Freud widened the conception of sexuality by, on the one hand, disproving its exclusive attachment to the reproductive process and the genital organs, and on the other, linking it up with the whole question of tenderness and the expression of affection. Sexuality, he maintained, manifested itself quite clearly immediately after birth, chiefly in the pleasure-giving function of the erogenous zones of the body (*"Funktion der Lustgewinnung aus Körperzonen"*). Later on, this function was subordinated to the reproductive powers, but without these two things becoming entirely identical. Freud's ideas about infantile sexuality were originally derived from data given by the analysis of *adults*. He arrived at "direct proof," to use his own words (*"direkte Bestätigung"*), when, in 1908, he began a similar analysis of children.

Freud's first discovery in the field of infantile sexuality lies fundamentally in his having established the existence of a number of analogies between various manifestations of sexual life in children, on the one hand, and adult forms of behavior generally looked upon as deviations from the normal—sexual perversions—on the other. For instance, he discovers an analogy between anal sexuality and the feelings of pleasure experienced by children in defecating. The child normally passes through different stages, during each of which a different area of the body is the centre of the stimulation of pleasure; and usually these stages evolve without

hindrance and develop imperceptibly until the normal adult form
of sexuality is reached.

It sometimes happens, however, that a certain amount of *sexual
energy*, i.e. a certain quantity of *libido, remains attached* to one
of the in-between stages, and it is in this way that *fixations* occur.
These fixations have the following consequence: the people who
suffer from them are found *disposed* to manifest their repressed
desires in this fixed form of sexuality; and when the libido, in the
course of its development, comes up against obstacles to its satisfaction, it quickly *reverts* to these past forms of sexuality. This is
the phenomenon known as *regression*.

2. THE DEVELOPMENT OF THE LIBIDO

Confining ourselves to a purely schematic description, we can
say that Freud distinguishes three main periods in the normal
development of infantile sexuality. The first, which extends from
birth to about the end of the fifth year, at which point it reaches
its climax, is a period of active sexual experiences. After this follows a latent period, situated approximately between the sixth
and ninth years. During this period, any expression of sex is
repressed and dismissed from the mind (infantile amnesia). Finally,
at puberty, the period of adult sexuality begins to develop. If this
is so, man's sexual development has two starting-points, the first
at birth and the second at puberty.

According to psychoanalysis, the first is the more important
period. It is in this period, stretching from birth to the sixth year,
says Freud, that the source of all neurosis is to be found, even
though the symptoms may not show themselves until much later.
In his later works Freud distinguishes three phases in this first
period, characterized by the fact that the mouth (*oral* phase),
defecation (*anal* phase), and the reproductive organ (*phallic*
phase) in turn become the child's centre of interest and his pleas-
ure-stimuli. After the latent period—i.e., in the third period—comes
the fourth phase in the development of the libido, the *genital*
phase. But the way the libido develops during this final phase is
always determined by what took place during the first period.

In its primitive state the libido is directed towards the *ego*
(primary narcissism and *ego-libido* or "*Ichlibido*"). It is also the

child's own body which—after its mother's breast—forms the first object of the libido (auto-eroticism). Soon, however, the libido seizes upon other "objects"—other people, for example. This is *object-libido* (*"Objectlibido"*).

It is during the third stage, i.e., the phallic phase, which stretches from the second or third year to the end of the fifth, that the first important choice of objects presents itself. The boy begins to feel an increasing bond with his mother: the mother becomes the object of the libido. According to Freud, it is not only the data given by analysis which reveal this special connection with the mother but the child's normal behaviour as well.

It is easy to see that the little man wants his mother all to himself, finds his father in the way, becomes restive when the latter takes upon himself to caress her, and shows his satisfaction when the father goes away or is absent. He often expresses his feelings directly in words and promises his mother that he will marry her; this may not seem much. . . . One might try to object that the little boy's behaviour is due to egoistic motives and does not justify the conception of an erotic complex; the mother looks after all the child's needs, and consequently it is to the child's interest that she should trouble herself about no one else. This too is quite correct; but it is soon clear that in this, as in similar dependent situations, egoistic interests only provide the occasion on which the erotic impulses seize. When the little boy shows the most open sexual curiosity about his mother, wants to sleep with her at night, insists on being in the room while she is dressing, or even attempts physical acts of seduction—as the mother so often observes and laughingly relates—the erotic nature of this attachment to her is established without a doubt.[1]

Along with the special love for the mother there goes, says Freud, a rival feeling of hostility towards the father. The relationship with the father is, however, dual: besides the above-mentioned hostility, the boy often has a great feeling of veneration for his father and shows every sign of affection. This choice of the mother by the boy's libido, with the accompanying ambivalent attitude towards the father, Freud called the *Oedipus complex*—a reference to the legend about Oedipus, who killed his father and married his mother.[2] A girl will have a similar erotic attitude towards her father.

[1] Cf. Freud, *"Vorlesungen zur Einführung in die Psychoanalyse."* See *Vorlesung* No. 21, *Gesammelte Werke*, XI.
[2] The general meaning given by psychoanalysis to the word "complex"

The Oedipus complex occupies a central place in Freud's explanation not only of neurosis, but of human activity in general—in particular, human culture. The data given by analysis are said to show that "every neurotic is himself an Oedipus, or what amounts to the same thing, has become a Hamlet in his reaction to the complex."[1] The development of the Oedipus complex and the bond with the mother are therefore of the greatest importance as regards the later love-relationships of the normal man.

The development of the libido towards the final genital phase is suddenly interrupted at the end of the phallic stage. Freud thinks that the shocks and disillusionments experienced by the child with regard to his Oedipian hopes, and especially the fear of being castrated—which often appears during this phase, when the child is concerned with his genital organs (castration complex)—have the effect of distracting his attention from sex. And with this the latent period begins.[2]

At this moment in the development of the libido Freud considers that certain processes come into existence in the child which are of the highest importance for his moral and cultural development. The Oedipus complex is resolved and desexualized by *a process of identification.* "If," Freud says, "one has lost a love-object or has had to give it up, one often compensates oneself *by identifying oneself* with it; one sets it up again inside one's ego."[3]

---

is as follows: a totality of contents or situations which as a result of special experiences in childhood are highly charged with emotion for the subject and produce their effects consciously or unconsciously in the course of the development of psychic life. These effects result from the fact that the situations or images in question produce strong emotional reactions in the subject.

As regards the Oedipus complex we should like to draw attention to the fact that autobiographical literature contains a great amount of testimony to erotic accounts of this kind—for example, in French literature, Stendhal's *Vie de Henri Brulard,* and the passages quoted by J. Paulus, *"Les deux visages de Stendhal,"* in *Miscellanea Psychologica Albert Michotte* (Louvain, Ed. de l'Institut Superieur de Philosophie, 1947), p. 431.

[1] Cf. Freud, *"Vorlesungen zur Einführung in die Psychoanalyse."* See *Vorlesung* No. 21, *Gesammelte Werke,* XI.

[2] Cf. Freud, *"Der Untergang des OidipusKomplexes"* (first edition 1924), *Gesammelte Werke,* XIII, pp. 395-402.

[3] Cf. Freud, *"Neue Folge der Vorlesungen zur Einführung in die Psychoanalyse,"* *Gesammelte Werke,* XV, p. 69.

This phenomenon takes place in the child's relationships with its parents. But here a difficulty arises; for when the Oedipus complex is resolved and desexualized, the boy normally identifies himself *with his father*, not, as one would expect, with his mother, who is the real "lost object."[1] This, as Freud confesses, is why "I am myself not at all satisfied with this account of identification."[2]

This did not, however, prevent Freud from elaborating, on the basis of this process of identification, theories and conclusions which had considerable repercussions.

To explain why the boy tends to identify himself with his father and not with his mother, new mechanisms have been suggested. In the first place, it is said to be impossible, considering the biological factors which are involved, for any far-reaching identification to be realized between the boy and his mother. Such a process would depend particularly on the degree of femininity in the boy. Again, in a cultural environment of a patriarchal type like ours, the father is the most important source of frustrations for the boy. Now the child does not only identify himself with the love-object which he is unable to attain, but also with the thing which constitutes the obstacle to the realization of his desires—i.e., in this particular case, the father. The value of these seemingly contradictory explanations of the process of identification lies in the fact that in the course of his practice the therapist does in fact discover these various kinds of identification taking place. It has been ascertained, in fact, that identification is also an ego-defence mechanism. To conquer his misery the boy can, in fact, identify himself with the person who appears to him as a rival and a source of danger with regard to his mother.[3]

With regard to the problem of the super-ego, it is sufficient to take the word "identification" as meaning the child's desire to behave and be like his parents, particularly his father. The father

---

[1] Cf. Freud, *"Das Ich und das Überich (Ichideal),"* *Gesammelte Werke*, XIII, p. 261: "These identifications do not correspond to our expectations: they do not in fact establish the lost object in the ego."

[2] Cf. Freud, *"Neue Folge der Vorlesungen zur Einführung in die Psychoanalyse,"* *Gesammelte Werke*, XV, p. 70.

[3] Re this question see Anna Freud, *The Ego and the Mechanisms of Defence*, Chapter IX, "Identification with the Aggressor" (London, Hogarth Press, 1937).

is thus "interiorized" in the child's ego as an "ego-ideal." This is the mechanism known as "introjection." This process implies here that the father becomes an object towards which the child tends; his drive to self-realization proceeds in the direction of "being like father." The father, who is thus "introjected," is his father with all his severity, his commands, his law and his omnipotence.

The starting-point of this idea of Freud's concerning introjection is to be found in a concrete fact of the child's psychic development. It is indeed a well-known fact that at a certain stage of his development a child will do what he has been told to do by his parents, and respect their prohibitions, even when they are not there. Their laws and standards of conduct thus become effective even when they are not directly imposed from outside, and the child therefore endeavours to be like his parents, particularly his father, by making their standards and ideals "his own."

This process seems from the evidence to be a very important phenomenon, but it can be interpreted in more than one way.

Identification means here that the child *wishes to be like* his parents, or rather, like his father. Thus the father is "introjected" in the *ego* as the *ego-ideal*, the father with his severity, his authority, his absolute law, his omnipotence. This image of the father becomes a "precipitate" in the ego. "No doubt this ego-ideal is a precipitate of the old idea of the parents, an expression of the admiration which the child felt for the perfection which it at that time ascribed to them."[1] This "precipitate" now occupies a special place in the ego, constituting what Freud calls the *super-ego*.[2] According to psychoanalysis this *super-ego* or *ego-ideal* is the starting-point for religion and the moral conscience, and indeed for human culture as a whole.[3]

These developments and applications of Freud's doctrine were only made step by step. Several times Freud modified his position on certain points. Moreover, some theories developed as a result of the collaboration of his followers. The whole theoretical edifice,

[1] Cf. Freud, *"Neue Folge der Vorlesungen zur Einführung in die Psychoanalyse," Gesammelte Werke,* XV, p. 70.
[2] Cf. Freud, *"Das Ich und das Überich (Ichideal)," Gesammelte Werke,* XIII, p. 262.
[3] See our chapter, "Psychoanalysis as a Science and a Theory of Life."

by which psychoanalysis claimed to explain all human activity, was made possible by the development of the analytical *method*, and it was the application of the method of free association to the *analysis of dreams* which very soon became for Freud the method par excellence of investigating the human subconscious. It is this analysis and interpretation of dreams that we must now discuss.

Development of the Method: The Analysis of Dreams

1. THE MEANING OF DREAMS

The method of free association did not merely allow Freud to build up his cardinal theory of repression; it also gave him access to the richest source of psychoanalytical material—the world of dreams. In its study of dreams psychoanalysis was able to give free rein to its "interpretative art," and it did not always utilize "conjectures" and "reconstruction" with the required critical sense. Nevertheless there can be no doubt that many interesting facts, containing a high degree of plausibility, have been discovered in this field too.[1]

By a happy "intuition" Freud came to look upon dreams as the kind of phenomena which, like the symptoms of neurosis, apparently incoherent and devoid of meaning, can nevertheless reveal on closer scrutiny a more profound meaning and coherence. It was from this point of view that Freud soon began to apply his method of association to the exploration of dreams.

When the patient had unburdened himself of the apparent, or surface, content of his dream, Freud would extract certain special images as a starting-point for the subject's free association. By "interpreting" a number of associations acquired in this way, he

---

[1] On the Freudian interpretation of dreams see especially *"Traumdeutung,"* which, according to the author himself (*Gesammelte Werke*, X, pp. 60–61), was settled in all its essential details as early as 1896 but not printed until 1899. It was published in 1900. (*"Traumdeutung"* forms Volumes II and III of the *Gesammelte Werke*.) As regards modifications of the Freudian theory of dreams see, further, *"Neue Folge der Vorlesungen zur Einführung in die Psychoanalyse,"* Vorlesung No. 29: *Revision der Traumlehre, Gesammelte Werke*, XV, pp. 6–31.

was able to reconstruct a significant psychic event which he called
the *latent* content of the dream, of which the apparent content
was a deformed version.

2. THE VALUE OF DREAM-SYMBOLISM AND FREE ASSOCIATION

The associations made by the subject do not directly supply
the key to the symbolic meaning to be attributed to the surface
content of the dream, but they do lead to certain situations and
representations which make "conjectures" and "reconstruction"
possible, and it was under these conditions that a *psychoanalytical
dream-symbolism* was gradually developed, according to which
certain well-defined dream-images acquired a fixed meaning.[1] This
fixing of the symbolic value of certain dream-representations was
helped especially by what Freud calls "extraordinarily transparent
dreams" and by the interpretation of free associations. This symbolic interpretation was then confirmed by the converging testimony of all sorts of signs discovered again and again in the analysis
of the subject. The natural similarity between the symbol and
the thing signified played a similar part. Thus lengthened objects,
for example, are symbols of the penis.[2]

When one comes to examine this method critically, however,
the symbolic meaning which has been erected on the basis of all
these converging signs and testimonies does not seem so firmly
based as it appears to be at first sight. For instance, when *flowers*
appearing in a dream are regularly given a sexual significance, this
is done in the belief that the *total* interpretation of the facts *gives
grounds for assuming* the existence of sexual desires and imaginings in the patient. And yet these desires and imaginings are said
to exist in the patient *unconsciously*—and so they can *not* at the
same time be considered absolute facts.

As dream-symbolism was so important in the development of
psychoanalytical theory, let us for a moment examine this process
of interpretation, and its foundation in fact, a little more closely.

It is held that apparently neutral objects like flowers are open
to a sexual interpretation, on the basis of "data" obtained through

[1] Cf. Freud, *"Traumdeutung,"* Chapter VI. On this point Freud was
inspired by the work of Scherner.
[2] *Ibid.*

free association, and which the psychoanalyst "interprets" afterwards. When, for example, an English woman patient dreams of
violets and then goes on to associate with "violet" the word "vio-
late," which has almost the same pronunciation, this is a sign
which, along with others of a similar nature, brings out the
"sexual setting" of the dream.[1]

If we now inquire into the value of such interpretations, we
find that this rests on Freud's theory that the "ideas" that arise
in free association are determined by the tensions between the
libido and the situation of conflict.[2] The facts of experimental
psychology, however, make this a highly debatable point. Associations—that is to say, the content of the ideas that rise up in the
mind—are certainly influenced by the fundamental dispositions of
the subject; but these may be no more than particular *conscious
attitudes or orientations which have been taken up at the very
moment of the association.* Experiments made by both Ach and
Lewin have shown that a particular orientation of mind, created
for instance by some task which has been imposed, influences the
nature of the associations or ideas that come to the surface.[3]

By the method of free association, it is true, every effort is made
to eliminate any conscious tension or mind-direction from the
subject; but an active orientation, identical in nature with the
tension created by the task in Lewin's experiments, takes place
spontaneously as soon as the subject's interest or attention is directed to a particular topic. Now there can be no doubt that this
actually happens during psychoanalytical treatment: the general
orientation of the patient's mind tends increasingly towards the
field of sex and eroticism. With many patients, the *particular* frame
of mind that results from this can have a considerable influence
on the nature of their associations.

[1] Cf. Freud, "*Traumdeutung,*" *Gesammelte Werke*, II, pp. 378–382.
[2] Cf. above, p. 9.
[3] Cf. Kurt Lewin, "*Das problem der Willensmessung und das Grundge-
setz der Assoziation,*" I, *Psychologische Forschung*, 1922, I, pp. 191–302; II,
ibid.. II, pp. 65–140. Compare also, on this point, the recent article by Elliott
McGinnies, "Personal Values as Determinants of Word Association," *The
Journal of Abnormal and Social Psychology*, 1950, LXV, pp. 28–36; also
the experiments by Sanford, in which it is shown that the actual need of
food has an influence on the contents of association (*Journal of Psychology*,
1936 and 1937, II and III).

Such being the case, the hypotheses about the dynamic origin and the profound significance of these associations seem debatable, in certain instances at least. This fact is of the highest importance as regards the value of the psychoanalytical interpretations of the material provided by the method of free association.

This does not mean, however, that in a great number of cases the sexual orientation which is revealed in the content of the association may not in fact be linked to deeper dynamic bases. That it is, is occasionally confirmed by all kinds of indications supplied by the situation as a whole. But it often happens that every element in the complex of associations or in the dream gets interpreted in a sexual sense *because of the analyst's a priori atti-tude* towards the case. Thus, in the example quoted, the word "vio-late" is looked upon as a sign of deep sexual impulses because the analyst's general attitude towards the dream is orientated towards a sexual interpretation; for this association could also be interpreted as a quite ordinary reaction based on the assonance of the two words. The analyst's general tendency towards a sexual interpre-tation of the dream as a whole has as its only justification the fact that the patient replies to the leading-word, "violet," by making an association that is *sexual in nature* ("violate").

We see, therefore, that the sexual interpretation of the associated word depends above all on the analyst's general attitude towards the dream, an attitude which is itself based on a sexual interpreta-tion of this very association.

If it is objected that, in the interpretation of a certain case, one can point to innumerable "data" provided by earlier analyses and to a whole tradition in this field, it should nevertheless still be remembered that this appeal to past experience does little to alter the kind of circular argument in which one is involved. All these "data" are in fact based on the same assumption: only a *sanatio in radice* could consolidate the structure as a whole.

Our criticism, based on the preceding example, may therefore be summarized as follows:

1. The sexual nature of the association in question is not proved, since it may depend on the *assonance* of the word "violate" rather than on its sexual significance. To speak more generally, the sexual nature and significance of associations are often simply a result

of the analyst's general mental attitude towards the case, which is sexual; whilst this attitude of mind tries to justify itself by the sexual nature of the associations.

2. Assuming that the particular association is really of a sexual nature, it still remains to be discovered, in each case, whether this association derives in fact from repressed unconscious dynamisms or whether it is simply the consequence of a *more immediate orientation of the mind,* adopted by the patient during the course of the analysis itself.

These criticisms do not by any means imply that psychoanalysis has not, by such obviously imperfect methods, arrived at *certain* conceptions in which it is only just to recognize a high degree of truth. But it is nevertheless important not to lose sight of the methodological shakiness of the construction as a whole.

In Freud's ideas on the symbolic meaning of dreams is to be found the germ of the theory of the *collective* unconscious. Symbols are in fact unconscious transpositions which are valid for the human race as a whole. The theory of the collective unconscious was, as is well known, developed independently by Carl G. Jung, who broke away from Freud.

3. DREAM-CONTENTS AND REPRESSED DESIRES

The problem of dreams, for psychoanalysis, lay in discovering why they were what they were, and in explaining the transformation of their content. The solution which Freud brought to this problem lay simply in applying to dreams the doctrine derived from neurosis.

According to Freud one can deduce from the latent content of the dream the repressed desire from which it takes its birth. During sleep the "censorship" exerted by the *ego* or the *super-ego* is weaker, but it is not on that account completely done away with. In these conditions the repressed unconscious desire manifests itself in a compromised form, as the symbolic, and by no means "transparent" story, constituted by the surface content of the dream. "The dream," says Freud, "is the camouflaged realization of a repressed desire."

The most important modification which Freud introduced into his conception of dreams lies in the fact that, according to his

later conception, a dream does not necessarily mean the *fulfilment*
of a desire; it may mean an *effort towards the realization of a
desire*, an effort which sometimes does not succeed. Thus the
same traumatic scene can be repeated again and again in a dream;
in this case the dream has not succeeded in suppressing the painful
situation by a realization of the suppressed desires.[1]

The material which the repressed libido uses for the surface
content of the dream often has as its starting-point facts or events
of normal conscious life. When, however, the true meaning of the
dream threatens to become "transparent" under this disguise, the
subject wakes up suddenly in fright.

The Development of Psychoanalysis into a Philosophy of Culture

The interpretation of dreams—that royal road to the realm of
the unconscious, as Freud called it—supplied psychoanalysis with
such a vast amount of material that from being a simple method
of psychotherapeutic treatment it became a *general system of
human psychology* and even developed into a *philosophy of human
culture*.

Psychoanalysis rediscovers the sexual dream-symbolism in cultural products like mythology, poetry, folklore, etc. These discoveries were to lead psychoanalysts to look upon such cultural activities as deformed or "sublimated" manifestations of repressed
libido.

Freud's analysis of the Oedipus complex and its development
enabled him, as we have seen above, to elaborate his theory of the
super-ego. Using the *super-ego* as a psychic fact and the results
of dream-analysis as material, Freud and his disciples developed an
interpretation of human culture and the human mind which, with
the exception of certain highly suggestive hints, belongs to the
shakiest part of psychoanalysis (cf. Chapter 1).

On the other hand, his analysis of dream-processes enabled him
to acquire an idea of the mechanism and the *functioning of man's
unconscious psychic life*.

[1] Cf. Freud, "*Neue Folge der Vorlesungen zur Einführung in die Psychoanalyse*," *Gesammelte Werke*, XV, pp. 29–31.

Freud calls the process whereby repressed thoughts and desires are *transformed* by censorship, "dream-work" (*Traumarbeit*). On the basis of this, he built up a new theory of the way the unconscious functions, and this work was to give a new form and meaning to the Freudian conception of man's psychic structure and mechanism *in its totality*. As a matter of fact, the structure and mechanism of psychic life, which he discovered as a result of his work on dreams were *no longer restricted to abnormal psychic life*, but concerned the mode of functioning of psychic life generally. For dreams are a phenomenon of *normal* life. Freud believed that dreams are constructed, and come into existence, in exactly the same way as neurotic symptoms. Both are deformed manifestations of repressed libido. This was to draw the attention of psychoanalysts to the hypothesis that *the forces active in normal psychic life are the same as those at work in abnormal or neurotic psychic life*. The same forces, in both cases, repress the desires and objects of the libido, and similar mechanisms transform this repressed energy and allow it to appear in substitute forms.

Thus Freud equates neurosis, perversion, dreams, and every kind of cultural activity: all these different phenomena are ways in which the libido manifests itself in psychic life. To the difference between normal and abnormal, he "gives merely a conventional value. And for this reason," he adds, "*it is quite legitimate to claim to understand normal psychic life from the basis of abnormal states.*"[1]

Later Freud found *confirmation* for his theory of the homogeneity of normality and abnormality in the psychoanalytical explanation of omissions, lapses of memory, absent-mindedness, etc. Assuming that his theory simply widens the field of application of the Freudian conception, without adding any strictly new elements, we can content ourselves here with a simple example.

[1] These are Freud's words in the very last of his works, published in the "*Schriften aus dem Nachlass.*" Cf. *Gesammelte Werke*, XVII, p. 125. The Freudian doctrine of the structure of the psyche (the *id, ego* and *super-ego*) is discussed in the following chapter of this book, in which the reader will also find a fuller account of various essential parts of psychoanalytical doctrine, taken as "general psychology"—such as the doctrine of instincts (*Sexual-triebe, Ich-triebe und Destruktionstriebe*) and sublimation. The fundamental theory of the "unconscious" is described in detail in Chapter III.

When, at the beginning of a parliamentary session which he was to declare open, the President of the Austrian Chamber expressed himself in these words: "I declare the session *closed*," Freud took this lapse of memory as an expression of the President's wish to see the session over.[1] These apparently fortuitous acts (like the ideas communicated by the patient by the method of free association) are really *determined by an inner dynamic force.* Here, too, whatever the subject does or says reveals a compromise between a desire and an opposing force. Similarly absent-mindedness or the inability to find something is the result of a repression. In every act, however insignificant, there are the same forces manifesting themselves through the same mechanism.

Psychoanalysis as a Therapeutic Method

Psychoanalysis in the Freudian sense has quite a different aim from Breuer's cathartic method. Breuer aimed at freeing the patient from his emotions by a kind of emotional release. The aim of the new method was to *bring into consciousness* psychic contents which, because of their connection with the libido, were repressed into the unconscious by the censorship of the *ego*. This *bringing into consciousness of the repressed unconscious* lies at the very heart of the psychoanalytical therapeutic process. Assuming that neurosis is a manifestation of repressed libido, what has been repressed must be made conscious, so that neurotic symptoms may be got rid of at the root. Moreover, this idea was gradually to undergo a certain development; other components of the therapeutic process were to be emphasized. Besides the interpretation and elimination of the patient's *resistance*, there are two further processes which require our attention: *transference* and the *re-education* of the patient in the course of treatment.

It was in his analysis of the patient Dora that Freud first mentioned the concept of "transference" (*Übertragung*). He had completed his analysis of this patient in 1899, but the results were

[1] Cf. Freud, *"Zur Psychopathologie des Alltagslebens"* (1st edition, 1904).

not published until 1905.[1] From then onwards, the principle of transference was to play an increasingly important part in therapy.

What exactly is involved in this idea of transference? The word has a number of meanings. It is used not only in psychoanalysis but also in general psychology. In the strict, specifically psycho-analytical sense, it means the patient's attitude and behaviour towards the analyst, not as the latter exists in himself but in so far as people who have played a part in the patient's past, and particularly during his childhood, come to life in him again. Freud, in fact, seemed to perceive that the patient did not adopt the same attitude towards the therapist as he would towards a helper or adviser or doctor. The therapist seemed, in the eyes of the patient, to be the reincarnation of someone who had been the object of his libido during the first period of his development, e.g. one of his parents. The same feelings now seemed to be transferred to the therapist (*Übertragung*). These feelings could be either positive or negative (ambivalence): the patient could feel either love or hatred for the analyst. For Freud these emotions were, in either case, libidinous in nature. These fundamental ideas have been confirmed by subsequent research and constitute one of the most valuable discoveries made by psychoanalysis as a therapeutic method.

There is a certain amount of malice in the delighted way in which Freud asserts that his friend Breuer's first patient, whose case, according to Breuer himself, contained absolutely no sexual element at all, harboured feelings towards her therapist whose nature, according to Freud, was obviously sexual.[2]

For Freud the erotic aspect of this transference was final proof (*unerschütterlichste Beweis*) of the theory that the forces at the base of neurosis derive from sexual life.[3] Freud argues as follows. Given that the feelings for the doctor are simply a transference of pathogenic attitudes deriving from the patient's early childhood, and given, again, that the feelings transferred to the doctor are

[1] See *"Bruchstück einer Hysterie-Analyse," Monatschrift für Psychiatrie und Neurologie;* also in *Gesammelte Werke,* V.

[2] Cf. Freud, *"Zur Geschichte der psychoanalytischen Bewegung," Gesammelte Werke,* X, p. 49.

[3] *Ibid.,* p. 50.

erotic, then neurosis itself is bound to be "libidinous." The critical reader, however, feels obliged to add a few question marks to certain elements of this "final proof."

What in fact is said here to be "given" is indeed nothing more than a number of interpretations which have been made rather too hastily.

It is a fact of great importance for the therapeutic value of the transference that in the course of the analysis the patient re-lives the childhood experiences which have generated disturbances (transference-neurosis). This new experience, however, is now realized fragmentarily and in less tragic circumstances than was the case in childhood. The transference can nevertheless lead to dramatic scenes between patient and therapist. The most important fact about this new experience of the traumatic situations is that it takes place under more favourable conditions, assuming that the analyst adopts a more broad-minded and more understanding attitude towards the patient, or reacts more adequately.

When, as a result of these more favourable conditions, the patient succeeds in overcoming his neurotic conflicts, and thus frees himself from them, an important stage has been reached on the road to recovery.

To achieve this the analyst has also to interpret the phenomena involved in the transference. He has to make clear to the patient the deeper meaning of his feelings and behaviour. Thus once again we come across the fundamental principle of *consciousness of the unconscious*. In the present case this principle means that the analyst provides the patient with a clear perception of the meaning and significance of his acts and conscious experiences, which, left to himself, he would never be able to reach.

As a result of this new experience, realized fragmentarily under favourable conditions, the patient succeeds in overcoming his neurotic attitudes. According to some more recent trends in psychoanalysis the processes of transference, and their utilization by the analyst, lie at the very heart of therapy.

One of the therapist's most delicate and difficult tasks in the later stages of analysis consists precisely in this effort to "solve" the problem of the emotional relationship which has developed as a result of the transference. It is through this, particularly, that the patient's complete liberation can be attained. It will be realized that this central process of emotional transference, a process which takes place in one way or another in every kind of therapy and indeed in many varieties of "direction," lays special obligations on the therapist. It is well to remember this in each concrete case.

To achieve the final aim of the therapeutic process it is not sufficient, however, for the analyst to supply the patient with an interpretation of the phenomena involved in the transference. In many cases the patient complains that although he grasps the meaning of the processes quite clearly, he nevertheless finds it impossible to escape from the infantile feelings under which he labours. Here, too, clear perception or conscious awareness is not enough. The important final stage which remains to be gone through involves a *"reconstruction" of the patient's conscious ego*. Only this "reconstruction" can enable the patient to find a positive solution to the emotional conflicts of his daily life. This process will develop chiefly as a result of new and favourable emotional experiences which the patient goes through in the course of treatment and in the ordinary situations of his life. In concrete circumstances the patient discovers other attitudes to adopt towards certain people and certain situations, and thanks to this he also acquires a new experience of himself.

Freud did not sufficiently emphasize the importance of this side of therapy. It was left to Rank and Ferenczi particularly, amongst his former followers, to realize its value. They were so engrossed with it that they attached far less importance to the therapeutic value of an intellectual *conscious awareness* of the genesis of disturbances. On the other hand, they assigned a preponderating influence to the new emotional experiences felt by the patient in the course of the treatment. When in 1924 Ferenczi and Rank published their ideas, these provoked little response.[1] Nevertheless, other therapists soon appeared to emphasize the process of "reconstruction" in therapeutic treatment. Since then more attention has

[1] See S. Ferenczi and O. Rank, *"Entwicklungsziele der Psychoanalyse,"* No. 1 (Wien, Internationaler Psychoanalytischer Verlag, 1924). See also the interesting account of this work by F. Alexander in Volume XI of the *Internationale Zeitschrift für ärtzliche Psychoanalyse*, pp. 113–122. Alexander himself was later to develop this trend particularly.

been given to this side of the therapeutic process, even in psycho-analytical circles.

We cannot here describe in detail the analytical technique; we wish, however, to draw attention to another point of the therapeutic process.

In his first method of treatment Freud simply gave his patients his interpretation of the data discovered in the unconscious, i.e. what had been repressed; but he soon realized that they were not always ready to accept his interpretation. When this fact first became evident Freud became rather annoyed.[1] It was only later that he discovered the mechanism of the dynamic factors at work in the patient which fight against accepting the interpretation. He then came to the conclusion that a preliminary analysis of the *mechanisms of resistance* put in motion by the patient was necessary before the latter could succeed in becoming conscious of the repressed contents. An important contribution to the analysis of *character resistances* was made by Wilhelm Reich in his *Character Analysis.*[2]

Freud applied his idea of emotional resistance to all who rejected his theories or considered them false: such unconscious resistance was simply an obstacle to admitting the truth of psychoanalysis. Psychoanalysts have, perhaps, overworked this simple argument a little.

In the final stages of his theoretical system, Freud saw in the patient's resistance to the therapeutic process of seeing the facts as they were—which meant resistance to his own cure—a manifestation of the instinct for death or destruction. But the whole mass of ideas about this instinct for destruction (*Destruktionstrieb*) constitute a very shaky structure. Still, there can be no doubt that his patients frequently did resist their own cure. Adler, as is well known, gave a different explanation of this resistance, and one which is possibly nearer the truth.[3]

According to Freud's own ideas, the psychoanalytical method is particularly effective in the treatment of hysteria, obsessional

[1] Cf. the interpretation of the patient Irma's dream.

[2] Wilhelm Reich, *Der Triebhafte Charakter* (Wien, 1925). See also on this subject Thomas M. French, "Ego Analysis as a Guide to Therapy," *The Yearbook of Psychoanalysis,* 1946, II, p. 49 (New York, International Universities Press).

[3] See the remark of the patient quoted in this connection, p. 169.

neurosis, phobias, pathological inhibitions, malformation of character, sexual perversions and sexual problems in general. The patients should not be too old, and a certain moral and intellectual level is also requisite.[1]

On the basis of suggestions which he found in the work of Jelliffe, Groddeck and Felix Deutsch, Freud foresaw that psychoanalysis could prove useful in the treatment of organic illnesses, too, because of the part which certain psychic factors often seem to play in organic complaints. This aspect of the psychoanalytical movement has of late developed very considerably under the name of "psychosomatism," especially in America. Groddeck is known to have been the first to apply Freud's discoveries and hypotheses to organic illnesses. Psychosomatism, though it does not derive from psychoanalysis alone (it was influenced particularly by Pavlov's experiments) nevertheless remains dominated by Freudian psychology.[2]

Let us conclude this introduction by quoting Freud's advice to his followers: ["The analyst respects his patient's personality; he does not try to mould it according to his own personal ideas; *he is satisfied when instead of giving advice he can obtain his results by arousing the patient's own initiative.*"[3]]

This remark of Freud's, which we should like to emphasize, appears highly significant in connection with contemporary developments in psychotherapy. Unlike psychoanalysis, the method known as *non-directive* or client-centred therapy has made the patient's *initiative* the central factor in treatment.[4] The first point Freud makes, his advice to the analyst to respect the nature of the patient and to avoid forming it according to his own ideals, is a principle too often forgotten by analysts, and it is the failure to observe this dictum which justifies what is perhaps the most important complaint that can be made against psychoanalytical treatment as applied by certain psychoanalysts to patients with a religious background.

[1] Cf. Freud, *"Die Freudische psychoanalytische Methode"*; also *"Über Psychotherapie"*; both in the *Gesammelte Werke*, V, pp. 3–26.
[2] See especially French and Alexander, *Psychosomatic Medicine* (New York, Harper, 1948); also the review *Psychosomatic Medicine*.
[3] See Freud's article in the *Handwörterbuch der Sexualwissenschaften*, s.v. *"Psychoanalyse"* (1923), *Gesammelte Werke*, XIII, p. 227.
[4] Cf. Chap. II, p. 91.

PART I

PSYCHOANALYSIS

AND THE PSYCHOLOGY OF MAN

CHAPTER I

PSYCHOANALYSIS AS A SCIENCE AND AS A PHILOSOPHY OF MAN

It seems to us quite right and proper that anyone interested in human behaviour should at the moment be especially interested in psychoanalysis, and should use it as a means of subjecting his own attitude and ideas on this subject to a deeper critical inspection.

During the last few years, indeed, psychoanalysis has entered on a new phase of development. Freudian doctrine and Freudian methods had been widely known for a long time, but until recently it could still be said that psychoanalysts were a relatively closed circle, forming essentially a *school apart*.

One of the revelations that awaited European psychologists on the renewal of contact with America in 1945 was the discovery that psychoanalysis had *penetrated deeply into the spirit of the whole of psychotherapy and clinical psychology*. Academic psychologists, on their side, have taken it up and discussed it in their textbooks. Finally, important branches of experimental psychology, notably that centring round the late Kurt Lewin, have been inspired by psychoanalytical ideas.

This may be considered a gratifying situation from several points of view. Formerly, the human personality was studied rather as the *meeting-point of abstract processes;* now, thanks to this recent development particularly, experimental psychology in America is once again beginning to look upon man as possessing, at the core of his personality, a *dynamic centre*. In Europe psychoanalysis is still considered a comparatively closed system; but *living* psychoanalysis tends more and more to be integrated with the development of psychology in general. Such a situation makes it desirable that both partisans and opponents of the system should embark on a revision of their attitudes.[1]

1. The Attitude of the Spiritually Minded Psychologist towards Psychoanalysis[2]

\In these conditions, the first question we wish to raise is this: is there any problem as to what attitude doctors and psychologists of a spiritual persuasion should adopt towards psychoanalysis?

Our reply to this question is quite simple. Psychoanalysis is a theory, *belonging to the realm of science*. The first question that a man of science, whether he be spiritually minded or not, must ask himself about such a theory, is, what is its *scientific value?* This means examining the critical bases of the explanations given, and inquiring whether the theory in question takes all the facts into account. /

Such is the attitude of the spiritually minded psychologist towards any system which claims to supply an explanation of the established facts, and such is our attitude towards psychoanalysis. When tackling the Freudian theory, which has frequently been criticized from other angles altogether, it is important to state these general principles of healthy scientific criticism at the outset.

---

[1] It should be remarked that in German-speaking countries, too, a certain *rapprochement* has been observed during recent years between the various schools of psychology (i.e., the schools of Freud, Adler and Jung). See on this subject W. Kemper, *"Le développement actuel de la psychanalyse en Allemagne,"* *Psyche*, 1948, III, pp. 826–833. We do not discuss, in this book, the progress of psychoanalysis in *European* countries, because one does not find in them the *rapprochement* with *experimental* psychology which specially concerns us here.

[2] By the term "spiritually minded psychologist" we mean the psychologist who is convinced that the so-called "higher" or *specifically human* elements in the psychic activities of man are not to be *reduced* to the "lower" levels of behaviour. Cf. our Preface.

⌊It may, however, be objected that psychoanalysis is not a scientific theory like any other. By this is meant that it is not *only* a scientific theory but that it has developed into a *conception of life* and a *philosophy of man.* This is perfectly true. And it is for this very reason that the positive facts discovered by Freud and his followers have remained until recently *absolutely riddled with theoretical philosophical interpretations.* That is why, when we state our own attitude towards psychoanalysis, we shall have to distinguish very carefully between all the different elements in the system. It is a fundamental rule of all scientific criticism to distinguish, in the first place, the *established facts* from the *theoretical constructions* developed to *interpret* these facts.⌋

Established facts have their own value, which they cannot lose; and they are eventually clarified by later research; whereas theories are sometimes very shaky constructions and are always, in any case, provisional arrangements which the development of the science obliges us to broaden or modify incessantly.

This rule, valid for all the sciences, is especially relevant in the case of psychoanalysis, which, though one of the youngest branches of science, has developed far too rapidly, and overstepped the boundaries of psychological science. It must be clearly realized, in fact, that though he started with certain important discoveries of an empirical nature, Freud felt himself obliged to develop, not merely a scientific theory, but a definite *Weltanschauung:* a complete picture of man and human life. This *Weltanschauung* element, added to the facts and the *theories* or *hypotheses* which are scientifically verifiable, makes a third component which it is important to distinguish in psychoanalytical doctrine.

Until recently psychology had not succeeded in separating sufficiently the *objective data* and the scientific *hypotheses* furnished by psychoanalysis, from this suggested *Weltanschauung.* In Europe psychoanalysis is still often treated as a system which must be either accepted or rejected *in toto.* This situation is largely due to the fact that until latterly, as we have seen, Freud's doctrine was the doctrine of a whole school. Furthermore, as a result of the attacks and insults that were directed against it, it had taken on a mystical character and become for its followers a kind of faith.

But now this period of conflict is over and the time has come *to approach psychoanalysis as an ordinary scientific system*, and with the necessary critical acumen. This means that we must not neglect the important objective data which it supplies, simply because its scheme of interpretation often seems to overstep the limits of reasonable explanation, or because its total conception of man does not agree with our own. It also means that, despite its new and impressive facts, we shall not feel obliged to accept the whole framework of interpretation within which these facts were acquired. This position, we believe, represents a reasonable attitude for the spiritually minded psychologist to adopt towards psychoanalysis. It is a purely *scientific* attitude.

When we come to examine psychoanalysis critically in this perspective, we find that the things which seem unacceptable according to our conception of life are exactly those things which have nothing in common with well-attested psychological science. We now propose to make these ideas clearer by means of a short analysis of the contents of the psychoanalytical system. To anyone who knows psychoanalysis as a *clinical* psychology such a critical analysis will inevitably seem insufficient, and to be an abstract and arbitrary truncation of the whole system. One finds the real value and significance of psychoanalytic ideas in the framework of the therapeutic technique. We are perfectly aware of the impoverishment which is bound to be involved in this separation of psychoanalytical ideas from clinical practice. But when the Freudian system is not content merely to supply an explanation and method of treatment of psychic conflicts, but goes on to claim to be a *general psychology of man* as well, it is obliged, as a scientific system, to submit to a critical examination of its ideas and theories. Nevertheless it must not be forgotten that psychoanalysis remains in the first place a clinical technique and is only secondarily a system of general psychology. In psychoanalysis as a *system of doctrine* we distinguish three different elements:

1. Freudism as a *Weltanschauung*, and especially its global conception of man;
2. the body of facts in psychoanalysis;
3. the working hypotheses and psychological theories which remain within sound scientific limits.

As for psychoanalysis *as a method of therapy*, we shall endeavour to place it within present-day trends in psychotherapy in Chapter II of this work.

2. The Idea of Man in Freud's Weltanschauung

(1) THE STRUCTURE OF PERSONALITY: THE ID (ES), THE EGO (ICH) AND THE SUPER-EGO (ÜBER-ICH)

Freud rejects the word *pansexualism* as a description of his system.[1] It is nevertheless a fact that the three "domains" or sectors which Freud distinguished in the structure of human personality, as in the whole of man's *constructive* psychic activity, are rooted in the energy of the libido, i.e. in the energy of the sexual instinct. We shall show briefly that this is so.

The deepest root of psychic life is found in what Freud calls the "id." The "id" contains "everything (in the field of psychic life) which is transmitted, everything that comes with birth and is involved in the constitution of the body—hence, above all, the instincts (*Triebe*) rooted in the bodily organism."[2]

These instincts, rooted in the physical organism, are on the one hand the death-instinct, which is *by nature destructive*, and on the other hand Eros or libido, the one *constructive* force in man. For Freud the basis of psychic life, or the "id," is nothing but *unconscious and unorganized libido;* it contains the impulses and desires which are not accepted in conscious life or which have been expelled from it (repressed). This area of psychic life, as is universally recognized, is obviously "libidinous" in nature.

Freud presents the "ego"—which contains particularly the functions of conscious knowledge—as a simple "part" of the "id." The idea that the "ego" is that part of the "id" which has been modified by contact with, and under the influence of, the external world

[1] See, for example, the introduction to the fourth edition of his *"Three Essays on the Theory of Sexuality," Gesammelte Werke*, V, p. 32: "In dem Bedürfnis nach volltönenden Schlagworten ist man soweit gegangen von dem 'Pansexualismus' der Psychoanalyse zu reden und ihr den unsinnigen Vorwurf zu machen, sie erkläre 'alles' aus der Sexualität." The term "pansexualism" comes from Bleuler.

[2] See Freud's last work in the *"Nachlass," Gesammelte Werke*, XVII, pp. 67–68.

hardly needs to be proved, according to Freud.[1] Knowledge, and the conscious activity of the human mind, are simply a "buffer" between blind instinct and external reality. Without this "buffer" the "id," in its urge towards satisfaction, would be shattered against reality. This is the reason why life raises up the conscious "ego" to make contact with the external world.

The "ego" watches over the transition from instinct to act; it interposes thought-activity as a sort of suspension bridge between need and action. Thus *reality* is the supreme law of the conscious ego (principle of reality). This law is no longer, therefore, that of pleasure, as it was for the "id." Nevertheless, the whole mechanism is no more than an instrument in the service of the "id"— "*zum Heil des Es*," as Freud says—of which the "ego" is fundamentally "a part."[2]

Freud's ideas on the intellectual functions in man are typical of the superficial way in which he gets rid of certain essential mental activities. It is almost inconceivable that Freud could simply reduce the activity of judgment to the level of pure libido and the death-instinct, when one considers the profound analysis and examination which its complex, specific nature has received from the world's greatest philosophers.[3]

In his study of negation Freud writes: "The study of the

[1] Cf. "*Neue Folge der Vorlesungen zur Einführung in die Psychoanalyse*," *Gesammelte Werke*, XV, pp. 82–83. "Die Auffassung bedarf kaum einer Rechtfertigung, dass das *Ich* jener Teil des Es ist, der durch die Nähe und den Einfluss der Aussenwelt modifiziert wurde, zur Reizaufnahme und zum Reizschutz eingerichtet . . . Das *Ich* ist doch nur ein Stück vom *Es*, ein durch die Nähe der gefahrdrohenden Aussenwelt zweckmässig verändertes Stück. In dynamischer Hinsicht ist es schwach, *seine Energien hat es dem Es entlehnt*." (My italics.) Groddeck expresses himself still more forcibly when he says "dass das was wir unser *Ich* heissen, sich im Leben wesentlich passiv verhält, dass wir . . . 'gelebt' werden von unbekannten, unbeherrschbaren Mächten" (i.e., the id). Cf. *Gesammelte Werke*, XIII, p. 251.

[2] *Ibid.*; cf. also "*Das Ich und das Es*," *Gesammelte Werke*, XIII.

[3] The real philosophical problems about cognitive functions in man—as examined, for instance, by Kant—seem not to have been fully understood by most psychoanalysts. One is astonished to see that even Franz Alexander could write in an excellent recent book: "Psychoanalysis has deflated the Kantian categories by explaining them as products of the adjustment to the physical environment." The author seems to reduce the whole problem to a question of logic. This certainly does not apply to the "*Kritik der reinen Vernunft*." See Franz Alexander, *Fundamentals of Psychoanalysis* (New York, Norton, 1948), p. 17.

judgment leads us for perhaps the first time to consider *the growth of an intellectual function from the play of primary instinctive impulses*. The judgment is the useful later development of what is originally admitted into or expelled from the ego, and realized according to the pleasure principle. The polarity in the faculty of judgment seems to correspond to the opposition between the two groups of instincts which we have accepted as existing: affirmation, as a substitute for union, belongs to Eros; negation, the result of expulsion, belongs to the destructive instinct."[1]

It is quite true that dynamic forces such as love and hate exert a powerful influence on the faculty of judgment and on the whole of man's cognitive life. Freud is quite right to insist on this. What is so astonishing is to find him asserting, on the basis of this *influence* of dynamic forces on some branch of human activity, *that the activity itself is nothing but the manifestation of this dynamism, i.e. of libido*. The passage from Freud quoted above mentions, in fact, "the growth of an intellectual function (the judgment) from the play of primary instinctive impulses."

Thus the "ego" is looked upon as a "part" which has evolved from the "id" and which has no energy of its own; and its most complex activities, such as the faculty of judgment, take their "birth" from the libido. This idea of the ego has, however, undergone a very important development in the psychoanalytical system. Both in therapy and in the theoretical system itself the ego has come to occupy an increasingly important place. This phase in the evolution of the system began in the twenties, but its foundations were laid in one of Ferenczi's most important essays, published in 1913: *Entwicklungsstufen des Wirklichkeitssinnes*.[2] The works of Franz Alexander, amongst others, have made a notable contribution to this development.[3]

According to psychoanalysis, the third sector of the human

[1] Cf. Freud, *"Die Verneinung," Gesammelte Werke*, XIV, p. 15. (My italics.) There is another example of the superficial way in which Freud treats the conscious, cognitive functions of the ego in *"Das Ich und das Es," Gesammelte Werke*, XIII, p. 246–249.

[2] This essay was first published in the *Internationale Zeitschrift für ärztliche Psychoanalyse*, 1913, I, pp. 124–138.

[3] See his *Psychoanalyse der Gesamtpersonlichkeit*. Neun Vorlesungen über die Anwendung von Freuds Ichtheorie auf die Neurosenlehre (Wien, Internationaler Psychoanalytischer Verlag, 1927). English translation: *The*

personality, i.e. the *super-ego* (*Über-Ich*), including the higher
moral and cultural human activities, comes into existence and
develops from the Oedipus complex. In this way, the libido is
equally responsible for bringing into existence the so-called
"higher" levels of human psychic life.

As this part of Freud's doctrine is highly important, we shall
quote a few relevant passages: "The broad general outcome of
the sexual phase governed by the Oedipus complex may, therefore, be taken to be the forming of a precipitate in the ego. . . .
This modification of the ego retains its special position; it stands
in contrast to the other constituents of the ego in the form of an
ego-ideal or a super-ego."[1] This passage shows, in a few words,
the obvious sexual origin of the *super-ego*, which in its turn is
the source of man's higher cultural achievements.

As regards this higher cultural activity, Freud begins with the
view that everything belonging to the field of mythology, poetry,
and art is a "substitute satisfaction for repressed desires which
are alive in the soul of everyone from childhood." He goes on:
"But then it became clear that a third and very important part
of psychic activity—i.e., that which has created the great institutions of religion, law, morality and all forms of public life—aims
fundamentally to enable the individual to overcome his Oedipus
complex and *transfer his libido* from infantile to social relationships—the only ones ultimately worth keeping."[2]

The English psychoanalyst Ernest Jones, an orthodox exponent
of Freud's ideas, expresses this even more clearly when he writes:
"The shift from the original sexual object to a secondary social
object is not only a substitution of the one for the other, but
rather a canalization of the primitive sexual energy in a new direction. To state it exactly, one should speak about *displacement*
and not about substitution or *replacement*."[3]

Psychoanalysis of the Total Personality (Nervous and Mental Disease Monographs, No. 52, New York, 1929).

[1] *"Das Ich und das Es," Gesammelte Werke*, XIII, p. 262 ("precipitate"
= Niederschlag).

[2] Cf. Freud. *"Kurzer Abriss der Psychoanalyse," Gesammelte Werke*,
XIII, pp. 425–426 (our italics).

[3] E. Jones, *Theory and Practice of Psychoanalysis*. The quotation is

In the more specialized domain of artistic activity and sensitiveness to the beautiful, Freud states: "There is to my mind no doubt that the concept of 'beautiful' has its roots in sexual excitation and that its original meaning was 'sexually stimulating.' It can, however, be diverted ('sublimated') in the direction of art, if its interest can be shifted away from the genitals to the shape of the body as a whole. . . . This is related to the fact that we never regard the genitals themselves, which produce the strongest sexual excitation, as really 'beautiful.' "[1] Thus it appears that the activities of the *ego* and the *super-ego,* as well as of the unconscious layers of the "id," are rooted in the libido as the only constructive force in the human personality.

(2) SUBLIMATION

Freud gives the name of *sublimation* to the process by which sexual energy, or libido, is transformed into "higher" spiritual or cultural activity. His doctrine, however, does not make clear the actual nature of this process; but since the significance of Freud's conception of man and his whole philosophy of culture depend partly on the nature of this process, we must examine it more closely.

The term "sublimation" covers two essentially different ideas:

1. The first of these is to some extent based on known facts that have been objectively established. There are well-known cases, for example, of children with sadistic tendencies experiencing what may be called sexual feelings on hearing or seeing someone being beaten. A child of this kind may develop a great liking for all the details of stories about wars and battles, and later make an intensive study of history, particularly military history. He may acquire an astonishing capacity for this branch of study. In this case the individual's *inclination* for *certain specialized studies* is probably due to sexual tendencies which have *directed his attention towards* the higher reaches of his subject.

---

made from the French translation of Jones' work by Jankélévitch (Paris, Payot, 1925); cf. p. 768.

[1] Cf. Freud, *"Drei Abhandlungen Zur Sexualtheorie," Gesammelte Werke,* V, p. 55, note 1.

Similarly, it happens that some people (by what is on the whole an unconscious transposition) express sexual impressions or imaginings in drawing or painting. The sexual theme can become an obsession, and be represented endlessly, with tireless effort and perseverance, in a thousand different forms. In this way may be born great artistic skill whose starting-point and dynamic force seem to derive from sexual tendencies or complexes.

Facts of this kind can be interpreted in different ways. It may be said that a tendency which is sexual in nature simply causes an interest in certain activities and acts as a stimulant to a certain kind of activity. These activities, which are found interesting and so practised frequently, thus reach a high level of development. Thus any tendency or motive—greed, for example—can become the source of a more intensive practice of activities which satisfy this tendency.

Our own opinion is that sexuality, like the desire to prove one's worth, secretly nourishes many different kinds of human activity. This is not the psychoanalytical interpretation of this process, however, when it talks about "sublimation"; for this term always implies that *the sexual need itself is manifested and released in the "higher"* activity which it has called into being. It is to the extent that sexual energy finds a *way of escape* in an interest in military history or drawing that there is any question of "sublimation" of the libido.

The interpretation of artistic or intellectual activity contained in the examples quoted above involves all sorts of immediate theoretical implications which at the present moment are not by any means proved. It is assumed, in the first place, that a given sexual tendency can be looked on as a potential of so much energy, and preserves its activating power as long as it does not give rise to any particular activity. This conception of psychic energy lies behind all Freud's explanations of the effects of repressing any tendency. The unsatisfied tendency is simply so much energy, which remains active until it is released, either by way of an omission, or a dream, or a sublimated act. One is then asked to believe that this potential energy can be released *through activities of an utterly different nature.*

Let us briefly examine what modern psychology allows us to

say about the transformation and abreaction of a given need into an activity of a different nature.

Certain pathological facts seem at first sight to favour the idea of such a transformation. It has been established, for instance, that certain forms of behaviour which seem at first sight to have no connection with the satisfaction of sexual need must nevertheless be considered perverted or pathological manifestations of this need. It is in this way that the sexual fetichist is able to gratify his sexual instinct by collecting women's shoes and the like. It should be observed, however, that in these pathological cases we are concerned with a perversion of *the need itself*. The need does not first show itself in a desire for a normal sexual object, to be converted later into a different kind of activity (collecting shoes). The sexual need, as it appears at any given moment, is directed immediately towards the activity mentioned. One is not therefore witnessing, in this case, a transformation or conversion of the energy implied in the manifestation of a need. Only a study of the origin of the perversion itself could give us any information as to whether there had been any transformation of normal sexual energy in the past.

In the field of objective psychology there are results from several branches of research which can help us to elucidate our problem. It has been established by experiment that certain kinds of activity can provide a substitute satisfaction of needs originally orientated towards other kinds of activity.[1] These experiments prove only that the psychic tension created by one kind of activity can disappear when the subject finds satisfaction in a field of activity that is connected with the one in which he was originally involved. This satisfaction compensates for the frustration that was felt when the first kind of activity failed to achieve the required object. It is in this way that the substitute satisfaction is born. But this fact does not prove that a *certain kind of energy can be discharged* by releasing another kind of activity.

[1] Cf. K. Lissner, *"Die Entspannung von Bedürfnissen durch Ersatzhandlungen,"* Psychologische Forschung, 1938, XVIII, pp. 218–250; W. Mahler, *"Ersatzhandlungen verschiedenen Realitäts-grades,"* Psychologische Forschung, 1938, XVIII, pp. 27–89; M. Ovsiankina, *"Die Wiederaufnahme unterbrochener Handlungen,"* Psychologische Forschung, 1928, XI, pp. 302–379.

It is the state of tension in general, created by an activity already at work, that disappears.

The problem of the "displacement" of energy from one activity to another has been more directly studied experimentally by Neal Miller in his recent experiments at Yale University. He shows that in rats a certain need—hunger, for instance—to a certain extent *stimulates* another kind of activity—drinking—when the need for food cannot be satisfied.[1] The need for food, therefore, is to a certain extent "transformed" into the stimulation of another activity. Or, more exactly, the two needs are comparable as functions. Miller's experiments, which have been carried out very ingeniously and with the utmost care, are the most direct attack on the problem of the transformation or displacement of the energy of a need which have yet been made. But, as the author himself has shown, the theoretical explanation of these facts can just as easily be conceived in terms of conditioning (according to the "generalization" of stimuli) as in terms of psychoanalytical theory ("displacement"). But it has not yet been established to what extent experiments of this kind can be of assistance in solving the problems of sublimation.

More relevant to these problems—though not so well substantiated—are the facts concerning the stimulation of appetite arising from unsatisfied sexual needs. Saul describes particularly the case of a young woman who felt a very strong desire for incredible quantities of delicacies whenever she suffered from emotional or erotic frustration.[2] We too have come across a boy in whom the longing for tenderness and affection seemed in moments of frustration or loneliness to seek compensation in greediness. We are inclined to think, on the basis of several pieces of evidence of this kind, that such facts are by no means exceptional. But they seem susceptible of a more satisfactory explanation than that of sublimation in the strict sense of the word. The vague sense of

[1] Cf. Neal Miller, "Theory and Experiment Relating Psychoanalytic Displacement to Stimulus-response Generalization," *The Journal of Abnormal and Social Psychology*, 1948, XLIII, pp. 155–178.

[2] L. J. Saul, "Physiological Effects of Emotional Tension," in *Personality and the Behavior Disorders*, ed. J. McV. Hunt (New York, The Ronald Press, 1944), p. 273; and J. H. Coriat, "Sex and Hunger," in *Psychological Review*, 1921, VIII, pp. 375–381.

unrest which accompanies erotic need—as it does other psycho-physical needs—seems able to be calmed as well by any kind of sensual satisfaction (such as eating sweets) as by a general activity of the organism. If this is so, it is not a case of a certain *specific* energy being converted into another activity but simply a case of a *general state of organic tension*—such as accompanies any psychic need—being relaxed by any kind of organic satisfaction or activity. We shall be returning to this point shortly.

The problem as posed by the American zoologist Kinsey is still more closely related to this whole question of sexual sublimation.[1] He too, discussing the problem of man's sexual behaviour in terms of zoology, in which he specializes, raises the question whether any sublimation of the sexual instinct is possible. Kinsey asks whether the individual can transform his sexual energy into "higher" forms of activity such as art, literature, science and all the other accomplishments that have a social value.

Kinsey is of the opinion that the idea of sublimation is considerably older than Freudism: he considers that it is to be found in religion and asceticism, particularly in Christian asceticism. This idea, however, does not seem to us to be quite tenable. Christian *ascesis*, as regards sexuality, does not depend on the possibility of a *transformation* of sexual energy into higher forms of activity. The reason for certain kinds of sexual abstinence recommended in the books of the New Testament is a good deal simpler. It is directly bound up with the cardinal notion of *mortification*, which does not imply the idea of a possible conversion of lower into higher, but something which is the exact opposite of this. According to Christian asceticism, there are some things in man which must "die" to make way for the action of other "dynamic forces"—grace and divine inspiration. These have no connection with the former things. Moreover, the counsels of asceticism merely imply that sexual relationships *direct man's interest* and preoccupation along certain lines which the Scriptures consider of secondary importance. This is what St. Paul means when he says that a married woman thinks how to please

[1] Cf. A. C. Kinsey, W. B. Pomeroy and C. E. Martin, *Sexual Behavior in the Human Male* (Philadelphia and London, W. B. Saunders Company, 1948), pp. 205–213.

her husband, while she who is unmarried thinks rather of pleasing God. It would therefore be a mistake, in our opinion, to imagine that Christian asceticism is inspired by such notions as sublimation, in the strict sense of the word. It is simply adding to the confusion which already surrounds this word, to see in it an expression of the fact that a certain mastery over the instincts can be favourable to the growth of other forms of activity. It is this meaning of the word, however, which has become current in certain circles: it is looked upon simply as a mechanism by which man manages to master his instinctive impulses by busying himself with things which are socially more acceptable. The complex activity which produced this development in man is not clarified in the slightest degree by giving it the courtesy-title of "sublimation."

Authors like Kinsey are opposed to the idea of sublimation because they believe that from the zoological point of view sexual energy can find a simpler and much healthier abreaction through direct forms of "sexual outlet." On the other hand, authors who look at human behaviour from the opposite point of view, and are primarily interested in the spiritual aspect of human accomplishment, are equally hostile to the concept of sublimation because they find it hard to accept the idea that artistic, scientific and other forms of activity are only outlets for the release of sexual energy.

Thus it is clear why the notion of sublimation is received with disfavour by authors of these two extreme schools of thought. Nevertheless, only positive research can supply us with a solution of the problem whether there can be any transference or "displacement" of sexual energy.

Kinsey's way of dealing with this problem of sexual sublimation is not, however, of a kind to elucidate the problem. Consider, for instance, the spirit in which he has presented and examined the problem.

Kinsey chooses a group of a hundred and seventy-nine men, all under thirty-five years of age, who show very little sign of sexual activity. It is, of course, amongst young men who show a level of sexual activity below the normal that the problem whether unspent sexual energy manages to transform itself into the stimulation of other kinds of activity must be examined.

Kinsey first proceeds to sort out the members of his group. In it are contained, he says, several different categories of individuals physically or mentally deficient, and for these the problem of sublimation does not arise; people with no sexuality to sublimate, because they feel few sexual impulses and on the whole desire very little activity. The group also contains a category of men whom Kinsey describes as "shy" or "inhibited," who "are afraid" of socially prohibited forms of sexual behaviour. Kinsey found amongst these people paranoiac cases, cases of attempted suicide, etc. But this category also includes normal people of a highly educated type and even a number of psychologists and psychiatrists. These are the people whose field of activity one would have expected Kinsey to examine—not that we believe that such an examination could have led to positive results as regards sublimation, but it is the obvious group to look to for an answer to the problem as the author presents it. But he avoids the problem entirely, and this, quite clearly, as a result of his prejudices as a zoologist. His opinion is quite simply that all these people harbour all kinds of "prejudice" in the matter of sexual behaviour—prejudices which to the zoologist seem incomprehensible. What he means is that these perfectly normal intellectuals observe certain moral laws of sexual behaviour. This is sufficient to brand them, from the zoologist's point of view, as "inhibited" animals. On the assumption of such pathological inhibitions, any further examination is considered superfluous. Kinsey contents himself with a few remarks which are worth quoting:

If they are better-educated persons, and especially if they have some command of psychology, these inhibited persons rationalize more adroitly, admit that masturbation does no physical harm, but reason that it is bad to continue a habit that may subsequently make one unfit for normal marital relations, decide that pre-marital intercourse similarly unfits one for making satisfactory sexual adjustments in marriage, that the homosexual is a biologic abnormality, and that extra-marital intercourse inevitably destroys homes. Even among scientifically trained persons, these propositions are offered as excuses for their sexual inactivity. Of 58 male psychologists who have contributed histories to the present study, 57 have defended one or more of these theses, in spite of the fact that no one of these conclusions has ever been justified by objective data that would satisfy scientists in any field that did not have a moral (traditional) implication. Out of 74 male psychiatrists who have contributed, 70 defend one or more of these same prejudices. These are all rationalizations, *clutched at in support of a sexual suppression that is too often mistaken for sublimation.*[1]

Kinsey therefore considers all moral laws governing the sexual behaviour of these psychologists and psychiatrists as so many *excuses for the inactivity* of people sexually *inhibited.* There was a time when people used to look for excuses for "activity," not "inactivity," in this field!

We are afraid that the problem of human sexuality cannot be understood from this "zoological" point of view.

Other branches of research and other schemes of thought, such as those presented by Taylor and Levey, are equally opposed to the idea of "sublimation."[2]

We can formulate as follows the conclusions arrived at by our consideration of the studies made in this domain. On the one hand, the exact mechanism whereby, in certain cases, sexuality manifests itself in artistic or similar activities is not yet sufficiently clear.[3] On the other hand, the possibility of sublimation in the sense of a "transformation" of the *sexual energy itself* into activities of another order remains a hypothesis which is not sufficiently confirmed by the facts.

It is common human knowledge, of course, that a great utilization of energy in one field can reduce the need for activity in

[1] Cf. Kinsey, *op. cit.*, p. 211. (My italics.)

[2] Cf. H. B. Levey, "A Theory Concerning Free Creation in the Inventive Arts," *Psychiatry* (Baltimore, W. A. W. Psychiatric Foundation), 1940, III, pp. 229–293. W. S. Taylor, "A Critique of Sublimation in Males: A Study of Forty Superior Single Men," *Genetic Psychology Monographs*, 1923, XIII, No. 1.

[3] See particularly the descriptions by Freud, "*Eine Kindheitserinnerung des Leonardo da Vinci*," *Gesammelte Werke*, VIII, pp. 128–211; and C. Baudouin, *Etudes de Psychanalyse* (Paris and Neuchâtel, 1922); *Psychanalyse de l'Art* (Paris, Alcan, 1929). The facts described in these books could be explained in various ways. None could claim at the moment to be more than a hypothesis.

others. Contrariwise, as we have shown, a given need can find release through satisfaction experienced in an adjacent field of activity. The need for sex can also direct a person's interest towards a special field, and this leads to higher accomplishments in this domain. Each of these processes can ultimately account for certain phenomena known as "sublimation," but there is not one which proves that *a certain kind of psychic energy* can be "transformed" or "displaced" and manifest itself *as such* in other forms of activity. A still deeper question which has not been solved lies at the very root of the problem: it is the question of what exactly is meant by the vague concept, "sexual energy," and how psychic energy in general is to be conceived.

There is no objection in principle, or philosophically, to the idea of sublimation which we have been discussing. We must simply consider it as a working hypothesis which remains to be confirmed by research. Personally, we are convinced that the facts explained in psychoanalysis by the process of sublimation are to be explained by different psychological mechanisms already more or less known.

Another process which, in our opinion, can play an important part in this matter is that of *emotional transference*. The following example will help to show how.

We have had occasion to study in detail the case of a young man who showed a very strong liking for yellow. He had also, from his earliest years, made a special study of the yellow races. Analysis of this case revealed that the boy was haunted by yellow for reasons which had a sexual origin. In the first years of his life anything that was yellow had gradually become an object of special liking for him. When the news of the war in the East drew his attention to the yellow races he took a special delight in reading about these people. The pleasure experienced from contact with his first sexual "object" had surrounded the colour yellow with a special attraction for him. This pleasure and this attraction had gradually extended to all objects having the characteristic of yellow.

In the same way, a person's name can have a special attraction for someone without his knowing why, because a pleasant experience is connected with somebody of the same name; or certain characteristics of a particular place can exercise a fascination over us because of their being part of a pleasurable experience; and the same characteristics, discovered elsewhere, can make us feel very favourably disposed towards the object or the person possessing them. This is the process by which the attraction or the pleasure which has been experienced overflows on to characteristics which have happened to be associated with it, and it is known as *emotional transference.*[1] It accounts for many cases when we seem to take a spontaneous liking or dislike for something.

In the light of these facts we are inclined to consider the activity of the boy who studies the history of the yellow races not as a sublimation of his sexual instinct but simply as the effect of an emotional transference. Anything yellow has a certain attraction for him, and the boy likes to be occupied with things that please him; thus he becomes very competent in the field to which his interest leads him. But it is difficult to see in what way this study can be described as a release of sexual energy, and difficult to see what exactly this could mean. The whole phenomenon is sufficiently explained if it is admitted that the sexual attraction of his first "libidinal object" had made everything yellow attractive to him, and that his intellectual curiosity—which is a different thing entirely from the libido—prefers what is most pleasing. Similar sexual associations made the boy especially fond of rain and, contrariwise, horrified of anything round. He took care not to live amongst or occupy himself with round shapes, just as he loved playing with yellow things and watching the rain. The process of emotional transference is sufficient to account for these phenomena; it could in our opinion explain equally well many facts of so-called artistic or literary sublimation. (Compare the examples given on page 45.)

What is known as sublimation is therefore neither a unique process nor a specific mechanism. We have mentioned in the course of this discussion several processes which could ultimately

[1] The reader will note the difference between the meaning of the expression "emotional transference" as employed here and in experimental psychology in general, compared with the meaning it has been given in psychoanalysis. As it is used here, "emotional transference" is a form of emotional *conditioning*.

explain many of the facts described as cases of sublimation. Three of these processes seem to us particularly important—firstly, emotional transference; secondly, the release, which comes through any kind of activity or satisfaction, of the diffused tension created by any kind of need (including therefore the erotic or sexual need); thirdly, the atrophy of certain forms of need through the canalizing of their activity into other directions.

The root of the problem lies in the psychoanalytical conception of the conversion of sexual energy. Freud is of the opinion that an unsatisfied need necessarily persists in the form of a fixed potential of energy which has to find an outlet. We shall see that it is possible to take quite a different view of the development of some dynamisms at least, in the evolution of the human personality. Certain tendencies atrophy as the result of a new orientation, through which man brings into existence other kinds of needs and satisfies them. It is in the light of such a theory of the development of personality that one part of the problem of sublimation will find a positive solution (Chapter IV).

2. The word *sublimation* has, however, a second meaning not always clearly distinguished from the previous meaning, although it is very different. There are a number of passages in Freud showing that he often considers the *"higher" psychic activities, as such, to be brought into being* through sexual activity, and *to be nothing but disguised manifestations of this activity*. In this case it is no longer a question of the *activation* or *stimulation* of a *pre-existing psychic function* by a transformation or "displacement" of sexual energy; here the psychic activity itself is nothing but the creation of, or a form of, the libido. The "higher" activity is a way of escape *created* by the libido. In this case the "higher" activity is ultimately of the same nature as the libido itself.

The logical conclusion from this idea is that all man's higher psychic activity is a *substitute* for sexual libido. Freud *did not explicitly* push his ideas to such extreme limits, however. We find in his writings statements which can hardly be interpreted in any other sense than this, along with repeated protestations when his opponents attribute this theory to him in its explicit form. When

Freud makes these protests he prefers to adopt a vague intermediary position, whose exact meaning is difficult to divine.

3. A few quotations will show that both these ideas of sublimation are in fact to be met with in Freud. The first idea is clearly formulated in his well-known work, *Leonardo da Vinci*. In that book he expresses himself as follows: "Observation of daily life shows us that most persons have the capacity to direct a very tangible part of their sexual motive-powers to their professional or business activities. The sexual impulse is particularly suited to yield such contributions because it is endowed with the capacity of sublimation, i.e. it has the power to exchange its nearest aim for others of higher value which are not sexual."[1]

To this statement we can reply briefly as follows. It is quite clear that "the common observation" of which Freud here speaks is hardly sufficient to determine the existence and the conditions of this important process. We believe, as we have already suggested, that the facts of daily life, interpreted as sublimation in the first meaning of the word, form part of quite a different process from that of the transposition of one kind of energy into a different form of activity.

It is in Freud's theories on the philosophy of culture, from which we have already quoted a few passages, that we find his second idea of sublimation.[2] For a particularly clear example we should like to recall there the Freudian conception of the source of the faculty of knowledge, and more particularly of the *judgment*. According to Freud, the faculty of judgment *is born* through the play of primary instincts.[3]

After what has been already said, we can give our own opinion on this matter quite briefly. The sex-instinct is, quite simply, utterly different in nature from the functions of knowledge. It is to be a dupe of verbal analogies to make of the union of the two concepts in an affirmative judgment a process of the same

[1] Cf. Freud: *"Eine Kindheitserinnerung des Leonardo da Vinci,"* Gesammelte Werke, VIII, p. 145.

[2] See particularly p. 44; see also the Freudian interpretation of the human impulse towards progress, p. 177.

[3] See quotation *supra*, p. 43.

nature as the union of love. The parallel drawn between negative judgment and the instinct for destruction is open to the same criticism. Freud was never able to account for the particularity involved in an act of judgment by his appeal to instinctive attraction and union. Problems of a philosophic nature are involved here, problems concerning the very nature and character and the fundamental implications of certain mental activities. It will suffice to recall Kant's penetrating analysis of the implications of man's cognitive activity, to show that the problem of judgment is not to be solved by reference to emotional attraction and repulsion.

If one considers the problem *genetically*, there is no more reason for saying that the faculties of knowledge and judgment come from the libido. In this matter Freud managed, on the basis of vague analogies with sexual union and repulsion, to develop theories which amaze the psychologist as much as they do the philosopher. In any case, the assumption that the libido develops genetically into higher psychic functions means that *active higher potentialities of development are given;* in which case, it is quite impossible to trace these potentialities back to the libido.

(3) THE THEORY OF INSTINCTS: THE SEXUAL INSTINCT, THE EGO-
    INSTINCT AND THE DESTRUCTIVE INSTINCT

Besides the sex-instinct (*Sexualtriebe*), Freud originally kept a place for "all those instinct-directions—not better known to us—which can be distinguished from the sexual instincts."[1]

He maintained that these instinctive forces make up the "ego-instinct" (*Ich-triebe*), which is opposed to the sexual libido. Freud's ideas about this ego-instinct changed, however, and he eventually came to consider it as deriving from the same origin as the sex-instinct. In the end he maintained in fact that it was a manifestation of *narcissism*.

When Adler showed that the will to power was the central dynamic force in psychic life, Freud devoted more attention to the *ego-instinct*. He embarked on an elaboration of his own system in the light of the new facts, clearly trying to integrate

---

[1] "Alle jene von uns nicht näher gekannten Triebrichtungen die sich von den . . . Sexualtrieben abscheiden lassen." Cf. *"Jenseits des Lustprinzips,"* *Gesammelte Werke,* XIII, p. 66.

Adler's ideas into the scheme of his own libido-theory. But he simply joined up the *ego-instinct* with the sex-instinct, as Adler had connected it with the will to power. Narcissism, i.e. the libido as directed towards its own ego, served as go-between. Thus we find him talking about *"narzissistischen Selbsterhaltungstriebe,"* which "therefore had now to be reckoned among the libidinous sexual instincts. The contrast between *egoistic* and *sexual instincts* was now converted into one between *egoistic* and *object-instincts, both libidinous in nature."*[1]

It will suffice to observe here that the reduction of the human "will to self-preservation" (which we shall describe later) to narcissism and sexuality seems quite unfounded. There are in Freud's work several remarks directed against Adler's theory, which seems to show that Freud had tried desperately to integrate Adler's conceptions into his own system, but without very happy results.[2]

Having integrated the ego-instinct into the libido, Freud, in his "philosophic view" of man, developed a new antithesis. This time he recognizes the existence of another instinct besides the *constructive* sex-instinct: an instinct of destruction, or *death-instinct*.[3] He says that in addition to the constructive powers which one can see in nature and in life, a powerful destructive force can also be seen at work everywhere—i.e., a fatal evolution towards death and inertia. This force manifests itself in psychic life in the form of a *destructive instinct* which is directed in the first place against the ego itself but which at the same time manifests itself in the form of *destructive aggressiveness* towards others.

Freud's descriptions of the death-instinct belong to the most "speculative" part of his work, and the theory was received very

---

[1] Cf. *"Jenseits des Lustprinzips"* (1920), *Gesammelte Werke*, VIII, p. 66, note 1; ("which are both by nature libidinous"—my italics). Freud later (1932) repeats the same thing in his *"Neue Folge"*: "Unserer Libido-theorie lag zunächst der Gegensatz von Ichtrieben und Sexualtrieben zu Grunde. Als wir dann später begannen das Ich selbst näher zu studieren und den Gesichtspunkt des Narzismus erfassten, verlor diese Unterscheidung selbst ihren Boden." Cf. *Gesammelte Werke*, XV, p. 109.

[2] Cf., for example, *"Neue Folge der Vorlesungen," Gesammelte Werke*, XV, pp. 71–72. Also *"Zur Einführung des Narzismus," Gesammelte Werke*, X, pp. 159–167; and *"Zur Geschichte der Psychoanalystischen Bewegung," Gesammelte Werke*, X, pp. 91 et seq.

[3] Cf. *"Jenseits des Lustprinzips"* (1920).

sceptically even by psychoanalysts, whose belief in him was otherwise unbounded. It is worth remembering, too, that Freud himself describes his doctrine of instincts as the *mythological part
of his system.*

Subsequently Freud came to consider many important phenomena as manifestations of this self-destructive instinct. It lies,
for instance, behind the resistance to being cured which often
appears during the treatment of neurotics. The desire for punishment and penitence and the "unconscious" feeling of guilt come
from the same source;[1] whilst destructive aggressiveness towards
others is shown, for example, in war.

In short, besides a constructive force, an impulse towards
destruction is to be found at work in man. The only constructive
force in life is Eros—libido or the sex-instinct—in the Freudian
meaning of the word. Whatever in culture or individual life has
anything more than a purely sexual aim is nothing but this same
sex-instinct "sublimated," as a repressed force, into higher forms.
And "the restless striving towards further perfection which may
be observed in a minority of human beings is easily explicable as
the result of that repression of instinct upon which what is most
valuable in human culture is built."[2]

Such is the psychoanalytical view of man and human culture.
The three sectors of the human personality, the "id," the "ego,"
and the "super-ego" all come from the libido; the ego-instinct,
too, is libidinous; so that all man's constructive activity comes from
the libido. The only thing which cannot be reduced to Eros is
the destructive instinct. Sublimation is the process whereby the
libido is converted into specifically human activities.

Such, in its main outlines, is the Freudian conception of man,
which was not built up in a strictly methodical fashion on the
basis of facts, but, on the contrary, frequently supplied the frame
of reference for the interpretation of the facts out of their true
perspective. This pansexualist scheme of interpretation caused the
most distinguished of Freud's followers—Jung and Adler—to break
with psychoanalysis. This theory of human personality and cul-

[1] See particularly Freud, "*Neue Folge der Vorlesungen zur Einführung
in die Psychoanalyse,*" *Gesammelte Werke,* XV, pp. 115–117.
[2] Cf. "*Jenseits des Lustprinzips,*" *Gesammelte Werke,* XIII, p. 44.

ture is the part of psychoanalysis which seems to us least acceptable, either as a *Weltanschauung* (or *philosophy*) or as a *scientific
theory.*

We do not mean, however, that the theory has not shed light
on several highly suggestive *aspects* of personality and culture.
It will be necessary to take these new, if partial, views into account
in any general theory of man and his cultural development. We
shall be able to show later, with the fullest documentary evidence,
that the presence of sexual elements must certainly be recognized
in the most elevated human activities. This will nevertheless receive
a totally different explanation from that of simply reducing such
activities to the libido.

3. The Body of Facts in Psychoanalysis

The most important element in psychoanalysis is its rich body
of facts concerning the content and mechanisms of psychic life,
discovered by the study of depth-psychology. These facts have
led to a considerable enrichment of our knowledge of the dynamic
factors in human behaviour.

The person to whom we are indebted for what is perhaps the
most important of these discoveries is the Viennese doctor Breuer,
the precursor of psychoanalysis: it concerns the fact that neurotic
symptoms, and all kinds of abnormal conduct which seem at first
sight to be entirely lacking in coherence and sense, can have a
significant content, i.e. a "meaning." This meaning is to be found
in the connection between the symptoms and an emotional or traumatic event in the patient's past life. We have already mentioned
the story of Breuer's woman patient and the meaning of her
hydrophobia.

This discovery of a connection between symptoms and the
subject's personal history has shed considerable light on a number
of facts about more or less abnormal forms of human behaviour
which formerly seemed meaningless and incomprehensible.

Similarly, the discovery of the pathogenic action exerted on
human psychic life by an *unresolved conflict* between fundamental
tendencies taking place *at an unconscious level* undoubtedly—
when expressed in these neutral terms—shed an important light

on the fundamental mechanisms of conduct and the motives behind conduct.

In addition to these fundamental insights, and others of the same kind, psychoanalysis has supplied us with a considerable body of facts drawn from the analysis of an enormous number of cases of neurosis. These facts have led to a considerable enrichment of our knowledge of human psychology. Although they have often been incorporated into schemes of reference whose foundations remain very dubious, so that it is difficult to define their exact objective significance, it is nevertheless true that many of them possess an undeniable psychological value. It is obvious that none of these facts can be ignored by a psychologist of a spiritual persuasion simply because some of the schemes of interpretation in which they are embedded are unacceptable. It is simply a case of letting the facts appear in their own light.

These new facts will certainly lead us to revise a number of elements in our "traditional" conception of psychic life. Such a revised view will form a most welcome complement to traditional psychology, which was based far too exclusively on intellectualist reflection, and which for that reason *isolated* the intellectual and spiritual level of our psychic life far too drastically from the "inferior" levels.

4. Scientific Theories and Explanations

Finally, Freudism, like any other scientific system, contains a number of ideas and theories which require closer examination before they can be accepted as firmly based on fact or rejected as unverified. There are several psychoanalytical theories which come into this category, and they amount to no more than working hypotheses whose verification varies considerably.

A great number of Freudian ideas regarding man's sexual *development* belong to this category, as may be illustrated by an example drawn from the Oedipus complex, considered *as a phase in the development of the libido.*[1]

---

[1] We are not, therefore, concerned here with the Oedipus complex as the starting-point of the psychoanalytical philosophy of culture; this belongs to the first category rather than here.

In Freud's opinion the Oedipus complex represents a stage in the development of the libido which is common to all men. But it has subsequently become clear that in the examination of this problem, as in many others, psychoanalysis failed to recognize the influence of *cultural* factors in the environment, which nevertheless play a very important part in the development of the human personality. Malinowski has shown that in certain kinds of cultural environment—he mentions especially the matriarchal society of the Trobriand Islands—the Oedipus complex does not appear in its Freudian form. Amongst these people are found relationships and complexes which both in the way they come into existence and the way they develop are utterly different from the Oedipus complex. In their society the sister takes the place of the mother and the uncle on the mother's side is more important than the father.[1]

But it is not only in cultural groups differing strongly from our own that the emotional relationships characteristic of the Oedipus complex are found to be missing. More progressive analysts like Fromm maintain that the Oedipus complex cannot be regarded as an unavoidable and universal stage of development but is dependent on particular social or family relationships; whilst Sears concludes his general survey of the factual investigations made in this field with the statement that though some authors claim to have come across the Oedipus complex there is nothing in the preference which children show for their parents to indicate any general existence of a *cross*-relationship (boy-mother, girl-father).[2]

These investigations into the Freudian hypothesis of the Oedipus complex illustrate how Freud, in his explanation of human development, took too unilateral a view of man as a being determined biologically by instinctive inner forces. The development of per-

---

[1] Cf. B. Malinowski, *La Sexualité et sa répression dans les sociétés primitives*, trs. Jankélévitch (Paris, Payot, 1923). See especially, pp. 68–74. E. Jones defended the Freudian theory against Malinowski, but to do this used psychoanalytical presuppositions rather than facts. Cf. E. Jones, "Mother-Right and the Sexual Ignorance of Savages," *International Journal of Psychoanalysis*, 1925, VI, pp. 109–130.

[2] Cf. R. R. Sears, *Survey of Objective Studies of Psychoanalytic Concepts* (Social Science Research Council, Bulletin 51, 1943).

sonality must be looked on as an interaction of inner factors and cultural factors. The cultural factor, with all its endless variety, was not emphasized sufficiently in Freud's theories; hence his many hasty generalizations.

The same criticism applies to the theory of a *castration complex*, which, according to Freud, profoundly affects the personality. It is true that it has now come to be generally recognized that signs of sexuality appear clearly in pre-genital forms (before puberty); and similarly the erotogenic[1] nature of the oral and anal zones has been confirmed. But the fear of castration (loss of the genitals) depends on particular social circumstances, and Sears concluded: "It seems probable that Freud's notions about children's attitudes toward sex were based on a small sample that was far from characteristic of contemporary American children."[2]

Freud's ideas regarding man's sexual development are not to be dismissed *a priori* on the ground that they conflict with traditional ideas on the subject. Only more exact scientific research can determine whether they will be confirmed or proved false. There are a number of facts in this field which Freud brought to light, that seem to contain an important element of truth, however much they may stand in need of further confirmation—as indeed is the case with any scientific theory.

The point at which Freud parted company most widely from proved fact was in his development of the idea of the Oedipus complex, and especially in his assertion that it lay at the root of the *super-ego*.[3] On this point Sears justly remarks: "Freud's notion of the universal Oedipus complex stands as a sharply etched grotesquerie against his otherwise informative description of sexual development."[4] This is exactly what we meant when we said earlier that Freud's philosophy of culture and view of man, based as they are on the Oedipus complex, were not developed in a strictly methodical fashion according to fact but on the contrary were outlines of a unilateral interpretation of

[1] The word "erotogenic" is used here in its Freudian sense, to mean "procuring pleasure."
[2] Sears, *ibid.*, p. 136.
[3] Cf. *supra*, p. 44.
[4] Sears, *ibid.*, p. 136.

man in which the facts themselves were considered out of their true perspective.

In the field of therapy too we find several different examples of Freudian hypotheses which have been made doubtful by more recent discoveries. In illustration of this fact we need only mention the emphasis Freud places on the discovery and deeper examination of the patient's *infantile conflicts and complexes*. As we shall see later in our discussion of psychoanalysis as a therapeutic method, this aspect of Freud's doctrine was brought into question by the psychoanalytic school of Chicago, where new methods which spent less time on a close examination into infant-life were successfully applied.[1]

More important still in this respect is the fact that recent studies and discoveries show increasingly that, generally speaking, Freud exaggerated the influence of infantile experiences on the later development of the personality.[2] According to Freud the experiences of the first five or six years prove ultimately to have a *determining* influence on the subsequent development of the personality and its conflicts, the later forms of the development of the libido being already implied in the events of the first years of life. This theory of the development of the personality excludes in effect any influence of a spiritual or autonomous kind on man. What can be affirmed on the basis of *facts* about the "determinants" of personality is considerably less, however, than the Freudian theory admits.[3]

What relationship do we find between this part of psychoanalytical doctrine (its scientific hypotheses and theories) and the Freudian *Weltanschauung* or concept of man? And as regards the

[1] Cf. Franz Alexander and Thomas French, *Psychoanalytic Therapy, Principles and Application* (New York, The Ronald Press, 1946). The Freudian position on this point is similarly questioned by Karen Horney, *New Ways in Psychoanalysis* (New York, Norton, 1939), p. 9. (Fuller information on this subject will be found in Chapter II, cf., *infra*, p. 85.)

[2] See particularly the survey of part of the literature on this subject by H. Orlansky, "Infant Care and Personality," *Psychological Bulletin*, 1949, XLVI, pp. 1-48.

[3] Cf. particularly Margaret A. Ribble, "Infantile Experience in Relation to Personality Development," in *Personality and the Behavior Disorders*, ed. J. McV. Hunt (New York, The Ronald Press, 1944), II, p. 646: "Precise and controlled evidence as to the permanence of these early infantile experiences in human beings is not yet available from direct observation."

other side of the problem, what will be the attitude of the spiritually minded psychologist towards this part of the Freudian
doctrine?

Working hypotheses and scientific theories, in contrast to any
total conception of man, which is always to some extent or other
a philosophical matter, belong to the domain of science and must
on that account be judged from the scientific point of view only;
nevertheless it is a fact that scientific hypotheses and theories,
especially when they centre round man, are not erected on the
basis of ascertained fact alone.

A scientist's philosophic idea of man indirectly influences the
direction which his theories and hypotheses take. Thus a psychologist like Freud, for example, who takes a determinist view of
psychic development—and this is a philosophical conception, not
a scientific theory—can easily build up a theory of the *dominant*
influence of the first years of life, to explain certain facts which
he has discovered. A psychologist with a religious outlook on
life will show himself more *open* to other possible lines of explanation; he will never forget that there are other factors in the
development of personality, such as, for instance, a certain measure of autonomous self-will; and for this reason his suggested
explanation of identical new facts will be presented differently.

This influence of philosophical ideas is not felt so strongly
when the objects of research are "philosophically neutral," as in
the case of inorganic matter, for example. But when it is a question
of man's psychic life and its meaning, every psychologist has
certain philosophical ideas which *help to determine the point of
view* from which the positive data are examined and explained.
Thus we can say that many of the scientific hypotheses made by
psychoanalysis rest on preconceptions which are anything but
religious. *But only objective psychological research and the proofs
supplied by the facts themselves* can allow us to take up our position with regard to these facts on the scientific level or oblige us to
develop new theories. It would be quite unjustified, from a methodological point of view, to dismiss these hypotheses *a priori*.

Thus the problem of the relationship, for example, between
certain forms of human behaviour and the sexual instinct must
be clarified progressively on the basis of facts, and in accordance

with the development of the psychological knowledge of man in his totality. It would be unsatisfactory to adopt a less comprehensive attitude towards certain aspects of human personality because of prejudice or the influence of traditional ideas.

5. Discrimination

The three kinds of material which we have distinguished, in accordance with scientific criticism, are often mixed indiscriminately in psychoanalytical literature. The actual facts are immediately envisaged from the psychoanalytical point of view and transposed into the perspective of Freudian theory. Many a thesis which seems to the critical reader to be a dubious hypothesis is presented as an interpretation that "hardly needs any justification."

The task for the spiritually minded psychologist is to extract the valid facts and ideas and sound working hypotheses from their setting in the psychoanalytical conception of man with its "metaphysical views." Some psychologists have declared this task to be impossible, on the grounds that psychoanalysis is a closed system, so that the facts only exist in the form in which they are interpreted by psychoanalysis. We do not share this opinion; and we should now like to show, by means of two examples, what exactly the task we have mentioned involves.

Psychoanalysis made an important discovery when it showed that a child's emotional relationships may have profound repercussions on its adult life. The "mother-son" relationship can affect the later "husband and wife" relationship and the whole process of a man's adaptation to his concrete situation. The Freudian data and ideas on this subject preserve their value even when isolated from the background of the generalized Oedipus complex against which Freud placed them. We are not justified in ignoring them simply because the whole theory of this complex, and the *philosophy of culture* with which it is involved, seem to be without any serious basis in fact.

Every philosopher of a critical cast of mind, even if he has no spiritual tendencies, will seek a sounder philosophical explanation of human life than is supplied by Freudian "speculation" on the Oedipus complex. We have a great deal to learn from Freud the *psychologist*, but, to speak frankly, Freud the *philosopher* shows little critical judgment in the way he treats the problems involved. Having made this reservation we can recognize the great importance of the emotional relationship of mother and child, emphasized by Freud in his discussion of the Oedipus complex—and restrict our attention to the psychological facts involved in this relationship and their influence on later life.

We may mention another example, drawn from the field of religion. In certain cases of obsessional neurosis, certain kinds of behaviour take place which seem to be caricatures of the ritual acts of religion: this discovery of Freud's is a well-attested fact. But instead of regarding these symptoms of obsessional neurosis as deviations from normal manifestations of ritual behaviour, Freud, as a direct result of his general attitude towards the problem, developed a theory which is the direct opposite of this: he considers religious behaviour a "deviation" from the usual case of neurosis. Religious behaviour becomes an obsessional neurosis which, from being so general, has become attenuated.[1]

Then, again, psychoanalysis discovers analogies between man's relationship with God and the "child-father" emotional relationships—which, again, are firmly attested facts—but it goes on to interpret any feeling for religion as a simple outgrowth from this emotional complex, claiming thus to have brought to light the deeper *emotional basis* of the "attenuated obsessional neurosis" known as religion.[2]

The main fault here from the methodological point of view lies in interpreting analogies between two kinds of phenomena by making one of them the source of the other. It seems on the contrary more likely—as we shall show later—that the two phenomena of religious feeling and the "father-child" relationship have a *common source lying at a deeper level still*. Finally, as regards this Freudian conception of religion, we must emphasize that the explanation proceeds, so to speak, in reverse: instead of beginning with the normal and going on from that to explain the abnormal,

[1] Cf. "*Kurzer Abriss der Psychoanalyse*," *Gesammelte Werke*, XIII, p. 423.

[2] *Ibid.*, pp. 423 *et seq.* The reader will find a fuller account of Freudian ideas on religion in Freud's three publications mentioned in the Suggestions for Bibliography.

Freud follows the opposite course. This, it seems to me, is one of the most important features of certain psychopathological theories; it will be discussed at greater length in the second part of this book.

We do not wish to deny that in the religious behaviour of neurotics *their obsessional thoughts and acts are revealed with exceptional clearness,* but the above are examples of what we had in mind when we spoke of valid psychological data being embedded in interpretative systems which are not clearly proved; and it is for this reason that we have insisted so strongly upon the importance of the discrimination which as men of science, and as spiritual believers, we have always to make in studying and utilizing psychoanalysis. Let us repeat that it would not be scientific to underestimate the importance of the data furnished by psychoanalysis because of its theoretic setting; but it is equally undesirable to accept the whole system uncritically because of the valuable elements to be found in it.

It is interesting to note that Freud himself, in his moments of critical reflection, set strict limits of exactly this kind to the significance of his facts and interpretations. Thus he writes in his *Kurzer Abriss* of 1924 that there is no use denying that psychoanalysis is unable to supply a complete explanation of things. He goes on to say that if one accepts the distinction made between the conscious *ego* and the instinctive *id,* then psychoanalysis seems to be the psychology of the *id,* and for this reason can only supply *contributions* towards the final truth, which must be completed by the psychology of the *ego.*[1] Elsewhere he writes: "When psychoanalysis, which as the science of the psychic unconscious has delimited its own field of activity, is accused of being biased, this is as mistaken as such an accusation would be against chemistry."[2]

In elaborating his own doctrine, however, Freud pays little attention to such critical limitations and modifications, for, as we have seen, *without seriously examining the part played by the*

[1] Cf. *Gesammelte Werke,* XIII, p. 427.
[2] Cf. *Handwörterbuch der Sexualwissenschaften, s.v., "Psychoanalyse"* (Bonn, Marcus under Weber, 1923); reprinted in *Gesammelte Werke,* XIII, pp. 227–228.

conscious ego he considers the activity of the id the only really important thing in the whole of man's psychic life.

But Freud has made it difficult for those who wish to formulate an *objective* judgment on his doctrine. He protests again and again against unscientific explanations of his system. Thus he writes: "The objections made against psychoanalysis even in scientific works have insufficient knowledge behind them, and this seems to be the result of emotional resistances to such knowledge. Thus it is a mistake to accuse psychoanalysis of 'pansexualism' and of being derived entirely from, and reducing all psychic phenomena to, sexuality. For from the beginning psychoanalysis distinguished sexual tendencies from other tendencies which it described provisionally as 'ego-instincts.' "[1]

In view of his statements of 1920 concerning the ego-instinct which we have already quoted (p. 58), one wonders how Freud in 1923 can pretend not to reduce the whole of our psychic life to the level of sex on the mere pretext of admitting to the existence of an ego-instinct as well as a sexual instinct; especially when he had said plainly in 1920, "both *are libidinous in nature.*" And later, too, he was to maintain, in his *Neue Folge,* for example (1923), that this distinction between ego-instincts and sexual instincts had lost all basis in fact.[2]

In his essay on the *resistance to psychoanalysis*[3] he again denied having contested the existence of nonsexual interests in man; but that did not prevent him from claiming elsewhere that the libido is the only constructive force in the psyche and the source of all psychic dynamism. Perhaps the saying "All too often a clear conscience is merely the result of a bad memory" is applicable to the father of the theory that absent-mindedness comes from repression?

In certain places, it is true, Freud speaks of "*a part of the ego-instinct*" as being "libidinous,"[4] but in the development of the theory he forgets all about the *other* part.

We do not doubt that Freud was sincere when he made his

---

[1] *Ibid., Gesammelte Werke,* XIII, p. 227.

[2] Cf. *Gesammelte Werke,* XV, p. 109.

[3] "*Die Widerstände gegen die Psychoanalyse,*" *Gesammelte Werke,* XIV, p. 105.

[4] "*Jenseits des Lustprinzips,*" *Gesammelte Werke,* XIII, p. 66.

protest and set these critical limits to the significance of psycho-analytical contributions. He keeps a vague little place in his mind free for "something *else*." But this other "child of his mind" is neglected to such an extent that when it comes to distributing the parts he is left out, and Freud only remembers his existence when he is asked whether he has forgotten one of the family. The "father complex" and the emotional "bond" uniting the father to the favourite child of his mind—i.e., sex—seem to have played a rather nasty trick on the father of the Oedipus complex just when he was constructing his system!

We find ourselves here faced with a phenomenon usually en-countered in authors who try to push a new idea to extremes. In the development of their own theories they ignore everything except what they have just discovered; but when it is pointed out to them that they are therefore exaggerating, they say that they have never denied these other factors or aspects of the problem. Thus Freud too replies very circumspectly to the criticisms made against him, speaking of "die *partielle* Ableitung der Kunst, Reli-gion und sozialer Ordnung der *Mitwirkung* sexueller Treib-kräfte."[1] But he forgets the two little words we have emphasized as soon as he has no opponents to reply to. These two little addi-tions are indeed so far from being integrated into Freud's thought that the very construction of the sentence seems to suffer from them; for in point of fact one cannot make an "*Ableitung*" from a "*Mitwirkung*."

To illustrate this tendency of Freud's to push certain new ideas to extremes, even though he realizes that in so doing he is going beyond the limits of reality, we will quote a passage from *Beyond the Pleasure Principle*, the work in which Freud gave the greatest scope to his taste for "speculation," especially as regards the death-instinct. In this account he describes the death-instinct as being, in general, an impulse tending to revert to a previous state, the state of infantile pleasure. He adds that this definition is perhaps not applicable to all the instincts. However, the new idea fascinates

---

[1] ". . . the *partial* deduction of art, religion and social order from the *collaboration* of the sexual instincts." Cf. Freud, *Die Widerstände gegen die Psychoanalyse* (Imago, 1925, XI). See also *Gesammelte Werke*, XIV, p. 105. (My italics.)

him so much that he cannot resist the temptation to push it to its extreme consequences. "But," he says, "we may first be tempted to follow to its final consequences the hypothesis that *all* instincts have as their aim the reinstatement of an earlier condition." The reader is then warned that he must realize that "what follows is the development of a sequence of ideas pushed to the extreme, and that its significance will be ultimately modified and rectified."[1]

It is necessary for us to realize that such was the state of mind of the founder of psychoanalysis, and to remember to take this into account when discussing psychoanalytical problems: it reveals an ambiguity in the Freudian conception of man which there is no need to stress any further. Two things remain indisputable. On the one hand, Freud recognizes only one constructive force when he is developing his theory itself: the libido; and he derives the whole structure of the personality from it. On the other hand, whenever he is faced explicitly with the extreme consequences of his ideas, he protests against them, declaring that he is quite prepared to reserve a place for other aspects of the subject.

To sum up: the Freudian philosophy, which derives every constructive power in man from the libido, can be looked upon—in Freud's own *mind*—as the exaggeration of a new and fascinating idea; this should not, however, prevent us either from accepting the valuable body of facts which can be extracted from their theoretical background or from going beyond this theoretic view of man to a conception embracing the normal human personality in its entirety.

[1] *Gesammelte Werke*, XIII, p. 39.

CHAPTER II

PSYCHOANALYSIS AND
PSYCHOTHERAPY

1. Statements of Principle

It is not our purpose in this chapter to describe psychoanalysis as a therapeutic technique. According to the main object of the first part of this book, we intend to "place" psychoanalysis in the framework of the many other contributions made to psychology and psychotherapy. For too many Freudians, psychoanalysis is synonymous with psychotherapy in general. In our opinion, psychoanalytic therapy as well as psychoanalytic psychology must not be isolated from the whole field of psychotherapy and psychological science. We therefore intend to describe, very briefly, a few recent trends which have developed either as a continuation of Freudian technique or in opposition to it.

The psychoanalytical method of treatment is at the present day applied in a more or less eclectic way by a great number of therapists; nevertheless, psychoanalysis in the strict sense of the word was until recently practised only by the followers of Freud, who all, in more or less orthodox fashion, accepted the *doctrinal system in its entirety*.

This connection between psychoanalytical *therapy* and the

72

Freudian *system as a whole* is the main reason for the attitude of suspicion which many people adopt towards this type of treatment. *In so far as it really exists*, this connection certainly obliges one to adopt the same attitude of critical reserve towards the therapeutic side of the system as towards the system as a whole.

Moreover, the therapist's treatment is not simply the application of a technique; it establishes between the therapist and the patient a personal relationship which plays an essential part in the actual process of treatment, and for this reason the *whole personality* of the therapist, with his life-conception and his whole way of looking at things, exerts an unavoidable influence on it.

The connection between analytical therapy and the system as a whole is an historical fact. Nevertheless, we are of the opinion that this method of treatment should not be considered as inseparably bound up with Freud's *Weltanschauung*. Analytical treatment, it is true, presupposes certain ideas about the mechanism of the psyche and its dynamic life; but it does not imply the whole of the Freudian philosophy of man. Furthermore, the development of psychoanalytical *therapy* itself shows an increasing independence of orthodox Freudian "dogma."

Leaving all superfluous theories aside, analytical therapy rests on the *presupposition* that a psychic conflict between, for example, sexual desires and moral or social requirements, leaves unconscious traces on psychic life which may exert a pathogenic influence. It is not absolutely necessary to see this as "repression" nor as determined in the first place by Freudian complexes.

In general and universally acceptable terms, the *fundamental principle* of this therapy consists in the fact that unravelling the tangled skein of the unconscious remains of psychic conflict (by some analytical technique or other) can have a salutary effect by enabling the patient to "see clearly" into the play of the conflicting forces.

The principle and presupposition of Freudian therapy are based on ascertained discoveries and working hypotheses which are not to be ignored. To the spiritually minded psychologist, too, they seem perfectly admissible, having revealed themselves in many cases to be highly efficacious.

Nor has Breuer's therapeutic method, which lies at the root of

Freud's ideas, lost its value. This so-called *cathartic* method assumes that in events which are highly charged with emotion the pathogenic element can arise from the fact that the emotion, instead of being fully released, remains "hemmed in," and so seeks an outlet along abnormal channels. The *fundamental principle* of this cathartic method, therefore, is that emotional release, if expressed freely, brings relief and a *catharsis.* This is a generalized statement of the fact established by Breuer that the "talking cure" or the "free-expression cure" brought relief to his patients or even a complete disappearance of the symptom. This method, moreover, is in complete harmony with many facts of every-day psychology.

The fact that in the therapist's opinion the patient should ultimately find "salvation" by *emancipating himself* from moral laws and restraints, rather than in recreating the balance of his moral forces, is a point which on the whole depends on the therapist's "philosophy" and not on the analytical method *as such.*

Freud has made this point quite clear himself: "It is a grave misunderstanding, only to be excused by ignorance, to pretend that psychoanalysis expects neurosis to be cured by sexual abandonment. On the contrary, the awareness, through analysis, of repressed sexual desires tends to encourage a mastery over those desires which could not be achieved by the old kinds of repression."[1]

It is therefore necessary to make a careful distinction between two quite different elements in psychoanalytical therapy. On the one hand, there is the *method* actually used; this is based on the idea of the pathogenic influence of certain mechanisms of conflict, and the salutary influence that comes from conscious realization of the forces at work. On the other hand, there are the *value-judgments* regarding these same forces of conflict.

Thus it is clear that words like "repression" and "censorship" imply certain theoretical assumptions of "value," but these are not essential parts of analytical therapy.

Nevertheless, because of the very nature of the therapeutic process one must point out the influence which the therapist's

[1] Cf. *"Psychoanalyse," Gesammelte Werke,* XIII, pp. 227–228.

personality can have on the patient's value-judgments—an influence which must certainly be taken into account in practice. In our opinion this does not mean that analysis should only be undertaken by a psychoanalyst who shares the same conception of life as the patient, but only that it is essential that the therapist should have a comprehensive knowledge of his patient's life-conception and a profound respect for it.

It is, however, a fact that a number of analysts attempt to make their patient adopt their own Freudian conception of life. This, as we have said already, is an abuse of the method and goes against Freud's own instructions.

The problem is often complicated, however, by certain circumstances inherent in the treatment. The moral and religious attitudes and ideas of people who are to undergo psychoanalytical treatment are frequently found to be based on unhealthy foundations. Neurotic elements of all kinds are mixed up in them. Religious practices often provide these people with an unhealthy solution of their frustrations and conflicts. Their morality may be influenced by neurotic feelings of anxiety and guilt. Now the therapeutic process can liberate the patient from these restraining or disturbing factors. Since the religion and morality of such people form a neurotic superstructure, they will be eliminated along with the neurosis itself. If the analyst has no sense of the moral and religious values which manifest themselves in the patient's personality in a neurotic and unbalanced form, he will be content to let these elements disappear. By proceeding in this way he is leaving out of account the positive work: the construction of part of the patient's personality. Now this involves an attitude which is undesirable even from the purely psychological point of view. Allowing the unbalanced forms in which the patient's morality and religion manifested themselves to disappear means leaving the normal need of these values unsatisfied. One may believe that from the psychological point of view this attitude has less harmful consequences for people whose education has not involved any contact with religion; but it can cause serious disturbances in patients in whose development religion, even in its neurotic forms, has played an important part. The building-up of a healthy religious attitude, on the other hand, is the best way of filling the gap which may exist in such people after the work of elimination has been accomplished. This is why it is often highly desirable that a neurotic person who holds a religious faith should address himself to an analyst who believes in the religious values of life.

It is by no means irrelevant to introduce into psychotherapy the religious conception of life and the moral attitude of patient and therapist. Today, the importance of this matter is no longer doubted by anyone—thanks to the practice of outstanding therapists like Jung, and to the discovery, in many different countries, that in a great number of cases of loss of psychic balance, the heart of the trouble has been found to be bound up with the problem of the *meaning* and *content* of life.[1]

In connection with this matter of analytical treatment, we must also emphasize certain matters of principle as regards *didactic analysis*. This is generally held to constitute an essential part of the training of the future analyst. There is no doubt that the fact of undergoing an analysis is so valuable a therapeutic experience that in most cases it can be considered the best sort of introduction to the practice of this method. The same is true, in fact, for most of the techniques of psychological treatment. In clinical psychology a personal experience of the methods used is the best kind of apprenticeship, for in this way the future clinicist gains personal experience of the processes involved in these methods. Nevertheless, from a purely methodological point of view there is no reason why this application of analysis to the clinicist should be considered an essential condition of serious training.[2] It seems likely

---

[1] As regards the general relationship that should be established between psychotherapy and the conception of man see also, particularly, L. van der Horst's interesting essay, "*Anthropologie und Psychotherapie*," in *Monatschrift für Psychiatrie und Neurologie*, 1947, CXIV, Nos. 1 and 2.

[2] In this connection it is interesting to quote also the opinion recently expressed by O. Mowrer: "Psychoanalytic therapists have taken a position at one extreme of a continuum, holding that treatment and training are not fundamentally different, hence the tradition of the didactic analysis. At the opposite extreme is the position that psychotherapy is something that can be done by anyone on the basis of a few simple rules, and without regard to the personal qualifications of the practitioner.

"It is unlikely that the latter position will long prove defensible, but neither is it certain that intensive didactic therapy is essential in all instances. *Rather than stress any fixed invariant training routine, what we need is a*

that less emphasis will be placed on this rule as psychoanalysis loses its esoteric character. There are cases in which there need be no fear that because of the analyst's lack of didactic analysis his personal complexes will have a pernicious influence on analytical practice. On the other hand, there are some new technical methods, e.g. the sound-mirror, which offer a whole range of new possibilities of direct participation in the therapeutic process. One can thus participate in an analysis without being a patient, and thus gain experience of the monotonous or dramatic phases of therapy. Obviously, to acquire concrete knowledge of analysis, and to be initiated into its technique, it is necessary to *participate* in it in some way or another. The method indicated may in certain cases make this possible.

We should like to point out here another use that can be made of sound-mirror apparatus in the training of the clinical psychologist and the psychoanalyst. It concerns a technique that can be used when the ordinary didactic analysis is considered unsuitable. Here is a brief description of the process. The young analyst, having already had sufficient training in psychoanalysis, lies down on a divan in his room alone. He then begins to make associations aloud, exactly as though he was taking part in an ordinary session. The only difference—and it is an essential difference, of course—lies in the fact that there is no analyst present. On a table behind him is the microphone of the sound apparatus. The apparatus itself should preferably be in the next room, so that the young analyst is not disturbed by the slight noise it makes. Thus, everything that is said by the "patient" during the session is recorded. At the end of a fairly long series of sessions, the "patient" may play back to himself the recordings that have been made and can thus be present as "analyst" at his own sessions. If it is considered advisable his teacher may also be present: this will enable a didactic interpretation to be made by the teacher in the presence of the analyst-to-be.

The essential difference between this and a real analysis is the absence of any transference, and this method may be used in those

---

trustworthy method of assaying something for which we have no better term than 'personal maturity.' " Cf. "Training in Psychotherapy," *Journal of Consulting Psychology*, 1951, XV, p. 274.

cases in which it is considered better not to instigate any transference. When combined with other kinds of instruction and training—for instance, the young analyst may be present at the reproduction of an analysis of another person, made by the teacher himself (always assuming that the person consents to his case being used didactically)—this technique can complete the kind of self-analysis that was practised by Freud. Even a fully trained analyst may adopt this method for the analysis of his own dreams, etc.

When attempting to solve this debatable question of didactic analysis it is worth while to remember also the objections of Kretschmer, the psychotherapist of Tübingen. He says that personally he holds to Freud's original point of view. It is known that Freud never allowed himself to be analysed; but he used to analyse his own dreams and omissions. Kretschmer also maintains that an important element in the training of the future therapist is an intensive study of his own dreams, and a comparison of them with the material supplied by the dreams of patients who are undergoing treatment under expert direction. Kretschmer is opposed to any didactic beyond that involved in the study of the method and laws of dream-symbolism. He recognizes, of course, the importance of the considerations that have led to the demand for didactic analysis, but he is not convinced that such an analysis is really indispensable, or even that it can be accepted at all.

In his course of lectures on this subject,[1] Kretschmer drew particular attention to the following dangers: "a superficial snobbery, the fragmentation of the personality, a deep disturbance of the feeling for 'tact' . . . and also the fixation and dogmatic contraction that are brought about by the prolonged action of transference-mechanisms."

Kretschmer says that these dangers are not, of course, "to be generalized in any way" but that nevertheless "they often come about in patients who have been analysed and in students of psychotherapy."

With regard to practice, it appears that "all the German schools of therapy have agreed to leave each clinic or institute to decide

[1] Cf. *Zeitschrift für Psychotherapie und medizinische Psychologie*, 1951, I, pp. 93–94.

for itself whether didactic analysis is a desirable condition of training. This important question is not to be solved by any dogmatic decision."[1]

We emphasize this point because we have discovered more than once, in a way that leaves no room for doubt, that didactic analysis can have a harmful influence on the future therapist. This is quite easy to understand. It is not good, in fact, for normal but weakly integrated personalities to have brought back into their consciousness traumatic scenes and events from their past life. Time has calmed the disturbances and healed the wounds, and there are some personalities for whom the activation of these centres of psychic infection can be highly dangerous. Such people need many long years before they can regain the internal state of relative equilibrium which they had reached, especially when the didactic analysis is interrupted by external circumstances such as the ending of a scholarship, etc. These are points which the student should consider before embarking on didactic analysis. It is a well-known fact that amongst the young men who are specially interested in clinical psychology and psychoanalysis there exist a certain number whose integration leaves much to be desired. For these people it is their personal "case" that lies behind their interest in these activities. Obviously, these are just the kind of people who stand most in need of analysis when they are preparing for psychoanalytical practice. Their own conflicts, if unsatisfactorily resolved, can have a bad influence on their relationships with their future patients. For this reason students of this kind seem to us to be unsuited not only to didactic analysis but also to psycho-analytical training as a whole. For a variety of reasons it is desirable that only well-balanced personalities should undertake the study and practice of psychotherapy. Quite rightly, in the question of the training of the therapist, the importance of a satisfactory apprenticeship is emphasized; but it is perhaps just as necessary to insist on the indispensable nature of the candidate's personal qualities.

Having thus separated—in principle—analytical *therapy* from the Freudian conception of man, the only question that remains is,

[1] *Ibid.*, p. 95.

once again, What is the *scientific, practical* value of the method, i.e. what is the proved and checked utility of this method in the treatment of certain neurotic troubles? Even the answer to the moral question as to the admissibility of certain parts of the treatment, in view of the moral dangers or disadvantages which may *accidentally* be involved, depends on this very point of knowing whether the particular treatment in question is the most useful or even the only one that will allow the patient to recover the great blessing of psychic balance.

The therapeutic value of analytical treatment can, of course, be the subject of scientific discussion. Two facts seem undeniable to anyone who is not blindly attached to any particular school.

It is unquestionable that at the present time all the methods of treatment are profiting from certain fundamental discoveries made by psychoanalytical therapy. As we have already said, a high proportion of modern psychotherapy, and clinical psychology in general, is riddled with analytical ideas. It is for this reason that every doctor and psychologist should have a clear understanding of the value of the ideas we have gained from depth-psychology. This applies to the systems of Adler and Jung as well as to psychoanalysis in the strict sense—though the student in psychology may perhaps reach a better understanding of what is new and valuable in psychotherapy if he studies various systems in an eclectical way rather than going into detail into all the works of orthodox Freudians.

The second indisputable fact is that the Freudian method must not be identified with psychotherapy proper—first, because some therapists *have broken away from this method* and developed new ideas and techniques which it would be unjust not to take into account; secondly, because there are other ideas and principles which have affected psychotherapy, introducing a number of valuable elements which may complete therapeutic theory and renew its practice.

We intend now to describe the most important facts supplied by these new lines of development.

Besides theories concerning the spiritual conception of man, we shall come across data which are important for all whose job it is to advise men or direct them. But this summary of the new ideas in psychotherapy will show us especially, in concrete fashion, the exact *position* of Freudian method today and the practical attitude it is proper to adopt towards it.

We do not intend to go *into detail* in our discussion of the ideas behind these new lines of thought, but will simply compare and contrast certain *ideas*, so as to throw more light on Freudian principles or make them more complete.

2. New Lines of Development in Psychoanalysis and Psychotherapy

During the last few years psychoanalysis has gone through a period of acute crisis, even in the opinion of the analysts themselves. The well-known New York psychoanalyst Gregory Zilboorg wrote recently: "That psychoanalysis is going through a crisis is a persistent impression in and outside the profession. This crisis [is] reflected in acute dissensions and schismatic undulations."[1]

(1) THE ASSIMILATION OF ADLERIAN IDEAS

One of these "movements of secession" includes the work of Karen Horney. This work has had a large public in America, and it is already spreading abroad—especially her well-known book, *New Ways in Psychoanalysis*, in which, after fifteen years of psychoanalytical practice, she makes the following confession:

I found that almost every patient offered problems for which our accepted psychoanalytical knowledge offered no means of solution, and which therefore remained unsolved.

As most analysts probably do, at first I attributed the resulting uncertainty to my own lack of experience, lack of understanding or blind spots. I remember pestering more experienced colleagues with questions . . . without, however, obtaining answers that seemed satisfactory.

I had my first active doubts as to the validity of psychoanalytical theories when I read Freud's concept of feminine psychology, doubts which were then strengthened by his postulate of the death instinct. . . .

. . . It is only through recognizing the debatable premises on which this

---

[1] Cf. G. Zilboorg, "Present Trends in Psychoanalytic Theory and Practice," p. 79; *The Yearbook of Psychoanalysis*, 1945 (New York, International Universities Press), I, pp. 79–84.

system is built that one acquires a clearer vision as to the sources of error contained in the individual theories. . . .

The resistance which many psychiatrists as well as laymen feel toward orthodox psychoanalysis is due not only to emotional sources, as is assumed, but also to the debatable character of many theories.

. . . I believe that the range of problems which can be understood is enlarged considerably if we cut loose from certain historically determined theoretical premises and discard the theories arising on that basis.

My conviction, expressed in a nutshell, is that psychoanalysis should outgrow the limitations set by its being an instinctivistic and a genetic psychology.[1]

This break-up of Freudian orthodoxy, so strikingly illustrated by Dr. Horney's case, depends largely on the fact that a very great number of psychoanalysts are coming more and more to realize that different points of view have been developed by distinguished followers of Freud who have broken away from him.

The fact that (as psychoanalysis developed) Freud adopted a purely negative attitude towards the "unorthodox" ideas of his best followers is important. The result of this narrow, negative attitude can be seen today in a widespread reaction which has opened up psychoanalytical doctrine to foreign elements, especially those deriving from the systems developed by Adler and Otto Rank. Jung's ideas affected psychoanalysis even earlier.

Freud's position—keeping strictly to a sexual interpretation of psychic phenomena and considering repression as the sole factor in pathogenesis, a *conscious awareness* of the repressed elements being the corresponding principle in therapy—prevented him from estimating at their true worth certain important ideas which were developed by his followers—a fact all the more surprising as the new ideas arose from discoveries made by the master himself. This is true of Adler as well as of Jung and Rank.[2]

Thus Freud discovered before Adler that neurotic symptoms may have an *intentional* character; that is to say, that the *ego* may use them for its own conscious ends.

---

[1] Cf. Karen Horney, *New Ways in Psychoanalysis* (New York, Norton, 1939), pp. 7–8.

[2] The pages that follow will show to what extent Freud had already published views that are generally attributed to Adler. As to Jung's "collective unconscious," this idea is implied in the universal system of symbols developed by Freud.

As early as 1906, Freud envisaged *"Motive zum Kranksein"* in an important work, *Bruchstück einer Hysterie-Analyse*. In this there are ideas that might easily be attributed to Adler, and as it contains an important passage that is very little known, we shall print it in full:

The child who longs to be loved and who resents sharing his parents' affection with his brothers and sisters, finds that he becomes the one object of their love when he arouses their concern through illness. Thus he discovers a means of attracting their affection, and he will use this means the moment he discovers a psychic method of bringing on sickness. When this child becomes a woman and finds herself, in direct contrast to her years of childhood, married to a man who has no consideration for her, who stifles her will, who ruthlessly exploits her capacity for work and who lacks all generosity, either spiritual or material, towards her, then illness becomes her one weapon of defence against life. It forces her husband to be indulgent towards her, to give her attention and more money, things he would never have done if she were well; he is obliged to be considerate of her when she is well again because of the danger of a relapse if he behaved otherwise.

The apparently unintentional nature of the illness—which the doctor too is obliged to accept as such—enables her to use the method which had worked so satisfactorily during her childhood without incurring any reproach. Nevertheless, the state of sickness is intentional. States of illness are habitually directed against some person or other, as is proved by the fact that when the person in question is absent the illness disappears.

The crudest and most commonplace comments that servants make about hysteria are in a certain sense true. It is quite true that anybody paralysed or bedridden would jump out of bed if his room caught fire, that a spoilt woman would immediately forget all her own sufferings if her child was ill or in danger of death, or if some other catastrophe threatened the household. There is only one thing wrong with such observations, and that is that they ignore the psychological distinction between conscious and unconscious—which is allowable in the case of children but not adults. This is why no amount of insisting that it is all a matter of will-power, no amount of encouragement or insult, can be of any use. The first thing is for the patient to be convinced herself, by means of analysis, that she wishes to be ill.[1]

This does not mean, however, that the ideas in Adler's system are simply developments of Freud's own discoveries. It was

---

[1] Cf. Freud, *"Bruchstück einer Hysterie-Analyse," Gesammelte Werke*, V. This passage appeared originally in the *Monatschrift für Psychiatrie und Neurologie*, 1906, XVIII, pp. 285–308 and 408–466; cf. p. 412.

chiefly by bringing out the social aspect of personality and show-ing the importance of the attitude adopted by the person towards himself and his position amongst others that Adler exerted an influence on depth-psychology and psychotherapy.

Dr. Horney incorporates some of Adler's ideas into her theory of psychic troubles, and so her system is more open to specifically human and social problems, especially those raised by the attitude of the personality towards itself and its own line of development. This widening of perspective is shown in her idea of neurosis, which she describes as "a disturbance in human relationship," the essential element of which she sees in a conflict of attitudes, "mov-ing towards," "moving against," and "moving away from people."[1]

This fusion of Adlerian and Freudian elements in Dr. Horney's system seems to us to represent a real advance. While Freud has undoubtedly increased our knowledge of the variety of the secret mechanisms in the human psyche far more than Adler, the latter has possibly developed a deeper conception of human personality as a whole. A union of these two systems, with their partial truths, might mean a considerable increase in our psychological knowl-edge of man. Jung is known to have attempted it as soon as the school broke up.

Another important gap in Freud's system is his neglect of *cul-tural* factors in psychic life in general and in the origin of neurosis in particular. There is obviously a close relationship between the *cultural* "determinant" and Adler's emphasis on the social aspect of the development of personality. We realize, of course, that it is through the social sciences, and particularly cultural anthropology —not through Adler's direct influence—that the *cultural* and the *social* factor has been emphasized in the present-day psychology of the personality; but the fact remains that orthodox Freudians are more interested in explaining cultural behaviour patterns in terms of psychoanalytic theory than in emphasizing cultural fac-tors in neurosis. On the contrary, psychologists open to Adler's ideas have managed to benefit from the social and cultural point of view in psychology. In this respect too Karen Horney has

[1] Cf. Karen Horney, *Our Inner Conflicts: A Constructive Theory of Neurosis* (New York, Norton; and London, Kegan, 1946). See also the book already mentioned, *New Ways in Psychoanalysis*.

introduced a new tone into the psychoanalytical movement. In her book *The Neurotic Personality of Our Time*,[1] she shows the importance of the cultural factor in neurotic tendencies and introduces this important aspect of personality into the field of psychoanalysis. The pioneer work of Sullivan in this field is well known.

(2) "SHORT" THERAPY

A further renewal that has developed as a result of the "movements of secession" comes from the psychoanalytical school in Chicago, directed by Franz Alexander and Thomas French, where another of Freud's followers, Otto Rank, has been one of the main influences.

In their important book *Psychoanalytic Therapy*[2] Alexander and French both insist that psychotherapy can only develop by *emancipating itself from stereotyped forms of psychoanalytical thought;* all accepted methods and ideas must be submitted to experiment.

On the basis of ten years' work and a study of about six hundred cases, these authors announce important modifications in psychotherapeutic theory and practice.

In the field of *practice* they show that psychoanalytical treatment can be considerably *shortened*. They abandon the "psychoanalytical dogma" that therapy is more effective, the more complete—and hence the more drawn-out—the analysis. It used to be considered that a proper analysis meant one session per day for at least two years. The first person to suggest and apply shorter methods of analysis was Wilhelm Stekel.[3] It is well known that Ferenczi and Rank wrote in the same sense. More recently, Alexander and French have obtained satisfactory results by means of a *short therapy* which involves only between one interview and six. The technique, too, is *adapted* to each individual case.

This short therapy is based on a number of new theories, particularly on the idea that *a minute analysis of the conflicts and difficulties of infancy is not essential to treatment.* It does in fact tend to be generally admitted that Freud overestimated the im-

[1] (New York, Norton, 1937.)
[2] (New York, Ronald, 1946.)
[3] Cf. Wilhelm Stekel, *Autobiography*.

portance of the events of infancy; a whole series of facts and many lines of research point to the same conclusion.[1]

For this reason the treatment centres more directly round the patient's *actual* difficulties of the moment, and analysis of the past is limited to *making clear* the nature of the actual conflict.

Alexander and French abandon the idea that the essential process in therapy is to become conscious of what is unconscious or repressed. Following Otto Rank, a former follower of Freud, they attach great importance to the process of emotional transference (*Übertragung*) which takes place between patient and therapist.

It is well known that this process of emotional transference was discovered by Freud himself. He showed that in the course of treatment an emotional relationship, either positive or negative (hostile), developed between the patient and the therapist, a relationship which did not derive from the situation of *the moment* but which was a *transference* to the therapist of emotional relationships experienced by the patient in infancy, as for example with his parents.

Freud no doubt realized the therapeutic value of this process, but it was Rank who put it *at the heart* of his theory and practice. By so doing, he gave the idea of transference a new meaning.

According to Rank, in fact, therapy no longer consists primarily in *becoming conscious of what is unconscious;* fundamentally, thanks chiefly to the therapist, the therapeutic process is a kind of apprenticeship in, and development of, a *new sort of social relationship.* The process of *transference* thus becomes an *apprenticeship in the realization of social relationships.*

Following up this idea, Alexander and French came to believe that the starting-point of the patient's pathological behaviour is to be found in past social relationships, or else has developed out of emotional conflicts which have ended disastrously. The essence of the treatment lies in the patient's experiencing this unsolved or badly solved conflict all over again in the setting of a new social relationship (with the therapist) and then finding a different solu-

[1] See particularly, for a general discussion of one aspect of the question, Harold Orlansky, "Infant Care and Personality," *Psychological Bulletin,* 1949, XLVI, pp. 1–48.

tion for it. Thus during the treatment the patient undergoes new and successful emotional experiences in the setting of personal relationships—only these new experiences being capable of suppressing, or at least mitigating, the evil consequences of the pathogenic emotional experiences caused by past relationships. Viewed in this light, therapy is a *process of apprenticeship:* the patient needing to *learn*, through a concrete social relationship with a particular person (the therapist), new forms of social relationship.

We should like to point out the practical importance of this therapeutic principle in the psychological direction of young people. It must be realized that a series of happy and successful experiences is often indispensable for the cure of certain psychic abnormalities; it is in these happy experiences that the individual finds an effective jumping-off ground and the courage to get himself right again. Social relationships with the person of the "director" may be for young people the first form of such happy and successful kinds of social experience.

(3) SOCIAL POINTS OF VIEW IN PSYCHOTHERAPY

It is important to emphasize the fact that the two lines of development in psychoanalysis which we have just described stress the *social* aspect of human behaviour and personality more than Freud did. Other lines of development in the field of psychotherapy bring out this fact even more clearly—especially *Relationship therapy* and *Group therapy*.

Relationship therapy is a development of the social aspect of Otto Rank's system by Jessie Taft, formerly an American social worker. In one of her early books, *The Dynamics of Therapy in a Controlled Relationship* (1933),[1] appear certain elements that were utilized by Alexander and French, and to which we have already alluded. We shall discover further elements taken from this book when we come to sketch Rogers' system.

Jessie Taft has translated various works by Rank into English, and, as we have said, has developed their social aspect in her own works. Even before Alexander and French, she emphasized the fact that it was not what the patient communicated or what the

[1] (New York, Macmillan.)

psychologist did or said that mattered in the therapeutic treatment, but the *kind of relationship that grew up* between them.[1]

Rank had previously drawn attention to the fact that the patient feels a need to dominate the therapist. He believed that this gave rise to a sort of conflict of wills between the therapist and the patient. Taft argued from this that nothing that the therapist *suggests to* or *forces upon* the patient can be of any help to him. *The therapist must not direct the patient,* must not force his will or opinions on him, but on the contrary, must enable him to discover his own independence.

This less "directive" conception of the therapist's rôle and the principle of social relationship are the two ideas which are helping to revitalize psychotherapy. Both derive from Rank, and we shall find the first being developed on a new basis in the *non-directive therapy* of Carl Rogers, which we shall be discussing shortly.

The most obvious respect in which the social point of view has influenced psychotherapy appears in what is known as *group therapy*. This term does not denote a special technique but is a general term covering a series of processes which have in common the fact that treatment takes place between groups of patients and therapists, who meet by chance or are selected so that the patients may discuss some of their problems and their attitude of mind towards their conflict-situations.

Another aspect of group therapy is the psychodrama developed by Moreno, which has been the subject of much debate. According to this method, the conflict which group discussion has revealed to be important is literally "played" in a dramatic form. When, for example, it is revealed that one of the members of the group has at a certain stage of his life had ideas of killing his wife,

[1] In the book by F. Allen, *Psychotherapy with Children* (New York, Norton, 1942), will be found information on the application of relationship therapy to children. In German literature, too, under Scheler's influence, the *"mitmenschliche Sein"* has been emphasized in the therapeutic situation. Cf. particularly L. Binswanger, *"Über Psychotherapie," Ausgewählte Vorträge und Aufsätze* (Bern, A. Franck, 1947; originally published in *Der Nervenarzt,* 1935).

and these ideas still seem to have some emotional power over him, the leader of the group intervenes in the discussion and suggests that these ideas be allowed full expression in a kind of improvised play. The "production" takes place forthwith. One of the women in the group takes the part of the wife. The scene includes an upper storey or balcony representing, for example, the bedroom. It is here that the quarrel breaks out between "man and wife." There comes a moment when the "husband" experiences all over again the desire to throw his wife out of the window. Everything is arranged as though the argument were actually taking place. At the critical moment the "wife" goes down from the upper storey and lays herself down below, as though she had just been thrown from the balcony. The patient can thus "live" the act of killing his wife as nearly as possible as though it was actually taking place. He rushes distractedly downstairs, hurls himself on the "body" of his wife and gives full vent to his feelings. Moreno thus manages to enact dramatic scenes which are really lived, and which it is hard to imagine simply by reading about them in a detached way. People who have taken part in them have been very deeply impressed by them.

The therapeutic principles involved in this method, and the powerful emotional release which it produces, will be readily perceived. The question arises, however, whether such highly emotional scenes, in which the lived past is re-enacted with such dramatic force, may not, in certain cases, have a dangerous effect. The exact influence of this kind of re-activation of traumatic events on the various kinds of psychic disturbances has not so far been systematically studied. The non-directive school, for example, has shown far more concern about the exact influence and development of the therapeutic process which it employs.

There is, however, a more experimental trend in the use of therapeutic and other group methods. We mean particularly the study of "group dynamics" in the late Kurt Lewin's School, developed particularly at the Tavistock Institute of Human Relations in London and the University of Michigan in the United States. These two groups publish in collaboration an important journal, *Human Relations*.

Group therapy, it is true, is still only in its infancy, but it seems to us important to emphasize the fact that psychic troubles are partly the result of imperfect adaptation to the social environment and an inability to grapple with the problems which are continually arising in the sphere of *human relationships*. It is for this reason that one can agree in principle that a cure can be achieved not merely by sorting out complexes and *past* difficulties but chiefly by the objectification and examination of present difficulties by means of an adaptation to life, in a real social setting. In this respect, *group therapy* seems a very promising development.

We must now show the connection between the social aspect of psychotherapy which we have emphasized and the *evolution of psychology in general in the direction of social psychology*.

In general psychology it is becoming recognized more and more clearly that human behaviour is not a matter of reacting to laboratory stimuli but means chiefly reacting to other people and adopting a certain kind of behaviour *towards one's equals*. The study of personality, too, is putting more and more emphasis on the social and cultural factors which play a part in the construction of the human personality.

This increasing emphasis on the social aspect of psychology means, generally speaking, an increasing breadth of ideas and methods. Besides its consequences for psychotherapy, we can recognize its influence on the methods used in diagnosing personal characteristics too. Obviously, by *watching a man in his relationships with his equals*, and the way he reacts to orders given to a whole group, we have a method that is better in many respects than the ordinary tests for gaining a full idea of the personality of the patient and the difficulties of adaptation which he experiences in daily life.[1]

This whole development shows that in the field of experiment, as in the fields of therapy and test method, the value of the social point of view is coming more and more to be appreciated.

[1] See particularly *The Work of Psychologists and Psychiatrists in the Services* (London, H. M. Stationery Office, 1947); and especially the remarkable account of experiences of social situations during the war in the American army: *Assessment of Men*, by the O.S.S. Assessment Staff (New York, Rinehart & Co., 1948). This work was done directly by H. Murray, the author of *Thematic Apperception Test* and *Explorations in Personality*.

(4) NON-DIRECTIVE OR CLIENT-CENTRED THERAPY

The last line of development in psychotherapy is on several points opposed to psychoanalysis. We shall treat it at greater length because of its relevance to personality theory. This is the "non-directive" or "client-centered" therapy of Cary Rogers.[1] Here what is emphasized is the fact that *it is up to the patient himself to construct his own personality*. The therapist, from this point of view, is simply the catalyst who facilitates the development of the growing process. Behind this new technique lies an important conception of personality.

While psychoanalysis emphasized the action of pathogenic destructive forces, such as repression, in man, Carl Rogers insists that healthy constructive forces of growth—Goldstein's *impulse to self-actualization*—lie at the heart of the personality. Rogers believes, in our opinion rightly, that these constructive forces must be the fundamental basis of therapeutic treatment.[2]

We have already mentioned several therapeutic principles, all of which have their value. Breuer believed that an *emotional release* had a cathartic action; Freud showed that a clear insight into the mechanisms of the psychic life itself—i.e., a *conscious awareness*

---

[1] See especially Carl Rogers, *Counseling and Psychotherapy: Newer Concepts in Practice* (Boston, Houghton Mifflin, 1942) and *Client-centered Therapy (ibidem*, 1951). See also Rogers' more recent contributions: "Significant Aspects of Client-centered Therapy," *The American Psychologist*, 1946, I, pp. 415–422; "Some Observations on the Organization of Personality," *The American Psychologist*, 1947, II, pp. 358–368.

[2] The reader will see in what follows that some of Rogers' fundamental ideas were already to be found in earlier German literature on the subject. What Rogers says about "self-ralization" seems to connect up, by way of Goldstein, with familiar biological theories of a vitalist tendency. Similarly, in the field of psychotherapy, there are ideas, especially in the work of A. Maeder, that we find in other forms in Rogers. See A. Maeder, *Die Richtung im Seelenleben* (Zürich, Rascher, 1928); also the article "*Régulation psychique et guérison*," in the *Archives suisses de neurologie et psychiatrie*, 1925, XVI, pp. 198–224; and the recent book *Selbsterhaltung und Selbstheilung* (Zürich, Rascher, 1949). We also find one of the principles of non-directive therapy in Rümke. He expresses it in almost the same way, in these words: "It is not the job [of the people who guide man's inner life] to impose an attitude, authoritatively, on the neurotic. This attitude might not be adapted to their personality. *But they have to discover the conditions in which the 'drive' to self-realization can reach*

of the contents of the unconscious—has a therapeutic value, when completely assimilated and accepted by the patient. Alexander and French held that the patient could be cured by a new experience of his conflict, an experience taking place in a *new social* relationship and having a *successful outcome*. All these principles can undoubtedly, *according to circumstance*, have an important therapeutic influence. But Rogers believes that the therapeutic power emanates ultimately from the *constructive forces* in the personality itself.

The origin of psychic troubles is to be found in the fact that *the normal construction of the personality has been hindered by unfavourable circumstances* or taken some unsatisfactory course. The disturbance then manifests itself in the fact that the individual is not satisfied with himself: *he has an unsatisfactory idea of himself and of others*. Thus the first aim of treatment will be to create a situation in which the patient comes *to "see" and experience his own personality, and other people's, in a new way*.

This is the point on which Rogers insists so strongly: that in therapy the most important thing is to give the patient a new *"perception" and a new experience of himself*. It is often thought that successful therapy is simply one that *solves problems*. "If a person had a marital problem, a vocational problem, a problem of educational adjustment, the obvious purpose of counseling or therapy was to solve that problem. But as we observe and study the recorded accounts of the conclusions of therapy, it is clear that the most characteristic outcome is not necessarily solution of problems, but a freedom from tension, a different feeling about, and perception of, self." Rogers goes on to quote observations made by his patients, the following being especially worth noting: "The happiest outcome of therapy has been a new feeling about myself. As I think of it, it might be the only outcome. Certainly it is basic to all the changes in my behavior that have resulted." . . .

---

a maximum in the person entrusted to their care" (our italics). Cf. *Studies en Voordrachten over Psychiatrie* (Amsterdam, 1943), p. 321.

Nevertheless, Rogers' great merit lies in his having developed a new technique opposed to current ideas and opening up new lines of thought for the psychology of the personality, both empirically and experimentally, on the basis of principles drawn from actual therapeutic practice.

"I am getting more happiness in being myself." "I approve of myself more, and I have so much less anxiety."[1]

The emphasis is therefore placed on *the subjective way in which the patient experiences himself* and others. This is why non-directive therapy tries to penetrate into the subjective world of each patient's experience and to express this world without using objective terms, without reference to a particular terminology. For such terms do not express the particular way in which the subject sees himself or the world.

This is the origin of a new development in Rogers' school towards what is known as the "phenomenological" study of the personality. This kind of study means that instead of trying to find out as much as possible *about* the patient, the effort is rather to see and experience the world exactly as he experiences it himself.[2]

Since the therapeutic process emanates from the constructive forces of growth in the personality itself, and since this process must above all things enable the person to reach a new conception of *himself*, the *therapist's function* is in the first place to create an atmosphere *in which the person can really be himself and in which the impulse to be himself can be released*. According to Rogers, this result can only be reached through an unlimited "acceptance" by the therapist of the patient's personality as it is.

Once this "warm" atmosphere of understanding has been created and the patient feels confident and protected against every kind of "attack"—when, in a word, he feels that he is accepted by the therapist as he is—then, in what is a new situation for him, a new

[1] Carl R. Rogers, "Some Observations on the Organization of Personality," p. 363; *The American Psychologist*, 1947, II, pp. 358–368.

[2] Cf. A. W. Combs, "Phenomenological Concepts in Non-directive Therapy," *Journal of Consulting Psychology*, 1948, XII, pp. 97–208; D. Snygg and A. W. Combs, *Individual Behavior: A New Frame of Reference for Psychology* (New York, Harper, 1949). In German psychotherapeutic literature, the phenomenological point of view in its strictest sense is represented in such publications as L. Binswanger, *Ausgewählte Vorträge und Aufsätze*, I (Bern, A. Franck, 1947); and the "comprehensive" method of K. Jaspers, *Allgemeine Psychopathologie*, 5th edition (Berlin, Springer, 1948). See particularly Chapters I and IV. The *Daseinsanalytik* of Martin Heidegger has had a decisive influence on the development of thought in this direction.

experience, the defence-mechanisms which he habitually raises against a world which does not "accept" him, and in which he is dissatisfied with himself, disappear. Generally speaking, this new situation will lead him to accept himself and others.

The further stages of this process may be briefly described as follows. In the warm atmosphere of acceptance the patient is able *to manifest and communicate spontaneously the deeper emotional attitudes* governing his behaviour. He is thus enabled to understand his own conduct and emotional attitudes and to see them in a different light; and in this atmosphere he is prepared to look at certain aspects which he had previously preferred to ignore. He thus gains a sounder idea of his own motive-forces.

Having done this, the patient himself takes the initiative in the endeavour to free himself from his situation, questioning himself and asking himself what is to be done. The personal solution which he thus forms, and the new aims he sets before himself, are signs of an impulse towards healthy growth and maturity.

Rogers maintains that the therapeutic process always evolves spontaneously in this way. In the new situation the patient feels able to express himself freely and to be "accepted" as he is. In this way he acquires a fuller idea of himself; and this gives rise to a more active phase, in which his spontaneous power of growth is manifested in new ways of personal development which he has himself devised.

According to this method, the therapist's function does not consist in applying a special therapeutic process *to the patient*. The patient cures himself—that is to say, his own growth leads him to overcome his difficulties. The therapist's function is simply to create the situation which enables the patient to set this process in motion.

This means that the therapist must adopt a certain attitude and a certain method. He must believe that the patient can be responsible for himself. There can be no question of a plain submission of patient to therapist. The therapist must simply make every effort he possibly can to "feel with," to "sym-pathise" with, the patient and understand him. He must "reflect" the patient's mental attitudes, and in doing so make these attitudes clearer to the patient. He neither approves nor condemns; asks no question, makes no suggestions; gives no interpretation, no advice. It is the patient himself who finds his own solution and puts it into effect.[1]

In this kind of therapy, *diagnosis*, as a separate preliminary stage, does not exist. The therapist does not "explore" the patient. Rogers considers it bad for the patient to feel that he is the object of the therapist's diagnosis or criticism. For Rogers, "diagnostic knowledge and skill is not necessary for good therapy." This he says, knowing full well that it will be looked upon as a heresy by many a therapist.[2]

Rogers' attitude towards psychological diagnosis is a direct result of his idea of what therapeutic treatment aims at. As we have already seen, the aim is not so much the solution of problems as a change in the patient's mode of "experiencing." To obtain this result I have no need of "*objective* information" about anybody, nor do I need to treat him from the outside as an object, or try to size him up. I simply have to try to penetrate to the inside of his personality and see things from there.

In a passage which has aroused much expostulation, Rogers expresses his ideas on the subject of diagnosis as follows:

. . . instead of elaborate case histories full of information about the person as an object, we would endeavor to develop ways of seeing his situation, his past, and himself, as these objects appear to him. We would try to see with him, rather than to evaluate him. It might mean the minimizing of the elaborate psychometric procedures by which we have endeavored to measure or value the individual from our own frame of reference. It might mean the minimizing or discarding of all the vast series of labels which we have painstakingly built up over the years. Paranoid, preschizophrenic, compulsive, constricted—terms such as these might become irrelevant because they are all based in thinking which takes an external frame of reference. They are not the ways in which the individual experiences himself. If we consistently studied each individual from the internal frame of reference of that individual, from within his

[1] A literal reproduction of non-directive interviews of this kind will be found in W. U. Snyder, *Casebook of Non-directive Counseling* (Boston, Houghton Mifflin, 1947); also in C. A. Curran, *Personality Factors in Counseling* (New York, Grune & Stratton, 1945).

[2] Cf. Rogers, "Significant Aspects of Client-centered Therapy," p. 421; *The American Psychologist*, I, pp. 415-422. See also Rogers, "Psychometric Tests and Client-centered Counseling," *Educational and Psychological Measurement*, 1946, VI, pp. 139-144; C. H. Patterson, "Is Psychotherapy Dependent upon Diagnosis?", *The American Psychologist*, 1948, III, pp. 155-159.

own perceptual field, it seems probable that we should find generalizations which could be made, and principles which were operative, but we may be very sure that they would be of a different order from these externally based judgments *about* individuals.[1]

It is not our intention to go into the value and significance of different methods of diagnosis here. Rogers's words obviously contain an important truth; but he probably goes too far in his general condemnation of diagnosis and all its methods. For the truth is that psychological diagnosis, in the best sense of the term, is the fundamental way of access to the patient's subjective *inner world*, and this on the basis of *objective data*. There is not an unbridgeable gap between these two worlds. The most that can be said is that diagnosis needs to be seen anew—in the way that the best psychiatrists have always seen it.

(5) A CRITICAL APPRECIATION OF THE NON-DIRECTIVE METHOD

The reader will realize that this therapeutic method has certain points in common with ideas that we have considered at length in the earlier pages of this book; it can nevertheless be genuinely described as new, and in certain respects as revolutionary. It differs not only from psychoanalytical technique but also from the *traditional* methods of direction, as currently applied by those who in a variety of fields have charge of souls.

Besides the theoretical bases which we have already outlined, this kind of treatment possibly has one of its psychological origins in the "democratic" principles of American education, according to which everyone should go his own way on his own responsibility, without "authoritarian guidance" or pressure from outside.

In our opinion there is an important fund of truth and valid ideas in this kind of therapy. Our own personal experience has shown us that certain groups of people who at first want to have their problems *solved* for them are afterwards grateful for being given the chance to solve their difficulties *themselves*. Recently we heard a young man complaining quite openly that he felt oppressed after every visit to his therapist. Each time he came away with the fixed impression that he *could do nothing for himself* and *was*

[1] "Some Observations on the Organization of Personality," *The American Psychologist*, 1947, II, p. 367.

completely dependent on the man. A little later, when this young man—who is a person of considerable intelligence—had been freed from the burden of this "strong direction" and grown convinced that he could save himself, he was well on the way to recovery.

Nevertheless, we consider that it would be a mistake to make this into *a general principle.* *"Non-directive" therapy* can be an excellent method in certain cases, and it is well to remember some of its ideas and methods in all kinds of treatment and direction of conscience, but in a variety of cases, at least at certain stages of the treatment, a more "directive" or at least a more "suggestive" influence seems desirable.[1] It seems to us, too, that there are characteristic features in such and such people or such and such a cultural group which can make this method more easy or more difficult to apply.

Rogers underestimates the stimulating, suggestive influence which in a number of cases emanates from the very personality of the therapist. The therapist is not content merely to "reflect" the patient's psychic image; perhaps even without his knowing it, his personality and his words can have a positive influence of a constructive nature on the patient. This fact is shown even in the practice of non-directive therapy. Snyder, for example, describes the way a patient thanked her therapist after a course of treatment, for the non-directive rôle he had played. But she adds: "Your silence, and your shrewd reflections, and your subtle important meanings have gained my utmost confidence. . . . *You always came through with some excellent things when they were needed.*"[2] This shows how, when the thing is seen from the individual's point of view, the patient "receives" a great deal from the therapist, even when he makes every effort not to "give" anything at all.

[1] William U. Snyder, Rogers' well-known follower, mentions that in one of the six cases he studied the patient rejected the non-directive method and strongly opposed its application. He adds that it would be interesting to examine the more fundamental reason for this attitude towards the method. See W. U. Snyder, "An Investigation of the Nature of Non-directive Therapy," *The Journal of General Psychology*, 1945, XXXIII, pp. 193–223.

[2] See the interesting reproduction of these non-directive interviews in W. U. Snyder, *Casebook of Non-directive Counseling* (Boston, Houghton Mifflin, 1947). (Italics mine.)

As regards the connection between non-directive therapy and so-called "directive" methods such as psychoanalysis, it is possible that, in his reaction against the latter, Rogers exaggerates the difference between them. A psychoanalyst would say in fact, that during a great part of the treatment, and especially in its initial stages, he adopts a non-directive attitude towards his patient. And it seems that, conversely, even in the non-directive method a certain directive influence, not intentional perhaps but nevertheless real, emanates from the therapist. This certainly does not mean that Rogers has not seized on "something new," something quite different from the psychoanalytical method by which the therapist explores and interprets the patient's "ego-defences" and shatters them when the patient refuses to accept his own ideas.[1]

We also think that Rogers exaggerates the significance of a total "acceptance" of the patient. When one talks about the therapist's accepting the patient as he is, and when one maintains that the patient in this way arrives at a *fuller acceptance of himself*, there is an essential difference between these two things. The patient arrives at a *fuller acceptance of himself*, but this is not simply self-acceptance. Rogers himself recognizes that this "acceptance" involves a search for *new* living objectives, and aims which shall be *more satisfying than the maladjusted goals* of the past.

What the patient has to accept is his basic psychic equipment and his fundamental characteristics, his potentialities, and the unchangeable reality of his being. But this does not mean that he must accept his mental attitudes and his development at the moment.

Similarly, the fundamental attitude required from the therapist is one of complete *understanding* but not *mere acceptance* of the patient's actual personality: it means accepting the patient in the sense of *not reacting against* or *attacking* or *criticizing*

---

[1] Our earlier remarks, concerning Freud's advice to let the patient take his own initiative, should nevertheless be borne in mind. (Cf. *supra*, p. 33.)

As regards the relationship between Rogers' ideas and those of Freud, Rank, Taft and Allen, see especially N. J. Raskin, "The Development of Non-directive Therapy," *Journal of Consulting Psychology*, 1948, pp. 92–110.

the person as he actually is, and it means also *fully* accepting his real potentialities and possibilities. It means accepting what he is as *a possible starting-point of new growth.*

This distinction makes no difference to the atmosphere of acceptance which the patient should feel in his contact with the therapist, but it is necessary to make this distinction to give a fuller idea of the total attitude of therapist and patient as it develops during treatment. For there is a more *dynamic* kind of attitude possible, an "acceptance" which from the very beginning implies the possibility of a change for the better in the personality of the patient and makes this possible—and this change is, after all, the primary aim of the treatment. Mere acceptance, and nothing else, involves an attitude that does not meet the demands of the total therapeutic situation, nor even those of the patient's actual personality. For the patient is essentially someone who wishes, or who should wish, to change. And it is not usually a case of *one simple* change, of simply consenting to everything that exists in the patient at the moment: that would mean that the cure was simply a matter of growing reconciled to the aberrations or deviations of an abnormal development of the personality.

It seems to us highly important to define clearly the meaning of this word "acceptance," since it is bound up with a more general problem. The thing which must be emphasized, in fact, is the difference between the moral and the therapeutic sides of this "acceptance." It is precisely this which Rogers seems to fail to do. He thinks it an unreservedly good thing if, as a result of the therapeutic process, the patient is reconciled to himself as he is— i.e., with all his old moral attitudes, good, bad or indifferent.

After treatment one of his patients said: "I've always tried to be what the others thought I should be, but now I am wondering whether I shouldn't just see that I am what I am. . . . I find that when I feel things, even when I feel hate, I don't care. I don't mind. I feel more free somehow. I don't feel guilty about things."[1]

Rogers considers it an unqualified benefit that the patient should have come to see herself "realistically," as she is.

[1] "Some Observations on the Organization of Personality," p. 363; *The American Psychologist*, 1947, II, pp. 358–368.

It is, of course, a well-known fact that people suffering from psychic troubles can set themselves "moral" problems which are in fact simply therapeutic ones. A great part of what they experience as "evil" requires no change in their behaviour or moral attitude. All that needs to be done is to banish the psychic troubles which are creating the obsession with evil and guilt. This is a psychological and not a moral problem.

We can even go further. Even when these unsatisfactory spiritual conditions of mind are really bad from the moral point of view, *some sort of emotional liberation from the moral aspect of his behaviour and state of mind* can often be a good thing for the patient in the early stages of treatment. But the treatment itself will not mean an absolute liberation from all ethical demands and the moral sense.

It cannot be too often emphasized that the real aim of therapy is not to make the patient incapable of feeling guilty, but to refashion his disturbed functions and lead him to a truly human and therefore *moral* condition of mind towards the absolute, towards his neighbour and towards himself.

Rogers' idea of a total acceptance of man *as he is* seems to us in need of qualification. It is a defect even from a *purely psychological point of view*. And the ultimate reason for this is that Rogers does not sufficiently take into account *the fundamental conflict that characterizes human personality dynamics*.[1]

The self-realization he talks about is not a force that *follows a simple one-track direction* in man; nor does it simply run parallel to the growth of the biological organism.

The impulse towards psychic development which characterizes the human personality is composed of a number of forces which give rise to conflict and very various potentialities. A choice has to be made between this multiplicity of possibilities in the actual building-up of the personality. Thus self-realization involves at every moment a kind of renunciation. At every moment there exist lines of development and tendencies which, taken as a whole, a man does not wish to follow. These forces and possibilities of development in themselves are not without value; but the per-

[1] Cf. Carl Rogers, *Client-centered Therapy* (Boston, Houghton Mifflin, 1951). Cf. Chapter XI, "A Theory of Personality and Behavior."

sonality refuses to follow them so as to achieve greater self-realization in the direction chosen, or in the direction rendered obligatory by circumstance or the past.

These aspirations or tendencies which a man refuses to satisfy are *accepted* by the balanced personality as *real elements in its psychic life*. But they are not *merely* accepted; they are not accepted as forms of self-realization; they are opposed, the personality "makes itself *other*." In this sense the balanced personality does not accept itself at all: personality is something which has to be *made*, not simply *accepted*. In this kind of self-realization the balanced person accepts his total being as *"given*," but he does not accept what is "given" as his destination; there will be potentialities in his psychic equipment which he will not use in any positive sense for his self-development or self-realization, and there may be some which he will do his best to eliminate.

This question of the acceptance or non-acceptance of the self is a crucial point in any theory of personality as well as in psychotherapy. The theory of acceptance in Rogers' sense loses sight of the *specifically constructive element* in the actualization of the personality, i.e. the conflict and tension at the heart of man's dynamic structure. Psychoanalysis has only seen this conflict from its destructive side. It is probably in reaction against this unilateral way of looking at it—which led psychoanalysis to its theory of *repression*—that Rogers established his theory of acceptance. We believe that it is possible to give a fuller idea of this conflict-situation in psychic dynamism. In Chapter IV we shall try to develop such an idea.

(6) NON-DIRECTIVE THERAPY AND THE IDEA OF MAN

The *theory of personality* developed on the basis of non-directive therapy seems to us as important as the *method*.

We have already pointed out one of its first essential elements: the emphasis on the *sound, constructive forces of growth* which exist in man. This change from the point of view which looks at man pathologically and in the light of his destructive processes, to one which sees him from the angle of normality and in his constructive processes, seems to us a most important development in the theory of human personality.

From our summary of Rogers' method it should be clear that his conception is not purely theoretical but permeates his whole method, and has been developed according to its results in practice.

We must now make clear a second element in this theory of personality.

Contemporary psychology tends to consider the development of personality simply as the resultant of two sorts of influences. On the one hand there are cultural circumstances and factors, the individual's environment and personal history; on the other, the physiological conditions of his organic constitution. The human individual is simply the meeting-place of these active forces.

In any individual one discovers a number of needs and tendencies: what appears of them in his behaviour and character is, in the final analysis, no more than the *resultant* of dynamic factors, like the vectorial sum in the parallelogram of forces.

On the other hand, the idea of a "personal," autonomous constructive force that cannot be reduced to external or physiological influences has been abandoned, or is looked upon as a pre-scientific idea. Even the idea of human "will" has more or less lost its real meaning in positive and pathological psychology.

One example from amongst thousands will suffice to illustrate the truth of this. In a work on "Child Guidance" a European psychologist, emigrated to America, mentioned the human will and maintained that moral problems were *problems of will*. This assertion provoked this highly typical reaction from an American critic:

I would not embarrass this author by asking him what he means by "*Will*." As a contemporary Behaviourist (who like all contemporary Behaviourists disbelieves most of what Watson professed) I would say that the normal child has the capacity to be trained in such a way that he comes to be attracted to goals other than the satisfaction of tissue need (e.g., music, philosophical and theological interests, etc.). These acquired needs can become so strong that he will prefer their satisfaction to the satisfaction of the so-called baser needs antagonistic to the so-called higher ones. When this occurs, one may say (if he cares to), "This child has *character*," or as Mr. Harms would say, "He has a strong *will*."[1]

Obviously, from this example, it is no longer recognized that human needs can to some extent at least be raised to a specifically

[1] *Psychological Bulletin*, 1948, XLV, p. 370.

human or spiritual level. Hunger, for instance, can exist as a fact of knowledge in the human consciousness. Thus raised to the level of consciousness, it becomes a new starting-point in the dynamic life of the *autonomous personality;* it no longer rises into the behaviour-mechanism directly by means of the neuro-muscular processes. The individual *adopts a certain attitude* towards this need and *decides* either to pursue the "value" which is its object or to follow some other value corresponding to some other dynamic orientation. *Will* is the name given to the psychic dynamism inasmuch as it undergoes this transformation in human consciousness and thus forms a new starting-point in the self-determination of the personality.

Rogers approaches such a conception of the self-determination of the person when, very impartially, he analyses the data implied in his own therapeutic ideas and discoveries. Here are his own words. His ideas form an element in American psychology approaching to the *traditional* philosophic idea of human personality:

The clinical experience could be summarized by saying that the behavior of the human organism may be determined by the influences to which it has been exposed, *but it may also be determined by the creative and integrative insight of the organism itself.* This ability of the person to discover new meaning in the forces which impinge upon him and in the past experiences which have been controlling him, and *the ability to alter consciously his behavior in the light of this new meaning,* has a profound significance for our thinking which has not been fully realized. We need to revise the philosophical basis of our work to a point where it can admit that forces exist within the individual which can exercise a spontaneous and significant influence upon behavior *which is not predictable through knowledge of prior influences* and conditionings. The forces released through a catalytic process of therapy are not adequately accounted for by a knowledge of the individual's previous conditionings, but only if we grant the presence of a *spontaneous force within the organism which has the capacity of integration and redirection.* This capacity for *volitional control* is a force which we must take into account in any psychological equation.[1]

It may prove significant for the spiritual conception of man in psychotherapy that such ideas should have been reached from data supplied by actual psychological treatment.

[1] "Significant Aspects of Client-centered Therapy," p. 422; *The American Psychologist,* 1946, I, pp. 415–422. (All but the first italics mine.)

It is a highly promising fact that client-centred therapy should be so active in the study of personality. Its studies are made by means of objective analyses of therapeutic material recorded *verbatim* in the course of the interview. The book by a follower of Rogers, Rev. C. A. Curran—*Personality Factors in Counseling*[1]—is an example of this kind of approach. It contains one chapter which is entirely devoted to the *theory* of personality in the light of therapeutic fact.

Another remarkable characteristic of this school is the important place it gives to *experimental* research on the actual therapeutic situation. The new and refreshing tendency in psychotherapy as a whole, including progressive psychoanalytical schools, is to liberate itself from subjective generalizations and dogmatic theories and to look to experiment as the means to progress. In America at the present moment clinical psychology and psychotherapy are a growing and active sector of experimental psychology.

This brief sketch should have sufficed to show that non-directive psychotherapy is a new development which both as a *theory* and as a *method* of treatment no one can afford to ignore.

(7) THE *rapprochement* BETWEEN CLINICAL PSYCHOLOGY AND EXPERIMENTAL PSYCHOLOGY

Having considered the importance of the *rapprochement* which can be seen taking place between clinical psychology on the one hand and general experimental psychology on the other, it now becomes necessary to show how exactly this contact is being realized.

We will first quote a few cases in which the "clinical situation" becomes the actual field of experiment.

It is generally recognized that patients at a psychological clinic are often people whose emotional life is unbalanced. This loss of emotional equilibrium shows itself, amongst other things, in the fact that in any particular set of circumstances the patient more easily feels *frustrated* than the normal person: furthermore, every frustrating situation causes an exaggerated *reaction* in him.

[1] (New York, Grune & Stratton, 1945.)

We can now examine how, *under the effect of the therapeutic treatment,* this exaggerated reaction to frustration evolves.

Before treatment, the patient is placed for the purposes of experiment in some frustrating situation. If, for example, he is a child, he is deprived of something that had been promised him. The force of his emotional reaction to this situation is then measured by recording physiological changes such as the psycho-galvanic reaction, changes in the circulation of the blood, and breathing. A control group consisting of normal persons is sub-mitted to the same frustrating experience, and the differences in the two kinds of reaction are noted.

At the end of the psychotherapeutic treatment the patient is again placed experimentally in a frustrating situation and his reactions again measured. A diminution in emotional reaction—i.e., a movement towards the normal reaction of the control group—is always observed in a patient who has been treated successfully. In this way it can be discovered by experiment what effect any particular method of therapy has on emotional reaction.

Here is another example. Backward children undergoing *play therapy* do nine forty-five-minute reading exercises during a month's treatment. It is said that the progress made during these nine periods combined with the play therapy is greater than would be achieved by a year's reading in school. Experiments of this kind point to highly significant facts, which will have to be taken into account in any general theory of the mechanisms of learning.

Systematic study has also been made of the relation between the new idea which the patient develops of himself during treat-ment and his way of "looking at" his fellow-men; and it has been established that both are intimately bound up with each other and develop favourably by non-directive treatment.[1]

Again, certain techniques in the use of diagnosis which are employed in clinical psychology—for example, Rorschach's test—are having a great amount of experimental research devoted to

[1] Cf. the Proceedings of the Annual Meeting of the American Psycho-logical Association, Boston, 1948, in the July 1948 number of *The American Psychologist;* also various contributions to *The Journal of Consulting Psy-chology,* 1949, XIII.

them. Rorschach's test has been examined for the laws of perception in general; the emotional shock produced by the coloured charts providing us with new ideas about the emotional value of colours, etc.

Another aspect of the *rapprochement* between clinical psychology and experimental psychology appears in the fact that systems and theories drawn from the field of the psychology of behaviour have supplied a basis of general ideas which clinical psychology has made great use of. Thus, at the meeting of the American Psychological Society in 1948, a symposium was prepared at members' request on the application of Clark Hull's theory of behaviour to psychological therapy. It may seem astonishing that a behaviourist system as rigid and mathematical as Hull's should tempt the clinicists.[1] But it must not be forgotten that the idea of *need reduction* which Hull uses to explain behaviour is a cardinal point in the explanation and treatment of psychic troubles.

On the other hand, some of the ideas of *general and social* psychology are being used increasingly to explain psychoanalytical processes. Thus, for instance, there is French's theory, in which *cognitive factors* and the process of *social integration* play an important part. This distinguished Chicago psychologist shows how the mere fact of conceiving *the possibility of achieving* the aim of an activity creates in the patient an attitude of hope about the satisfaction of his needs. According to French this attitude of hope transforms the "destructive" pathological tendencies of the patient into "erotic" or beneficent ones. As a result of this change in emotional attitude the individual succeeds in enlarging his capacity for understanding and also his capacity for social relationships.

In a young man who is trying as the result of an infantile need to gain his mother's love, the hope of realizing his aim lessens the psychological tension and turns his relationship with his sister into an erotic one. In this "optimistic" situation, he expresses his affection for his sister in dreams and gives proof of an affectionate understanding of her own needs. It is *with her*, and at the same time as her, that he now wins his mother's love and protection. A

[1] Cf. C. Clark Hull, *Principles of Behavior* (New York, Appleton-Century, 1943).

few days later, however, the realization of his aim seems impossible and he despairs of gaining his mother's love. This new situation is translated in another dream into destructive tendencies of hostility towards his sister and a total lack of understanding of her needs.[1]

We are here simply trying to extract the psychological value of the material used by French as a starting-point and proof of his theory, and it is sufficient for our purpose to show that factors of a cognitive and social nature are coming to play an essential part in this theory, which may be described, not as *psychoanalytical* but simply as *psychological*. The *rapprochement* between psychoanalytical problems and theories and those of Behaviorist psychology in general comes out still more clearly in the words with which this distinguished American psychoanalyst ended the article he contributed to the Chicago symposium of October, 1948: "The key to our next advances in psychodynamic understanding must be more systematic investigation of the *mechanisms that make possible goal-directed behavior*."[2]

In these words psychoanalysis as the doctrine of an esoteric school disappears, to become integrated with the general psychology of behaviour.

Another point that must be noted is the effort being made to submit certain cardinal ideas and processes in psychoanalysis to experimental control. Laboratory psychologists are endeavouring to establish connections between certain ideas of the psychology of behaviour and psychoanalytical explanations of human conduct.

One of the most suggestive researches on this subject—made by Neal Miller, whom we have already mentioned in a different context[3]—attempts by means of experiment to connect the idea of "generalization," well known in the theory of conditional reflexes,

---

[1] Cf. Thomas French, "The Integration of Social Behavior," *The Psychoanalytic Quarterly*, 1945, XIV, pp. 149–168. Compare also on this subject the ideas of De Greeff, as found in his important work, *Les instincts de défense et de sympathie* (Paris, Presses Universitaires de France, 1947).

[2] Cf. Thomas French, "Study of the Integrative Process, Its Importance for Psychiatric Theory," in *The Mooseheart Symposium on Feelings and Emotions*, ed. M. L. Reymert (New York, McGraw-Hill, 1950). See also, from the same author, *The Integration of Behavior* (The University of Chicago Press, 1952).

[3] Cf. *supra*, 48.

with the concept of "displacement," frequently employed in psychoanalysis.

It is said, for instance, that certain aggressive reactions set up in the child in the first place by the attitude of its parents, can be increasingly transferred on to its playmates—just as tendencies and activities which in real life are focussed on a particular person get transferred in dreams on to someone else. Moreover, this process of *displacement* plays a part in that *emotional transference* which is one of the essential mechanisms in psychoanalytical therapy.

On the other hand, study of the conditioned reflex has ascertained that behaviour caused by a special stimulus (such as a particular sound) can be provoked just as effectively by another auditory stimulus with a different wave-frequency from that of the first (the phenomenon of generalization). Here, as in the case cited above of parents and playmates, one stimulus has been displaced by another of a similar kind but nevertheless different.

There are great differences, however, between the two types of facts on which the ideas of *displacement* and *generalization* are based. More recently, therefore, efforts have been made to create experimental situations approaching more and more closely to the psychoanalytical idea of displacement but for which an explanation remains possible in terms of generalization. Thus we find that two rats, which have been trained to strike at each other as soon as an electric current is passed through the bars of their cage, attack a similar object—for example, a doll—when left alone in the cage.[1]

More important than this "displacement" of objects affecting behaviour is the fact that a transference can equally well be made from one need to another. For instance, there is the question whether sexual need can be alleviated by the satisfaction of other appetites, such as hunger or thirst.[2] In Behaviorist terminology this would mean that the *excitation systems* of different instinctive tendencies resemble each other, or overlap to such an extent that there can be a certain transference from one to the other.

[1] Neal E. Miller, "Theory and Experiment Relating Psychoanalytic Displacement to Stimulus-Response Generalization," *The Journal of Abnormal and Social Psychology*, 1948, XLIII, pp. 155–178.

[2] Cf. *supra*, p. 48.

This Behaviorist formula was tested experimentally as regards a possible transference from thirst to hunger. The results of the experiment showed that hunger and thirst possess a certain degree of functional equivalence, and that this can be equally well expressed either as "generalization" or in terms of "displacement."[1]

Research on the so-called "experimental neurosis" in animals is also supposed to throw light on some of the ideas and processes of psychopathology. The works of Masserman and Liddell are particularly important in this respect.[2]

All this research and much more of the same kind tends to have a most welcome influence, not only on the experimental psychology of human behaviour but on the development of psychoanalysis and clinical psychology in general. Anybody who ignored or neglected these currents in psychoanalysis would be quite rightly considered out of date as a psychologist.

3. Conclusions

From this sketch of the present condition of psychoanalytical method and psychotherapy in general it should be clear that there can be no question of a simple alternative between *accepting* and *rejecting* orthodox psychoanalysis *in toto*. Here as with Freudian *theory* it is wiser to adopt a more "open-minded," a more scientific attitude. This means seeing Freudian therapy as one method amongst many, and seeing it in its connections with psychotherapy as a whole. Thus, we maintain, there is no reason either to limit oneself to its technique or to reject it lock, stock and barrel.

There is no doubt that the application of orthodox analytical technique has frequently been successful in the field of therapy. It is equally certain that in a number of cases it has either produced no result at all or simply caused a temporary improvement in the patient's condition. This is shown particularly in the impartial inquiry which was carried out by Oberndorf into the results obtained by eighteen psychoanalysts over a period of at least

[1] Cf. Neal Miller, *loc. cit.*, p. 161.
[2] See the contributions of Jules Masserman and G. S. Liddell to the *Mooseheart Symposium on Feelings and Emotions* (New York, McGraw-Hill, 1950).

twenty years each. Further confirmation comes from the fact that of the thirty patients who in the course of two years applied to Oberndorf himself, thirty per-cent had already undergone a course of analytic treatment, without any success.[1]

The success obtained by the application of any particular method does not, of course, prove the validity of the theory behind it. The fact is that a great number of cases of neurosis can be interpreted according to vastly different theoretical systems—Adler's as well as Freud's, for example—and such cases would probably be treated successfully by any of the corresponding methods. Sometimes it is even sufficient for the case to be simply "treated"—for someone to concern himself with the patient by taking an interest in him, understanding him, or rousing his initiative.

Let us add that in practice every psychotherapist has to adopt an eclectic system in the construction and adaptation of the *technique* that best suits his own personality; and especially has to be skilful in varying and adapting his methods to suit the case he is dealing with.

The pathogenic factors and mechanisms in human psychic life are more diverse, both in origin and in nature, than Freud and Adler and many other theorists with their rigidly uniform systems are prepared to admit. The analytical method may suit one case, but another may require a different kind of treatment. In each case the way in which the therapist manages the interviews and guides the relationship between the patient and himself, or, again, the way he grasps the conflict as a whole, will bear the mark of his personality. No one will deny that besides the objective value of the method employed, the therapist's personal "stamp" is an important factor in psychotherapy, even when the method of treatment, as in *non-directive therapy*, is one in which he plays a comparatively passive part.

The uneasiness that is to be felt in the minds of a number of orthodox psychoanalysts is a direct result (as we have shown by examples) of the need they feel to free themselves from the narrow confines of Freudian doctrine.

[1] Cf. C. P. Oberndorf, "Results of Psychoanalytic Therapy," *International Journal of Psychoanalysis*, 1943, XXIV, pp. 107–114.

Besides this narrowness of view which prevents Freudian therapy from envisaging the wider human problems involved in psychic disturbances, the analytical method has practical disadvantages in the field of therapeutic technique. It is often a bad thing for a patient during treatment to concentrate for months on end on his own psychic life. Many neurotics need to be taken out of themselves and delivered from their egocentric state of mind. The *objective attitude* of the man who directs his psychic activity outwards towards "the world," and does not concentrate always and everywhere upon himself is perhaps the first characteristic of psychic health. For this reason a detailed investigation into his own past—which may involve months, even years, of looking into himself—can in some cases be bad for the patient.

The well-known Chicago psychoanalyst Franz Alexander has said that Freudian analysis encourages the *neurotic tendency to regression*. Even before Alexander, one of Freud's own followers, Wilhelm Stekel, had emphasized the danger of a protracted analysis. This is one of the reasons why the psychoanalytical school of Chicago (French and Alexander) adopted the abridged technique which, as we said earlier, attaches less importance to *genetic* analysis or a detailed investigation of the past. As soon as enough facts have been gathered to make it possible to identify the source of the traumatic experiences, treatment begins on the patient's *immediate* difficulties of adaptation. In our opinion, however, short therapy cannot be effective in all cases. The orthodox Freudian technique seems to be indicated in a number of instances. Therefore, in therapy as well as in psychoanalytic doctrine, *discrimination* should be the rule. Orthodox psychoanalysis is not to be thought of as simply synonymous with *psychotherapy*, but analytical therapy undoubtedly is and remains a basic therapeutic technique.

Moreover, psychoanalytical *therapy* is not inseparably connected with Freudian *theory*. Despite the fact that sexual disorders frequently lie behind the most disturbing symptoms in psychotherapy, some therapists have come to admit that sexual conflicts are by no means invariably the fundamental cause of these disorders. The actual sexual problem itself is often better understood in conjunction with other dynamic forces and conflicts involving the human personality *as a whole*, and which are bound up with the whole complex system of human tendencies and needs. From this point of view sex is merely the most vulnerable part of psychic life, where the total dislocation of the personality manifests itself in its most striking and, it may be, its most serious form.

For the psychiatrist or psychologist with a spiritual outlook who concerns himself with psychotherapy, the essential point is to go thoroughly into the matter and so reach a wide conception of human life and the needs which are at work there. The study of the teaching of one school only can never fulfil this requirement. This study should also involve that of the "spiritual," i.e. the *specifically human* aspects of personality, and the problems they engender, without, however, these being considered as isolated abstractions, unconnected with man's organic existence as a whole.

Needs and frustrations at the spiritual level are not, perhaps, as easy to discover as sexual aberrations; but the deepest reason why a person fails to adapt himself to existence is often to be found in a loss of spiritual balance, and the void thus created in the man of our time. Not infrequently it will be discovered that a revivification of the patient's spiritual potentialities will develop the energy which lies at the root of a balanced life.

Anyone who uses study and practice to delve ever more deeply into human personality as a whole can utilize the various psychotherapeutic techniques without danger. He will gain from them a wealth of insight and practical instruction, and thus develop a more concrete idea of psychic disorders without any risk of falling into one-sided generalizations.

Psychiatrists and psychotherapists possibly do not realize the value of a profounder study of the psychology of the normal man. We believe that the study of psychic aberration should come after the study of normal psychology, just as problems of pathological physiology are investigated only after a knowledge of *general* physiology has been acquired. "Individual" psychology, in the wider sense, as used by Alfred Binet—i.e., the study of the personality as a whole, and of the dynamics of behaviour within the framework of the psychology of behaviour—will be essential in the formation of the psychotherapist of the future in the field of general psychology.[1]

To sum up, then: this general survey of the present tendencies in psychotherapy shows the progress of psychoanalysis in clearer perspective. Secondly, it indicates that there is a greater *possibility* than there used to be of developing a spiritual conception of personality in psychotherapy. There are many signs which suggest this: first, *the tendency to use the vague notions of the unconscious and repression less narrowly.* Treatment is coming to be looked upon, for instance, more as an apprenticeship in a new kind of relationship with oneself and others, the acquisition of a new idea of oneself, with a consequent freeing of the forces of healthy growth.

Then there is the tendency to consider the *experiences of the first few years of life as less decisive* for the development of personality than they were formerly thought to be. According to Freud, the lines of personal development are laid down even before the awakening of the spiritual personality.

Finally, there is the emphasis on the *social aspects* of psychic life and the *forces of healthy growth,* rather than on *organic* impulses and *destructive* mechanisms. This means a wider and healthier conception of man's psychic life.

All this does not by any means imply that the present tendencies in psychotherapy are approaching a spiritual conception of human personality. To some extent the opposite process is at work. But there are some encouraging signs, and the present atmosphere is more propitious for the development of a broader conception of human personality than was that of the orthodox psychoanalytical school.

It is incumbent on spiritually minded psychologists to work towards this development. Nowhere else in psychology, perhaps, is it more disastrous to base one's ideas and one's activity on a truncated conception of human personality than in psychotherapy, where the essential thing to do is to remedy the malformations of man *in search of himself.*

[1] See for information about more profound studies of this subject the Suggestions for Bibliography.

CHAPTER III

PSYCHOANALYSIS AS THE PSYCHOLOGY OF THE UNCONSCIOUS (DEPTH-PSYCHOLOGY)

1. The Unconscious and the Idea of Man

From the time of Descartes *consciousness* was looked upon as the characteristic feature distinguishing psychological phenomena from the other manifestations of human life. Psychic life was practically taken to be the same thing as consciousness. In this life of consciousness, the chief parts were played by the functions of *knowledge* and *will*. Occasionally, of course, disturbing elements such as instincts and emotions gave signs of their existence, but the struggle between rational functions and these perturbing elements was always decided in the light of conscious life. Psychic life, with its passions and conflicts, was crystal-clear; the forces that were active there were *known*, and when the battle was over, the victor was felt to have won a clear-cut decision. Even now, we usually feel in our own hearts that the same judgment can be rendered in our own case.

In recent years depth-psychology has presented us with a different picture of psychic life. *In fact*, it is said, forces quite different from the *rational* faculties of understanding and will are in control. In their conflict with the "higher" tendencies, the "lower" ones or the "instincts" follow a secret strategy. In the open battle of consciousness the instinctive forces may frequently suffer defeat; they easily give in. Man then imagines that he can proceed along the way of reason towards the end that he has consciously set up for himself. But, says depth-psychology, the instinctive tendencies always attain their object. They govern our conduct; they are the real motive-force behind all behaviour. *But their activity goes on behind the screen of conscious life.*

It will be obvious that this emphasis on the action of unconscious forces profoundly modifies the traditionally held image of man as a spiritual being, especially as so much emphasis is laid on the so-called "inferior" needs.

At first this change of perspective was limited to the more or less pathological aspects of psychic life. But at the same time a line of investigation was developing in psychology and psychiatry which was increasingly narrowing the boundaries between the normal and the pathological, until finally there was only a *difference of degree* between the normal individual and the pathological case—the reason given being that the psychic life of both reveal the same fundamental mechanisms and conflicts.

Thus the *normal* man too was brought into the orbit of depth-psychology. The effects of unconscious dynamic forces were shown in the most insignificant manifestations of his psychic life—as, for instance, in his dreams and slips of the tongue. *It is precisely this extension of the unconscious from the pathological to the normal which has gradually but unmistakably caused such considerable change in our psychological picture of man.* In all kinds of manifestations of psychic life, disguised unconscious tendencies of a morbid nature have been shown, with a greater or less degree of probability, to exist.

Thus depth-psychology has brought crumbling down from its pedestal the Renaissance picture of man, the master and the "rational" man, the idol of the Enlightenment. Nowadays we are inclined to agree with Jacques de Lacretelle, who said, "Every human being is a madman who watches himself."[1]

[1] Jacques de Lacretelle in his preface to the French translation of Emily Brontë's *Wuthering Heights*, *Haute Plainte* (Paris, Gallimard).

These ideas, after successfully invading psychology, have now permeated everything, including the ideas of people who have no interest in psychology. We have all become far more sceptical and distrustful of the manifestations of our psychic life. Certain forms of piety and pretended sanctity, of humility and devotion, which were once openly admired, are now received with suspicion or reserve. We have become particularly suspicious of some illnesses and similar irregularities.

As regards such manifestations, even the man in the street talks—usually quite mistakenly—of *hysteria* and *neurosis*. These are simply vague words to him, but they do at least mean that behind such forms of behaviour he suspects the intervention of mysterious forces which do not reach as far as consciousness. Man has become mistrustful of the mystery which dwells within him. On all sides he suspects infiltrations from the pathological and the unconscious.

In public life, especially in courts of law, the judgments passed on man and his actions have become a good deal more tentative. Ideas like *irresponsibility* have become only too familiar. Here too is a feeling that unconscious pathological mechanisms are at work.

But it is especially in modern *literature* that the psychological picture of man bears the stamp of these new ideas. And it is, of course, this literature particularly which has helped to spread the new idea of man. Today we are far from the clear psychology of the classical writers, far even from the transparent, well-ordered passions of Racine. The Fate of classical tragedy, that mysterious tragic power which drove man *from outside*, has been transformed into an *inner* power, a force in the individual's own unconscious life. The man presented to us by contemporary literature is the man of depth-psychology. For both, the pathological and the unconscious are involved with the normal and with it form one tangled skein. As Groddeck put it, there are irrepressible unknown forces that live the human life in man. What we call the conscious *ego* plays rather a passive rôle in this drama between impersonal forces.[1]

The intellectual life of university men and men of science gives a most striking idea of the struggle which is being waged between two conceptions of man in our modern civilization. As a social

[1] Cf. Freud, *Gesammelte Werke*, XIII, p. 251.

being and a man of culture, the scientist still holds to the traditional view, regarding the human person as an autonomous being who is his own master, with an exceptional place in nature. But when he gets back to his laboratory or clinic he unconsciously changes the framework of his thinking; here the human personality is absorbed into the impersonal processes of nature, into the system of instinctive forces which together make up the dynamism of life.

This must suffice for the moment to show how the various psychoanalytical systems, as psychologies of the unconscious, have had such a profound influence on our conception of man.

We must now examine how the doctrine of the unconscious came to light in psychoanalysis.

2. The Unconscious and the Split Personality

The idea of the unconscious had been familiar in philosophy and literature for a long time.[1] Carus, the contemporary and friend of Goethe, had said that the key to psychic life was to be found in the unconscious. But the new psychoanalytical idea of the unconscious developed from studies of hypnosis, and more particularly theories about hysteria.

Hypnosis made the psychiatrist realize a highly significant fact, that the psychic life of any single human being has two separate zones of consciousness, so to speak. In a state of trance the patient can relate events which he is quite unable to remember in his ordinary daily life and which, therefore, are no longer conscious. Contrariwise, the events that take place under hypnosis do not enter into normal conscious life, so that the individual cannot remember them afterwards.

This discovery gave Charcot, and particularly his pupil Janet, the idea of *double consciousness* and the *dissociation of the personality*.

This idea of dissociation became the basis of a theory to explain hysteria. Charcot showed that by hypnotic suggestion hysterical symptoms could be created—as, for instance, paralysis of the arm.

[1] As to the various senses of the term "unconscious," see James G. Miller, *Unconsciousness* (New York, John Wiley, 1942).

This fact was interpreted according to the associationist ideas of the time: the "representation" or picture of a paralyzed arm that had been suggested during hypnosis became *inaccessible* to the thought-contents and associations emanating from the other state of consciousness, i.e. daily life, and for this reason the symptom could not disappear in normal life.

The hysterical personality was characterized by just such a dissociation of psychic life. The hysterical person cannot integrate into *a totality* the multiplicity of his psychic contents. Thus certain contents escape from the unity. The hysterical person finds himself, in Freud's familiar image, in the same situation as the woman who comes back from a shopping expedition carrying a heap of parcels. She cannot manage to hold them all, and every time she tries to pick up the one that has fallen down she drops another.

Hysterical paralysis of the arm, therefore, would mean being unable to connect this representation of the arm with the other associations of the conscious ego.

This theory of Janet's regarding the split personality lies at the root of the Freudian idea of the two zones of psychic life, the *conscious* and the *unconscious*. This connection is made clear by Freud himself. This is what he says: "We followed his example when we made mental splitting and the dissociation of personality the central points of our theory."[1]

It is interesting in this connection to note a passage from Freud dating from 1892. In this passage, speaking of a certain memory-content, he says: "This content is unconscious, or more precisely, it belongs to the *second state of consciousness*." Here we see a parallel drawn between the *unconscious* and a *second state of consciousness* separate from the first.[2] Freud's declaration of 1925, therefore—in a violent passage of his *Selbstdarstellung* which is aimed at Janet—hardly seems correct. "Historically," he wrote, "psychoanalysis is completely independent of Janet's discoveries."[3]

[1] Cf. "The Origin and Development of Psychoanalysis," *The American Journal of Psychology*, 1910, XXI, p. 191. See also *Gesammelte Werke*, VIII, p. 17.
[2] Cf. "*Zur Theorie des hysterischen Anfalles*," *Gesammelte Werke*, XVII, p. 11.
[3] Cf. "*Selbstdarstellung*," *Gesammelte Werke*, XIV, p. 56.

3. The Dynamic Idea of the Unconscious

However, Freud developed a different idea from Janet's about this split consciousness. According to Janet the dissociation of the personality is a result of a *congenital* weakness of the nervous system, which makes the individual incapable of synthesizing his psychic contents into a unity. Freud, on the other hand, using his new psychoanalytical method, directs his attention more and more towards the *psychic conflict* which reveals itself *between different tendencies*. The result of this conflict is that the objects of one tendency (in this case sexual) are *repressed out of the field* of consciousness. These psychic contents then become unconscious and thus form another kind of psychic content, what is called the *unconscious*.

In this conception, the division of psychic life into *conscious* and *unconscious* contents is essentially bound up with the *dynamic aspect* of psychic life and the theory of *repression*. Freud says this in so many words: "We see in psychic dissociation the result of an activity in which the two categories of psychic content rise up against each other."[1]

As Freud's ideas developed, the field of the unconscious extended further and further. Whereas in the early stages the *ego* was looked upon as the *field of consciousness*, as opposed to the unconscious and the repressed, ultimately it appeared that "large portions of the ego and super-ego can remain unconscious; are, in fact, normally unconscious."[2]

And he gradually defined more clearly the distinctions between the various meanings that the word *unconscious* had taken on in psychoanalysis.

Because of the importance which this notion of the unconscious assumes in our spiritual conception of man we must endeavour to appreciate at their just value the facts and theories which lie behind the psychoanalytical development of the idea.

In ordinary psychology the term *unconscious* is often used to

[1] Cf. Freud, "*Über Psychoanalyse,*" *Gesammelte Werke*, VIII, p. 23: "Wir . . . erkennen in ihr (die psychische Spaltung) das Ergebnis eines aktiven Straubens der beiden psychischen Gruppierungen gegeneinander."
[2] Cf. "*Neue Folge,*" *Gesammelte Werke*, XV, p. 76.

designate the *latent* form in which certain contents are present to the mind. It is in this way, for instance, that memories are present in the mind when they are not actually being remembered. Freud suggests that this kind of unconsciousness should be called "preconsciousness." This preconscious is not in fact conscious but, unlike the psychoanalytical unconscious, *it can easily become conscious*. This preconscious has no interest for depth-psychology.

It was Bernheim's discoveries concerning the phenomena of *post-hypnotic suggestion* which gave Freud the first hint of the meaning that the unconscious has since acquired in psychoanalysis.

Bernheim was a contemporary of Charcot, who practised hypnosis at Nancy. When his patients were in a state of trance he would give them an order—for example, to perform a certain act at a certain time. The patient was then roused from his sleep, and at the set time he would perform the action he had been told to do, without being in the least aware that he had been given any order to do so.

In Freud's opinion, these phenomena showed that the elements present latently or unconsciously in the psyche do not necessarily remain in a state of impotence and inactivity. An element can remain unconscious and yet intervene actively in behaviour.

Freud connects these facts, which reveal the "activity" of the unconscious, with his theory of repression. The only reason why certain contents or certain representations become active without coming into consciousness is because *access to consciousness is barred*. This is because *the content of these representations rouses tendencies* that are opposed by other forces dominating the consciousness. It is certain, says Freud, that the rejection of unconscious thoughts is caused by tendencies embodied in the content of these thoughts.[1]

Thus we come back to the Freudian conception of dissociation. Certain psychic contents are dismissed *because of their dynamic content:* this means that they cannot come into consciousness and so form a realm apart. But the meaning of the unconscious has been enriched by the addition of a new essential element. The unconscious is no longer simply repressed out of consciousness

[1] Cf. *"Einige Bemerkungen über den Begriff des Unbewussten," Gesammelte Werke*, VIII, p. 436.

because of a dynamic conflict: *it still continues to exert an active influence on conscious conduct even though it does not penetrate into consciousness.*

Such is the *dynamic, bilateral* idea of the unconscious in psycho-analytical doctrine. The unconscious, taken in this sense, says Freud, dominates the greater part of psychic life.

4. The Unconscious as a Principle of Interpretation

Besides meaning a dynamic factor of human behaviour, the word "unconscious" has a further meaning in psychoanalysis. It is used to designate a *part* of the *structure* of personality. On the basis of his analysis of dreams Freud turned the unconscious into something entirely different from a mysterious *property* of certain active elements in psychic life. He deduced from the mechanism of dreams a whole apparatus of processes and mechanisms previously unknown, which he looked upon as real, though unconscious, psychic activities. For this reason he proceeded to make the unconscious a "part" of psychic activity and a "sector" of the psyche, *in which* are to be discovered the "unconscious contents" in the dynamic sense of the term. The unconscious was now used in a *topical* sense to mean a "sector" or zone of the psychic life. In this zone a whole network of unconscious processes is at work, just as in the zone of consciousness there are all the usual psychic processes.[1] It was by ascribing this new meaning to the unconscious that psychoanalysis carried the dissociation of the personality to the extent of dividing the psyche into "two sectors."

In order to avoid confusion between the two meanings of "the unconscious," Freud in his later works used a new expression. He called the psychic "zone" or "sector" of the unconscious, i.e. the unconscious in its systematic and topical meaning, the "*Id.*" Nietzsche had previously given this name to all that is impersonal and "determined by nature" in man. As the result of a suggestion

[1] See particularly Freud, "*Einige Bemerkungen über den Begriff des Unbewussten in der Psychoanalyse,*" *Gesammelte Werke,* VIII, pp. 438–439; and on the subject of the "psychic topic": "*Das Unbewusste*" (1913), *Gesammelte Werke,* X, pp. 264–303.

by Groddeck, Freud adopted this term into his system.[1] He meant
by it that "dark, chaotic part" of our personality whence arise
our impulsive drives, and which contains the psychic contents
that cannot enter consciousness or that have been repressed out
of consciousness by the censorship exerted by the third sector of
the personality, the super-ego (*Über-ich*).

This change of terminology has a wider significance than appears at first sight. It means that gradually the *quality* of unconsciousness, in the dynamic sense of the term, is being recognized
in an increasing number of activities. In this way several processes
which were attributed in the first place to the ego or the super-
ego and considered as conscious were later declared to be unconscious.

The process of repression, for example, held at first to be a
conscious process emanating from the ego, was declared unconscious and attributed to a great extent to the super-ego. Repression
in fact was given such a large place in Freud's system that it
could no longer be looked upon as merely the effect of a *conscious*
conflict. Freud appealed to this process in many cases when the
individual had no knowledge of a conflict. By turning repression
into an *unconscious* process Freud increased the opportunities of
applying it considerably.

It is clear that the attribution of the *quality* of unconsciousness
to all kinds of activity belonging to many different zones of the
personality was bound to create confusion between the *unconscious* as the *zone proper* of certain contents and mechanisms discovered by Freud, and the *unconscious* as a *quality* inhering in
activities found in different zones. It is also evident that this
extension and overlapping of the unconscious means an extension
of the part played by "hypothesis" and "construction" in psychoanalysis. In fact, *"unconscious" is the name given to all those psychic elements whose existence is to be assumed in the development
of psychoanalytical theory, i.e. all the elements assumed by the
psychoanalytical interpretation of overt psychic phenomena.*

The unconscious thus became an element in theoretical "constructions" which psychoanalysis did not always use with the
utmost care. The consequence has been that the centre of gravity

[1] Cf. *"Das Ich und das Es"* (1923), *Gesammelte Werke*, XIII, pp. 246–255.

of psychic life has been shifted rather too hastily to obscure, irrational areas. It has become the fashion in popular parlance— and for some psychologists too—to "*explain*" all sorts of phenom- ena by a simple appeal to the unconscious. We shall see later that this idea of the *unconscious* may need to be qualified.

This *orientation towards the irrational in man* has been still further accentuated by other movements—by philosophical sys- tems like that of Klages, and by physiological explanations of psy- chic life such as Behaviorism.

5. The Unconscious and Freedom

Having presented the doctrine of the unconscious and shown the influence it has had on the psychological view of man, it remains for us to consider our central problem: to what extent is the influence of unconscious factors on conduct compatible with a spiritual belief in *the freedom of human acts?*

(1) POST-HYPNOTIC SUGGESTION

To begin with, let us consider the hypnotic phenomena, from the consideration of which Freud's ideas concerning the influence of the unconscious on conduct began.

Acts performed during hypnosis are not particularly relevant to our problem; for these acts do not form part of normal behav- iour. But it is known that a hypnotized person, *after* coming out of a trance—and therefore back *into a normal state of conscious- ness*—may perform acts ordered during the trance, and do this without knowing that he is obeying an order.

These are cases of post-hypnotic suggestion, a phenomenon studied particularly at the school in Nancy. Here is how the director, Dr. Bernheim, describes it:

The patient heard what I said to him while he was in the trance, but he remembers nothing about it, not even that I spoke to him. The sug- gested idea comes back into his mind when he wakes up; having forgotten where it came from, he believes it to be original. Facts of this kind have been proved by Bertrand, General Noiset, Dr. Liébault and Charles Richet. I have tried them out successfully again and again and am convinced that the people concerned are telling the truth.

At eleven o'clock I suggested to C. that at one o'clock in the afternoon he would be seized by an irresistible desire to go all the way up Stanislas Street and back again, twice. At one o'clock I saw him come out into the street, walk from one end to the other, and then come back again, stopping in front of the shop-windows as though he was just taking a stroll.[1]

The phenomenon can be taken as established. It has been studied experimentally and checked both for its length and for its effectiveness.[2] An order given during hypnosis may not only be obeyed immediately after the person concerned has wakened up; it may remain efficacious for many days and even for weeks afterwards.

For what concerns us, it must be assumed that the given order stays in existence *unconsciously* in the individual. Imagination of the act and the need to perform it rise into consciousness at a set moment, *but the source of the image and the need remains unconscious.* The act is performed as though it were a spontaneous achievement of the person himself.

It seems doubtful whether such an act, arising from the unconscious, can be called free, and, if this is so, whether any form of unconscious influence on action is compatible with freedom of behaviour.

The first important fact to realize when faced with this question is that *suggestions made during hypnosis are not invariably carried out.* Some authors have asserted the contrary and said that post-hypnotic suggestion is accomplished necessarily and invariably.

Thus Liébault, and after him Beaunis, declares, "One characteristic of actions performed a long time after the suggestion has been made is that the urge to do them seems to the individual to come from his own initiative; whereas in reality he goes towards his object under the influence of a decision which he has been made to take with the fatality of a falling stone, not as a result of that controlled and intentional effort which is the source of all our reasonable actions." "In short," adds Beaunis, "he thinks

---

[1] Cf. Bernheim, *De la suggestion* (2nd ed., Paris, Doin, 1888), pp. 45 and 47.

[2] See particularly E. R. Kellogg, "Duration of the Effects of Post-hypnotic Suggestion," *Journal of Experimental Psychology*, 1929, XII, pp. 502–514; also the recent account by A. W. Weitzenhoffer, "A Note on the Persistence of Hypnotic Suggestion," *The Journal of Abnormal and Social Psychology*, 1950, XLV, pp. 160–162.

himself free but he is not free. This is a 'direct hit' at the argument for free will which is drawn from our *feeling* of freedom."[1]

If this were so, post-hypnotic phenomena would provide an illustration of Spinoza's maxim. For Spinoza, our consciousness of freedom is simply ignorance of the causes that make us act.[2]

It seems quite certain that in *abnormal* cases such as hysteria and abulia, post-hypnotic suggestion produces its effect quite automatically, despite the occasional feeling of spontaneity and freedom. Beaunis himself stipulates one condition, to ensure the accomplishment of suggestion: the individual must have been frequently hypnotized by the same person. But this, as is well known, means a weakening in the force of resistance.

And it is quite certain that in some cases the individual fights hard against performing the act, when it goes against strong tendencies. Thus Bernheim admits, as Charcot has also admitted:

The effect of post-hypnotic suggestion is not absolutely a matter of fate; some people fight against it. . . . Here are a few examples. . . . To young G. I suggest that when he wakes up he must stand on the table. When he wakes up he looks at the table but he does not get up on to it. The desire to do so is no doubt there but respect for the people present gives him the strength to overcome the desire.[3]

Another case quoted by Bernheim brings out very clearly the inner conflict that can take place in the individual:

One day I told one of my hypnotized patients, a girl, to kiss one of the men on duty when she woke up. As soon as she woke up she went up to him and took hold of his hand; then she hesitated and looked round, seeming embarrassed by the attention that was being paid to her. She remained like this for a few moments, with an anxious look on her face, obviously experiencing the acutest distress. When she was questioned, she finally confessed that she wanted to kiss Mr. X but that she could never bring herself to behave so improperly.[4]

[1] Cf. J. Morand, *Hypnotisme et Suggestion* (Paris, 1889), pp. 322–323.

[2] Cf. Spinoza, Letter XXXII: "This is the human liberty of which men are so proud; fundamentally, it means that they are conscious of their appetites but not of the external causes which determine them."

[3] Cf. Bernheim, *De la suggestion,* pp. 52–53.

[4] This case is quoted from Dr. J. S. Morand, *Hypnotisme et Suggestion* (Paris, Garnier, 1889), p. 320.

(2) THE UNCONSCIOUS SOURCE OF NORMAL NEEDS

There are then three main points established by the study of post-hypnotic phenomena. First, the individual *experiences a conscious inclination* to perform an action. Second, this inclination emanates in actual fact from *psychic contents which are not conscious* (for example, from an order given previously), and the act which is performed rises from these unconscious contents. Third, the individual may, or may not, give way to his inclination.

The crucial point is this, that the inclination—and consequently the behaviour—*has an unconscious source,* i.e. derives from an *unconscious* order.

Now an analysis of human behaviour soon reveals that it is not at all unusual for an inclination to arise or start from the unconscious layers of the personality. Most of our tendencies and natural needs—hunger, thirst, sex—have their source in unconscious biological states of the organism. From these dynamisms a single thing emerges into consciousness: at a fixed moment, and in pursuance of the satisfaction of a need, we feel drawn or driven to perform an act whose image rises up in our mind. The source or basis of this desire is not immediately given to consciousness. Or, again, we may be mistaken about the source of our desires. What we take to be our real motives for being attracted towards a certain object may merely be pretexts for justifying our behaviour. The real source of a tendency can often only be discovered by scientific research into its antecedents and the factors which brought it into existence.

From this comparison with the process of normal need it should be clear that in both cases the problem of the unconscious is the same. Nevertheless there is an interesting difference between the two processes. In post-hypnotic suggestion it is a forgotten *psychic content*—the command or order received—which is the unconscious source of the image and need which rise up in the individual; whereas in natural needs the inclination emanates fundamentally from *physiological states* of the organism itself. Neither, however, is in itself *directly or fundamentally conscious.* Notice, finally, that the problem is the same both for Freud's dynamic unconscious and for post-hypnotic suggestion. In both cases unconscious psychic contents are the starting-point for images and inclinations which rise up into consciousness. And, as we have shown, it was in post-hypnotic phenomena that Freud found the prototype of his active unconscious.

(3) FREEDOM AND TENDENCIES RISING FROM THE UNCONSCIOUS

We have now to inquire whether facts such as these can be reconciled with activity that can properly be called free. But what exactly is the process known as a free act?

The fact that we are impelled by a certain need—which has its own *source*—towards such and such a form of behaviour, does not mean that the act is not free. It is not so much the *source* of the need, conscious or unconscious, that interests us, as the *felt need itself* and *the way it influences* behaviour.

When behaving freely, in fact, the individual takes up an attitude towards the different elements of "value"—the motives—which are *actually being lived* in the given situation, i.e. are being experienced. The "attractive power" or value of each motive depends on the power of the *aspirations and impulses which are being experienced at the moment*. The ultimate source of these aspirations and impulses does not come into it, either into any scrutiny of the motives or into the attitude which the individual may adopt towards them. In other words, *it is to the extent that they are actually "felt" that the "motives" are to be considered as forces influencing freedom of action*. Ignorance of their source does not alter the case at all.

Whether the act is free or determined will therefore depend on the way the dynamic factors which the individual experiences within himself release the activity. The act will *not* be free when the "motives" or motive forces cause a reaction which is like a link in a chain, materially determined by natural processes. On the other hand there *will be* a free act when the individual *faces motives as value-elements which he recognizes intellectually without being completely absorbed by them;* for in this case, in an act of full self-possession he transcends the impression or the attraction experienced *hic et nunc* and consents to motives to which *he himself gives a value, according to the concrete system of values which makes up his own personality*.

From this it should be clear, then, that because a certain act arises from an unconscious dynamic source, this does not raise any *special problem* as regards its freedom. As with all other acts, the freedom or necessity depends on whether the dynamism behind the act has developed and acted on the spiritual level. This depends on whether the individual *transcends* the actual impression he experiences or is simply "affected" by it. The question whether this spiritual level of activity exists in man, whether there is a certain element of freedom—i.e., spirituality—involved in human conduct, does not arise here. It is a question for philosophical psychology, and outside the scope of this treatise. Here it is sufficient to have shown that no *new* problem is raised by the fact that certain tendencies *derive from the unconscious*.

As we have said, there seem to be a great number of acts, arising out of unconscious tendencies or suggestions, which are *not* performed *automatically*. It can even happen that a person *fails to* perform the act he has been told to perform because of a tendency to respect propriety or the conventions. Occasionally, again, a compromise will be reached and the patient will simply shake hands with someone he has been told to kiss. In some cases, however, it really does seem as though certain acts—especially those performed as a result of post-hypnotic suggestion—can actually be performed just like so many *automatic reactions*. This is particularly true of certain hysterical and abulic cases which have been interestingly described by Janet.

Janet maintains that for some patients the performance of a voluntary act demands considerably more effort than the act of obeying a post-hypnotic suggestion. He maintains, for instance, that a woman patient suffering from abulia and lacking the willpower to perform a certain act which she had been asked to do, performed the same act without any effort as the result of an unconscious suggestion. After hypnotizing this patient Janet said to her: "When I knock on the table, take this hat and hang it on a peg." He goes on:

I woke her up. A little later I called her, as though I wanted her to do something for me. "Would you mind taking this hat? It is getting in my way while I am writing. Hang it up on the peg, will you?" "Of course I will," she replied. She tried to get up, shook herself and stretched out her arms, but her movements were uncoordinated, so she sat down; then she stood up again. This went on for twenty minutes. Then I knocked on the table. Immediately she got up, took hold of the hat, hung it up, and went and sat down again. The action had been done by suggestion in a moment; she had not been able to do it by an effort of will in twenty minutes.[1]

In cases of this kind the suggestion seems to act rather like a force of impulse and lead directly to the action without any interference from the individual concerned.

This kind of unconscious behaviour does not present any *special* problems either: such examples can be classed with ordinary automatic actions.

The conclusion seems to be that as regards this question everything depends on the psychic equilibrium of the person concerned. When he has no will at all—i.e., when the psychic powers do not appear at the spiritual level—the dynamism roused by an unconscious order is released automatically or impulsively in behaviour. But when the individual is normally balanced and has the normal psychic powers, *the tendency roused by suggestion does not have any different effect on behaviour from that of any of man's other tendencies which arise either from biochemical or physiological factors or ultimately, even, from cosmic forces.*

(4) FREEDOM AND UNCONSCIOUS SEXUALITY

The Freudian psychology of the unconscious does not merely claim that motives and inclinations may have their source in the "dark depths of personality." The thing that has so profoundly changed the picture of man that it presents to us is its thesis that conscious motives, as we experience them, are a *deception*. Even so-called higher motives are held to be nothing but disguised forms of libido, the only constructive power in human behaviour.

Hence when anybody follows any conscious motive he is quite simply deceived; what has happened is that impulses which he refused to follow in their naked reality now govern his behaviour in disguise.

In the next chapter, when we discuss the dynamic structure of personality, we shall examine the thesis that the libido is the only

[1] Cf. Pierre Janet, *Les Médications Psychologiques* (Paris, Alcan, 1925), I, p. 226.

driving-force in human personality. For the moment we need only concern ourselves with the problem of the connection between *unconscious transformations* and *disguised* tendencies, on the one hand, and freedom, on the other.

It is quite clear both from clinical data and from ordinary, every-day psychology that so-called lower or instinctive tendencies can motivate conduct in disguised ways. When we strip this idea of the theoretical trimmings which psychoanalysis has added to it, all we find is something that helps us towards a fuller view of the *complex dynamism* behind human activity.

Besides psychoanalysis, Adler's Individual Psychology has made important contributions to this field of knowledge. Individual Psychology shows that not only the libido but also the inferiority complex and the need for self-assertion can lurk, in a highly disguised form, behind "motivations" of human conduct.[1]

The fact that an individual can be completely mistaken about the real nature of the motives governing his conduct has not, as we have said, escaped the notice of every-day psychology. The positive contribution made by depth-psychology in this field lies simply in its having helped us towards deeper knowledge of the processes involved in such mistakes, and also in its attempt to uncover the mechanism of these processes. Their bias and their hasty generalizations have, however, done considerable harm to the new ideas which Adler and Freud introduced into this field.

The particular point about human freedom is that psychoanalysis, not content with showing how instinctive dynamisms affect all "higher" motivation, used the facts it had discovered to construct a theory that reduced *all such motivation* to a disguised form of libido.

The fact that in certain circumstances a person misunderstands the real character of the tendency by which he is being moved does not prevent the act itself, performed consciously as a result of this mistaken tendency, from being free. Here, as in the case of tendencies whose source is unconscious, what counts is the fact that the individual "personally" accepts the tendency as it presents itself to him. The only thing that would make freedom

[1] The word "motivation" is used here in the sense defined below, which it has acquired in contemporary psychology.

of behaviour an impossibility would be if all motivation *were essentially a disguised form of escape* for the libido.

When a man makes occasional mistakes about the nature of his motives the fact that he "personally" *agrees* to act in accordance with the mistaken motive implies that this inclination exists as a "value" for him at the spiritual level of his personality; otherwise he would not be able to adopt towards it a positive attitude reached by deliberation. Thus, when a man *consciously agrees* to bear his suffering for the love of God, this assumes that "doing something for the love of God" is for him an inclination or a value existing on the intellectual level of his personality. If on the other hand, to keep to the same case, it becomes obvious that the man *likes* to be ill *so as to assert himself*, it can be said that he is mistaken about the motive that impels him to "accept" his suffering. Nevertheless, the fact that the conscious motive of resignation to the will of God is *accepted* at the level of consciousness, *adds* to the unconscious dynamism of wanting to be noticed a new element which must be included in the *total* motivation behind this person's behaviour. This new element is the *conscious intention* of the person performing the act, which appears to the performer to be an act of resignation to the divine will. The total dynamism behind the person's behaviour will in this case be a complex of several dynamic elements.

If, on the other hand, the tendency to resign oneself in suffering to the will of God is held to be intrinsically mistaken, then man's whole dynamism is reduced to a process which excludes all spiritual development as a real dynamic factor.

After such theoretical considerations let us, with the help of a few examples, try to see more clearly into the concrete reality of the motives behind certain forms of behaviour. In this way it will become clearer that the real motivation is a *complex of several components* and not simply an unconscious mechanism. The real problem will then be reduced to seeing *how, in this context of complex motivation, freedom of behaviour is to be understood.*

Let us take as our first example the motives behind a generous acceptance of trials and suffering. This is in fact a central point in the Christian attitude to life.

It is certainly not only in abnormal cases that the motive-forces "recognized" in this acceptance of suffering *are found to be mixed with tendencies arising from deeper layers of the personality.*

To take one example from many: A young woman of about twenty-five had been unwell for several years with asthma, headaches, and so on. Weeks of illness would alternate with days of activity and relatively good health. This girl was a good influence on a number of other girls in the district, directing their work and being a great help to them in all sorts of difficulties.

A variety of circumstances led this invalid girl to develop a deeper insight into her psychic condition. Analysis of the events of her childhood brought to light the fact that her life at that time had been dominated by a conflict between an inner feeling of perversion (the result of childish sexual practices) and the general opinion of her both at school and at home, where she was held up as a model child from every point of view. This feeling of contradiction between her inner perversion and her social "perfection" she found agonizing. A number of fairly distressing events occurred to her during her childhood, and these she interpreted, in the light of this conflict, as punishments sent by God, and accepted them eagerly as an expiation of her sins.

Later, when she was about eighteen, she became ill, suffering a great deal from a feeling of neglect, of not being sufficiently surrounded with affection. Her feeling of inner perversion had in the meantime managed to create an attitude that encouraged her tendency to feel sure of "coming out on top," not so much by her *actual* virtues or moral perfection as through her penitence. During her two years' illness she had been told of the special value of sacrifice and suffering, by which man rises far above the easy perfection that is to be reached through the active life or the apostolate. About this she said later: "These words made such an impression on me that the years when I was ill in bed were the best years of my life."

Though she had been cured of her illness, she never recovered her health completely. This was the beginning of that invalid state we have already mentioned. During her course of psychotherapy, she came to see more clearly into some of the details of her condition and her behaviour; she began to understand certain things that had remained "vague" in her consciousness because she did not want to recognize them. Faced with the naked truth of the situation, she ended by making a kind of confession, very rarely obtained in such cases:

I had nothing positive in my life when so many others were getting so much. Sometimes I felt a secret satisfaction at the thought of being interesting and important because I was ill. In my deepest being I began to feel sorry when a new crisis did not arise. I was so self-engrossed in it all! . . . When I made an offering of my sufferings, that cost me very little because it flattered my own ego so much. With all my whole being I want to be cured, and yet I'm terribly afraid of it because my ego would lose so much by it. I am unhappy because I realize so clearly now that all this isn't as I would like it to be—and so I never dared confess it to myself. I wish I could change it all!

The important thing in this case is that we are concerned with someone who cannot simply be described as hysterical. Undoubtedly this person was of high moral worth, animated by a desire for sincerity that sometimes went very deep indeed. Her attitude towards her illness was not simply one of fraud; but her elevated feelings and noble motives were inextricably mixed up with all kinds of other forces. Such is the complex reality that we have to respect. This girl would not have felt so genuinely unhappy when she realized the duplicity of her feelings if she had not had aspirations of genuine nobility, utterly different from the mere desire of wanting to be "interesting." It is this *complex of elements* in the acceptance of suffering that needs to be emphasized; it would be wrong to reduce the whole thing to one component only.[1]

It is the same thing in those (usually less serious) cases one meets, of people living in a family or small community and always asking for special consideration because of their state of health: they always have to be an exception to the ordinary rules of life in some way or other. There can be no doubt that these people would like nothing better than to be able to behave like everyone else. They genuinely suffer from always having to be the exception. But on deeper examination one frequently discovers that the deepest desire of their personality is *to be different from others, not to be confused with the mass, not to be someone who does*

[1] As for the question of knowing whether it is right to describe these more obscure elements in motivation as *unconscious*, see pp. 197–201.

not count. When a personality is dominated by such a need, and
has been unable to find satisfaction in more positive ways, this
can be "arranged," as depth-psychology has shown, by unconscious mechanisms. On the one hand, there will always be something that is not going so well—physical health, for example—so
that they will simply have to behave in an exceptional way. And
then they will try to convince themselves on the conscious level
that they are doing all they can and would like nothing better
than to be able to behave like others; but "God has willed otherwise": they are prepared to bear their little trial courageously.
Thus the problem is solved: the desire to be different is satisfied,
and on the level of consciousness they may imagine themselves on
the way to holiness.[1]

Systems of depth-psychology have taught us to be so suspicious
of unconscious mechanisms of this kind that there is a real danger
of our overestimating their importance. Many doctors and psychologists are no longer able to see anything in abnegation or the
acceptance of suffering except a distorted way of satisfying some
unavowed need. The emphasis, as we have shown, should rather
be laid on the very diverse mixture of motives to be found at the
root of these complex attitudes.

Besides emphasizing the value of abnegation and self-sacrifice,
Christian philosophy has endeavoured to subjugate the sexual instincts in man. Here too there are other factors besides what is
called "virtue" that can "help" people to develop a purity sometimes described as *angelic;* and many manifestations that were
highly thought of in their day as signs of exceptional holiness seem
rather dubious to us now. Forms of psychic infantilism in matters
of sex and rather unhealthy inhibitions and defence-mechanisms
not infrequently lie behind attitudes once described as virtuous.

But here again depth-psychology has not always shown discretion. It has described as inhibition or repression or sublimation any
form of behaviour by means of which man in his spiritual aspira-

[1] On the subject of the theoretical foundation of this attitude, see the
account of Adlerian psychology in the Appendix.

tion has tried to subjugate or control the biological forces of the libido.

Moreover, as is well known, the presence of sexual elements in certain religious phenomena has made psychoanalysis conclude that all religious aspirations are fundamentally "libidinous." The theoretical aspect of this question will be examined later; here we need only consider the *admixture* of various dynamic factors in certain kinds of phenomena and behaviour connected with religion.

The presence of *sexual* elements in the *religious* delirium of some of the mentally sick is a thing sufficiently familiar in psychiatry; but it must be emphasized that in many cases which are more or less normal, sexuality seems to *prefer* to get involved with all kinds of religious elements. This raises a problem which we must briefly examine. How are we to explain the interpenetration of sexual and religious elements in the imagination of a great number of normal persons? Once again the question is to know whether it is sufficient to make *sublimation* account for the connection. It seems to us that other factors and processes, of a more concrete nature, must be advanced to explain the fact.

In several cases we have been able to ascertain that the connection originated in a *quite specific conflict* which had taken place between religion and sex in infancy. A child transposes everything connected with religion into an unreal celestial sphere and clothes saints, priests, etc. in the garb of angels. When the period arrives at which the genital organs and their attendant activities begin to interest the child, there is a rush of ideas that tends to connect these sexual characteristics with sacred persons and religious things. All kinds of questions then present themselves to the child. In his imagination he sees the sexual organs projected on to sacred scenes; sexual ideas about Jesus or the Virgin Mary trouble his mind, and he is tormented by all manner of questions. Some children who eventually show neurotic tendencies are so terrified by such thoughts and imaginings that they reject them with the utmost violence. They feel guilty about them, as though they had committed sacrilege. But it is precisely the strong emotional "charge" in these "forbidden" images, and the violence of the reactions they provoke, that makes the child unable to get rid of them. The more he tastes their prohibited and "mysterious" character, the more he is dominated by them; soon they become veritable obsessions. Every thought, every object connected with religion is as though sexually bewitched.

We know from experience that images in which religion and sex are intimately bound up sometimes continue to trouble adults and manifest themselves particularly in their dreams. In some cases of a more serious nature, in which the patient passes through crises of delirium, the same images appear.

These cases show clearly that there are no grounds for regarding the *connection* between religion and sex as a matter of *sublimation* or the reduction of one to the other. The explanation is to be found in concrete situations of conflict, in which the antithesis between the two elements, and their union in the *human forms* of religion, are the dominant factors.

There are other factors which play an equally important part in causing this remarkable connection between sexual images and religious ideas. The two fields probably have deep points of contact in the *experience of the mysterious*, that element of obscurity which exercises such a fascination over people. Similar points of contact are to be found, of course, in certain ancient cults and mysteries, and psychological observation and analysis provide equal proof of the fact. It often happens that a patient in the course of remembering certain childish sexual experiences, or relating his dream-contents, reveals what an impression of *mystery* sex had for him. To the child, sex is something inaccessible, a terrain jealously guarded by the grown-ups; *entrance into which is moreover forbidden by God.* This sexual activity thus comes to have an irresistible attraction for the child; it becomes a region which he longs to enter into possession of, so that he may free himself from the burden of the superior forces which, he feels, are trying to enslave him. One patient told us that when he decided to do what was "forbidden" he felt so big and powerful that it was like being like *God.* Another imagined that the veil of the temple hiding the holy of holies would be torn down and that he would thus enter into the sphere of the divine. With others (*as the result of very concrete circumstances and experiences*) the mysterious nature of the Eucharist and the host comes to be associated with sex and in this form continues to obsess the imagination.

These facts, which show that there are undoubtedly *points of contact* between sex and religion, do not, we repeat, give any grounds for concluding that there is any dynamic source common to both elements or any process of sublimation. In the cases just mentioned, it would be nearer the truth to say that to some extent the two meet in a *common sphere*, the sphere of the mysterious and the "great."

Religion and eroticism, moreover, possess certain elements in common because their dynamisms originate, not in the same layers of personality, but in *more general needs*, notably the needs for contact, integration and expansion, as we shall show later.[1]

What has been said of the spirit of sacrifice and acceptance of suffering is also true of the virtue of purity and religious matters in general; psychoanalysis has been too hasty in giving a uniform interpretation of the variety of the components involved, simply by reducing the whole to one of these components. Depth-psychology is suspicious of the psychological background of the most elevated manifestations, the most sublime outpourings of the spirit and grace, especially in the two delicate matters of purity and the acceptance of suffering. For these two matters are delicate indeed: it is very difficult to disentangle comparatively unhealthy excrescences and malformations from the noblest aspirations. Here, as in all his other actions, man is usually involved in an inextricable tangle of motives, an admixture of *higher* and *lower* on the moral level and of *conscious* and *unconscious* on the psychological level.

It is these *facts*, and not the theories based on them in any psychoanalytical scheme, which should supply our data for the problem of the connection between the sexual unconscious and freedom.

Therefore the essential problem as regards the freedom of human behaviour is to know *whether, and to what degree, man is deceiving himself when he imagines that he is consenting to conscious, rational motives.* When he believes his actions to be guided, for instance, by the spirit of abnegation, to what extent is he being moved by a disguised form of self-assertiveness? It is

[1] Cf. *infra*, Chapter IV.

not so much the unconscious *source* of these tendencies that we need to concern ourselves with, as the question whether the needs as felt and experienced, and as motives of action, do not completely hoodwink "rational man."

In answer to this question let us observe that a "transformed" motive, or a partly unconscious need, is not normally the *whole* dynamic force behind a man's actions: this has been shown plainly by our earlier analyses. His system of motivations is a complex whole of tendencies and values *to some extent or other* recognized in their real form and *to some extent or other* spiritually created. In the next chapter we shall be able to show in greater detail the *psychological foundations* of this complexity. Here the question is *whether this complexity of our system of motives makes impossible any idea of a free will intervening in our actions,* or whether, on the contrary, in any satisfactory theory of the freedom of behaviour, this complexity appears as the normal condition of human conduct.

Free will is not to be looked upon as a "spiritual force" separate from the complex dynamisms of the human psyche. As we have already remarked, free will means that these complex motive-forces do not release any kind of behaviour directly, or blindly, but only after they have been taken up into the transcendent individual *ego.*

An act that derives *at least partially* from such a grasp of the "motive-powers" by the transcendent *ego* is to that extent a *free act.* The element of freedom in such an act means that in concrete fact it is not the resultant pure and simple of a process governed by influences of environment and physiological factors but that there is also another principle behind it—the self-determination of a person.

Our actions always only *partially* derive from the activity of spiritual motive-forces. *People and things act upon us from all directions—physiological and psychological, conscious and unconscious—because our organism opens out upon the world in all directions. Any concrete situation affects us in all these ways at once and either invites or compels us to reply to it by means of some kind of reaction—which is our behaviour.*

Our behaviour is, therefore, a "reply" to an action which reaches us *by various ways.* In it the spiritual element is always one component only, because in *our very being* the spiritual element is simply one component amongst many. There is no such thing as a *purely spiritual* reply to the situations with which life presents us; there is only a "human" reply. *The action of the situation on the person, and the reply, are at once spiritual and material, like the person himself:* i.e., our activities are absorbed into a process of physical, biochemical and physiological reactions, but at the same time transcend this process to the extent that they are faced up to and consciously grasped by our *ego*.

Thus we can say that our behaviour is free to the extent that the situation and the reply are built up as a function of the autonomous personality of the individual. Freedom *varies* according to the *level* reached by any man in this kind of personal development of his activities.

Looked at from this psychological point of view, our behaviour cannot satisfactorily be divided into two categories, the free and the unfree. Freedom is not a static property of a few limited kinds of behaviour. On the contrary, all human activity is characterized by a certain degree of freedom, i.e. *a varying degree of spiritual activity.* There are very few kinds of behaviour, whether morally good or morally bad, which do not to a certain extent, at least, feel the influence of the transcendent activity of the human personality. This influence reveals itself somehow, even if only in the kind of check that sometimes prevents people from succumbing without scruple to irresistible impulse, or which moderates the enthusiasm with which they follow their instincts. It would, on the other hand, be just as much an illusion to imagine that any of our acts derive from *purely spiritual* activity, and that they do not have their dynamic origin in the vital centres and unconscious bases of our personality. These are levels of activity which contribute towards the attitude freely adopted in any given situation; physiological or unconscious layers of the personality which may be behind the irresolution that makes one hesitate to appreciate a value or the tendency of an argument, for example; but from these depths of the psyche may arise too the certainty that renders a conviction unshakable and the inspiration that takes the place of the will.

Seen in this way, freedom, like the spiritual element in our personality, is not so much a permanent possession as a *task* which each man fulfils in his behaviour to a greater or less degree throughout his life.

It is worth noting in this connection the complementary nature of the positions adopted by the Freudian theory and traditional psychology. Psychoanalysis reduces all dynamic activity to *impersonal* forces, so that man is dominated by the vital, unconscious force of the "id"; he does not govern or dispose of himself at all. Traditional psychology, on the other hand, concentrated on the other aspect of this dynamic activity and represents self-determination, or the conscious will, as a force which can govern human conduct in sovereign fashion absolutely. The real dynamism of human behaviour is, in fact, a varying combination of all these components, biological and spiritual, conscious and unconscious, known or disguised.

It is a task for the personality itself to increase its capacity for self-government and its knowledge of its own motives. It will best realize this aim by seeing ever more deeply into the complexity of the dynamic factors in its behaviour. The depth-psychology of Adler and Freud supplies us with *data* that can enrich our psychological insight. With its help we can rid ourselves of certain illusions about our freedom, and so become *more truly free* from the compulsions of the secret mechanisms in human nature through which men so often lose their real personality.

6. Freedom and Morals in Psychotherapy

We have shown that in human activity freedom is a spiritual component of behaviour which is not simply either present or absent. We have so far been concerned with the *purely psychological* idea of freedom, however. In morals, freedom has a somewhat different meaning. An act is described as morally "free" when the intervention of the spiritual element is such that the autonomous personality can be considered the "author" of its own actions and consequently responsible for them. The man who passes judgment on others must assume the existence (or absence) of responsibility, and this constitutes the moral aspect of the psychological idea of freedom.

Thus in certain cases the material factors will be found to have played such a direct part in an action that this must be considered as deriving *principally* from the non-spiritual elements. The intervention of the spiritual elements may have been limited to an inhibiting action which was not powerful enough to prevent the act. In this case the individual will not have been free and cannot therefore be held responsible for his action, since the spiritual element in his personality was not the *principal author* of the act.

It is clear that on the psychological level this idea of moral responsibility, like the idea of liberty, must be considered a much more tenuous and subtle matter than it is usually found to be on the ordinary level of morality.

The moral aspect of freedom plays an important part in therapy, chiefly in two ways. On the one hand, there is the moral sense of the patient who is obsessed by fear or the feeling of doing wrong, or who is tormented by a pathological longing for perfection. Can the therapist allow the patient to oppose certain tendencies because he feels them to be immoral, or thwart his desire for perfection? On the other hand, there is the question of the patient's real responsibility in everything concerning the means to be employed in curing him. Can the therapist recommend to an *irresponsible* patient actions that are objectively immoral but which would eventually have a therapeutic value?

We shall leave the solution of these delicate problems to the moralist, and confine ourselves to the *psychological* aspect of the problem—which indeed any moralist anxious to grasp the material object of his science—i.e., human behaviour as it exists in its psychological complexity—will also need to take into account.

The problem is not as simple as it may appear at first sight. It may be said that the therapist should certainly not counsel immoral acts if they are felt *subjectively* by the patient to be reprehensible; and that when irresponsible patients are involved, certain objectively immoral forms of behaviour may be prescribed for therapeutic reasons because of the simple fact that the patient cannot, subjectively, commit sin.

(1) PSEUDO-MORAL PROBLEMS

The solution, we repeat, is not so simple—firstly because many of the problems which present themselves to the patient as *moral* ones are fundamentally not moral but *psychological*.

An example may enable us to understand this better. The scrupulous patient, who never stops scrutinizing his behaviour for its hidden guilt, does not fundamentally present any moral problem at all. We do not mean that such a way of behaviour is not really culpable—on that point we pass no judgment—but we mean that the apparently moral attitude that dominates his way of looking at everything he does, is *not* fundamentally a moral attitude at all; it is probably a purely *psychological* attitude towards himself. This attitude can often be the result of a longing to outshine others, manifesting itself in the pathological form of a desire for absolute perfection and purity, with scrupulosity as a mere sickly symptom of these desires and longings. *The "moral" attitude of this kind of scrupulous individual is a psychological problem related to his thwarted longing to assert himself;* and it is to this, and not to the moral or non-moral aspect of his behaviour, that the therapist's attention should be directed.

Similarly, with a patient suffering from obsessional ideas leading to pollution, the therapist should not directly help the patient to overcome the tendency to masturbation. Even for the psychiatrist who looks upon therapeutic treatment, not only as a means of psychic equilibrium, but as a renewal of the moral and spiritual personality, the solution will not consist simply in reducing the number of pollutions, but in *remedying the patient's psychoasthenic dispositions* as a whole, and thus freeing him from all his obsessional ideas.

An important part of the treatment in both these cases would be to *detach* the patient *emotionally* from the kinds of behaviour in question, and especially *to relax his moral attitude towards them.* He would then come to realize that his scrupulosity or his tendency to masturbation is no more than a *form of psychological reaction,* and quite a different thing from sin. Often the pathological reaction will disappear, as the moral aspect of the conduct ceases to be an obsession; the moral preoccupation being simply one aspect of a psycho-pathological symptom.

We come here to a central problem, upon which moralists and psychotherapists are often sharply divided. Whereas the therapist aims to liberate the patient, the moralist emphasizes effort and self-control. For both morality and psychotherapy it is important that mutual understanding should be reached between the therapist and the moralist, both being concerned with human behaviour.

The moralist's attitude towards human behaviour is closely connected with his sense of the value of effort. This is for him a necessary condition of the struggle against impulsive tendencies and the establishment of an ideal of personality. Every culture and morality implies this ideal. It demands an effort to eliminate everything in a man's tendencies and modes of behaviour which may be opposed to it. By means of a continuous psychic effort man maintains himself in his specifically human condition. The moralist therefore considers any relaxing of psychic effort dangerous.

The moralist, however, must also think of the human condition as a whole, and consequently of the psychic aberrations which can appear in human behaviour. He must realize that effort and the pursuit of an ideal do not always fulfil the positive rôle ascribed to them. The pursuit of an ideal is the most constructive and also the most destructive force that can animate human psychic life.[1] The old adage applies here: *corruptio optimi pessima.* Nothing is more dangerous to human balance than the orientation of tensions towards the realization of an unsatisfactory form of personality-ideal, or the elimination of certain obstacles in pursuit of this ideal. In such cases indeed effort becomes paroxysmic and the tension is transformed into an obsession.

The therapist frequently finds himself confronted with such cases of loss of balance. The task which becomes necessary here to enable the patient to recover his moral human value puts this case at the antipodes of the processes which take place in the positive construction of the moral personality; for in this case the first thing to be done is to weaken the action of the inhibiting mecha-

---

[1] See particularly J. Nuttin, *"Séminaire et équilibre psychique"* in *Le Cardinal Mercier fondateur de Séminaire* (Louvain, Séminaire Léon XIII, 1951, pp. 133–149).

nisms, which, because of the conflict of tensions, make any kind of constructive action impossible.

The difference of opinion between the moralist and the therapist arises from the fact that when they defend their own ideas each has his own very different picture of man. The moralist judges therapeutic behaviour, and attitudes of mind prescribed in the course of treatment, as though they were the attitudes of behaviour of a normal person. But in one's estimation of any pharmaceutical product one does not adopt the same point of view as for an ordinary food or drink. We do not mean to suggest that moral standards cannot be universally applied, but it is obvious that a form of behaviour or a kind of treatment can only be judged for what it is. Before he makes any moral judgment on any particular mode of behaviour the moralist should endeavour to grasp its psychic reality. Let us take the case of a therapist who in his treatment of a particular patient advises him not to torment himself so much about the masturbation he has committed in the past, and not to be so afraid of such behaviour in the future. This advice, which enables the patient to modify his psychic attitude, means in the eyes of the therapist creating conditions which are more likely to enable the patient to free himself from obsessional attitudes. Such a process cannot be regarded as weakening the patient's moral sense; on the contrary, it means a liberation from a pathogenic condition. Both therapist and moralist have the same end in view, that of remedying certain aspects of the patient's sexual behaviour; but in any particular abnormal case a conscientious therapist may be of the opinion that the best way of obtaining this result does not lie in exacerbating and strengthening the patient's sense of responsibility, but rather in relaxing the exaggerated pathological tension which is preventing the activity of the spiritual personality.

Other cases may involve obsessions concerning the fulfilment of positive ordinances. Let us take the case of a Catholic who experiences this kind of difficulty about fasting before communion. A conscientious therapist who advises his patient not to pay any attention to it, and suggests that he should drink a glass of water every time the obsessive scruple attacks him when he is brushing his teeth, may not be prescribing anything immoral. In fact, when a conscientious therapist ascertains that the observance of the ordinance about fasting before communion, and the fact of not taking communion for fear of transgressing this law, together create an obsessional condition in the patient, one can admit that the observance of the ordinance is only possible with detriment to the patient's mental health. One who insists on the observance of a positive ordinance to the prejudice of a patient's health, reminds us of a well-known passage in the Gospels where such an attitude is condemned very severely.[1] The moralist must realize that it is for the therapist to judge what psychic effects the observance of the law or the fact of not taking communion are likely to have on the patient. It is then for the moralist to judge whether, when these consequences have been taken into account, the patient is really to be excused. It is certainly preferable, even from the therapeutic point of view, that the patient should have the therapist's advice confirmed by a priest. This will have the further advantage of giving the patient peace of mind, and prevent him from feeling that he is disobeying a commandment of the Church. This is why collaboration with a competent moralist is important in therapeutic work of this kind.[2]

Our aim in giving these few examples was not to provide an answer to the moral problem involved here. We do not even claim *formally* that the attitudes of the therapist which we have given as hypothetical examples are morally justified. A full discussion of this question lies outside the scope of this book. We have merely tried to show the actual psychological state of the problem, which the moralist should take into account when making his judgment. The difference in point of view between the moralist and the therapist does not always arise in fact from the therapist's lack of moral sense. In certain cases its origin can be found in the fact that when the moralist makes his judgment he does not take into account the *real* nature of the behaviour whose moral worth he is estimating. The standards of morality do not change, but the adoption of a psychological point of view changes the psychic reality of the actions which the moralist has to judge.

[1] Cf. Luke XIII, 11–17.
[2] This passage was written before the recent revision of the Church's law with regard to fasting before communion.

(2) THE THERAPEUTIC VALUE OF IMMORAL WAYS OF CONDUCT

The second problem, even more complex, is to know whether in the course of treatment the therapist whose outlook is based on moral values can prescribe forms of conduct which would be immoral for the normal man, when the patient concerned is more or less irresponsible.

There is no doubt that immoral kinds of behaviour can in certain circumstances help a patient to recover his *psychic equilibrium*. Thus for example somebody (who may be married) who has become neurotic as a result of enforced continence or unsatisfactory sexual relationships, can sometimes recover his lost or threatened balance through a love-affair which renews his whole life.

In such cases the task for any system of therapy based on moral principles does not consist merely in re-establishing the patient's psychic equilibrium; it must help him to re-establish his moral being in its integrity, as the patient himself conceives this. For this reason certain forms of *psychic* cure, which can only be achieved through a mutilation of the moral personality, cannot be considered *real* cures in this sense.

In such cases therapy finds itself faced with a large and difficult task, for what it has to do is *to help a moral and spiritual personality to keep itself alive.* The treatment must therefore aim to reinforce or re-establish the activity of the moral and spiritual elements in the unbalanced psyche. This may best be realized by helping the patient to discover a meaning or a new value in certain things or certain aspects of his life which have been neglected, or gradually atrophied. Thus, by giving new meaning to the patient's life, the therapist will enable him to use long-lost forces of physical and psychic activity.

Seen from a naturalistic and purely psychological point of view, the results of this kind of treatment may not seem very brilliant. It is a fact that *in certain circumstances* man would develop better biologically if he had only to become a beautiful, healthy animal.

The problem becomes still more complex where patients who must be considered morally irresponsible are concerned. It might be thought that in such cases the first stage in the reconstruction of the *moral* personality would be to restore the psyche to its natural equilibrium, it being only on such a restored basis that the moral personality could be rebuilt.

In psychotherapeutic practice, cases of this kind quite often occur, and with psychological ideas as they are today the therapist is tempted to put the cure of the psyche—ignoring the moral personality of the patient—before everything else.

But the therapist whose real aim is the reconstruction of the total personality, psychological and *moral*, will find that he is *very rarely called upon* to recommend a kind of behaviour that is "objectively" immoral *even for purely psychological reasons*. It is a very dubious method of treatment in any case.

It is in fact psychologically impossible to consider these immoral forms of behaviour as extrinsic to the personality. *Behaviour is the very expression of the personality which is to be rebuilt*. Hence, such means could never ultimately attain the desired end.

Nor is it possible, as we have already shown, to consider the spiritual components of the personality, and consequently the freedom and responsibility of the individual, as qualities which are either there or not there. Spiritual freedom is a reality which is built up *gradually*, during the course of treatment. That is why though under the influence of immoral kinds of behaviour the patient may develop a kind of personality which is *psychically healthy*, from the point of view of the ultimate aim it will be a *deformity*. To produce a building which is fundamentally ugly, as the result of incorporating materials of another "style," can hardly be considered a successful result of the *first stage* in any reconstruction. It means quite simply that there is some kind of fault there.

This is not pure theory, remote from the concrete reality of clinical practice, a fault of which even the spiritually minded therapist may easily be guilty through having conceived the *real aim* of his therapy too vaguely and abstractly, on the level of pure principle. In practice—since he is concerned with one thing only: the natural equilibrium of mental life—the fact of having destroyed certain aspects of the patient's moral personality is not always taken into consideration.

Of course the situation is quite different when what is involved is not something suggested by the psychiatrist as a remedy, but a seemingly "immoral" act *which is in fact a neurotic symptom* in the patient himself. In this case, which is analogous to those we have already discussed on p. 142, it will be necessary to reduce the "moral" problem to a predominantly psychological one. When a psychic deformity manifests itself as a moral aberration, it needs to be treated on the psychological level.

(3) THE MORAL ASPECT OF THE EMOTIONAL ABREACTION

A final problem remains to be examined: what is the moral value of the *emotional discharge* that usually accompanies a course of psychotherapy?

All therapeutic methods consider that free expression, the discharge of emotional attitudes (both positive and negative) may be absolutely essential in the case of certain people. The question arises whether it is permissible to allow feelings which, from the moral point of view, man should endeavour to control, to manifest themselves freely in the course of treatment. It is certainly not permissible to rouse feelings or signs of hatred or any other immoral emotion either in thought or word.

To answer this question we must first of all remind ourselves of the very nature of human behaviour. It is no use saying that therapeutic treatment cannot be compared with normal conditions because it only takes place outside them; if this were so, behaviour under treament would have to be looked upon as more or less *unreal*, and this would mean that the feelings released could not be looked upon as *real* feelings. The therapeutic situation is most certainly part of the individual's real development and must be seen in the context of real human conduct to which morality applies. It is, however, a very special sort of conduct.

We suggest that this difficult problem may be solved in the following way. The moral character of any particular act is obviously determined in the first place by the nature of the act, i.e. by *what* the person actually *does*. *What* the person really does we call the *inner significance* or the immediate *meaning* of the act. It is just this meaning which turns a totality of actions into an *act*. The same activities or parts of an action may be integrated as constituent components of very different kinds of behaviour. They thus acquire a totally different meaning and moral value, for the simple reason that they become different actions. The person who drinks a glass of beer really *does* something *different* from his neighbour who merely raises his glass from the table, for example, to clean the cloth underneath, even though the action of lifting a glass is part of the action of drinking. The mere addition of activities which intervene (as so many segments of an action) in the act of "drinking" does not determine this action, or its morality.

When in his life of relationship with others a man allows himself to be inspired or guided in his inner or verbal actions by emotional attitudes of mind of an immoral nature, this activity must be described as immoral. *The emotional release achieved in the therapeutic situation cannot, however, be regarded as this kind of behaviour.* To understand this point clearly it is necessary to make a careful analysis of the situation in which this behaviour takes place.

In this examination we shall only be concerned with people with a sense of responsibility and who adopt the standards of Christian morality. Under these conditions the situation can be described as follows. The patient's conscious responsible personality realizes that its psychic life is disturbed by various emotional experiences of the past. The person also understands—as a result of the ideas communicated by the therapist, for example—that a new experience of these traumatic events, along with the corresponding emotional reactions, is necessary to free his conscious personality from these disturbing factors. When in these conditions a person submits to treatment, and abandons himself to the emotional abreaction of different feelings about his parents or, by transference, about the therapist, *this kind of behaviour cannot be regarded as a habitual behaviour-pattern towards his parents or the therapist.* What the person formally does and agrees to do in this abreaction, is to eliminate from his psychic life the undigested remains of emotional experiences, by allowing them to appear in a therapeutic situation.

In this, which is a reasonable course of behaviour, the attitude of the conscious personality must be to eliminate as far as possible all conscious control. To this it is in fact impelled by the actual necessities of the technique of abreaction. The conscious personality keeps itself in the background, in order to allow the infantile elements of its psychic life as much play as possible in the actual process of abreaction. In other words, it is necessary to make a distinction between what the moral personality does, and the phenomena provoked by the patient's infantile or disturbed psychic functions. These functions simply cause the exteriorization of the emotions of love or hatred in the psyche which have not been abreacted. These emotions are real psychic elements, for which the patient's conscious moral personality is not responsible. They were in fact born in him in his infancy and developed according to the normal laws of human psychic life.

In his ordinary social life the patient has adopted an attitude of control and domination over these disturbing contents and mechanisms, but this attitude has not enabled him to build up a balanced personality or to reach the kind of integration which takes place in normal persons. The inner meaning of the therapeutic treatment as a form of behaviour is therefore the following: the provisional acceptance of an attitude towards certain real psychic facts which is totally different from the usual attitude, *under technical conditions and well-determined circumstances.* Instead of controlling and dominating these disturbing elements, it is a case of liquidating them in conditions which have been determined technically. The emotions expressed by the patient are not the result of emotional attitudes adopted by his moral personality. What the patient does is to free himself from undigested psychic "remains."

There is a passage in Westerman Holstijn which will help to make clear the difference between the two schemes of behaviour. "In the course of a well-conducted analysis," he writes, "the patient is not by any means in his ordinary psychic state, although he is often unaware of this. . . . Free association gives rise to a totally different state of consciousness. During the association the patient . . . is so 'far away' that when the session comes to an end he feels as though he has just wakened up." Holstijn adds that this phenomenon arises chiefly from the fact that the conscious, organized part of the personality, i.e. the ego, is operating more loosely and exerting less control.[1]

The abreacted behaviour adopted by the patient must therefore

[1] See A. J. Westerman Holstijn, *Grondbegrip der psychoanalyse* (Utrecht, Bijleveld, 1948²), p. 44.

be regarded in the light of his behaviour as a whole. Leaving aside the patient's personal intentions, *what we are faced with here is behaviour of a technical character*, i.e. a course of treatment. In this, the main thing is for the patient *to do something to his own personality*, i.e. to release the "brakes" which are being applied too hard, and thus produce a liberating release of different feelings of love or hatred, feelings which exist in him as a result of the action of the natural laws of human psychic life. This release, brought about by technical means, in which the emotions undergo various changes according to psychological laws and provoke emotional attitudes towards the therapist, is a process which exteriorizes the infantile or neurotic psyche. This process involves a revivification of some of the patient's attitudes as a "small child" towards his parents, for example. The conscious, reasonable personality of the patient, which has accepted the treatment, adopts a kind of behaviour which means suspending the excessive action of the old controls, in order to allow the natural processes to unfold and thus achieve the patient's liberation. This is certainly not the normal, direct way in which the moral personality develops, for this means conquering the "immoral" impulses and preserving personal control over oneself. But this normal process, which acts constructively in the person who is psychically healthy, has a pathogenic influence on one who is psychically ill. This is why recourse is had to a therapeutic treatment in which the higher functions, in so far as they have a restraining influence, disappear into the background, so that the lower mechanisms can manifest themselves in set reactions. This therapeutic intervention means allowing emotions which actually exist in the psyche, but which have been ignored, to manifest themselves and be transferred; for it is the ignoring of them which has involved harmful consequences for the personality as a whole. No doubt it would be unjustifiable to allow such a dissociation between the moral personality and the infantile or pathological mechanisms to take place in ordinary life, but here we are concerned with a technical treatment in the general framework of a therapeutic situation. Just like any medical treatment, this therapy is determined in the first place by the theory and technique of psychotherapy, and not by the standards which govern the life of social relationships.

The *material content* of this treatment, which involves formally a therapeutic auto-catharsis, can mean an expression of love or dislike for particular people. It is therefore quite clear that these feelings are directed towards other people. In the therapeutic situation the patient hates his mother or grows attached to his therapist. But we must insist that this is not *done by* the conscious personality which is allowing itself to be treated; all that is involved here in fact is a result of the action of various infantile mechanisms. It goes without saying that the patient is not necessarily aware of this while he is being treated. He is obviously completely absorbed by the situation. But this process has only been able to take place because the conscious ego which exercises the control agreed at the beginning of the therapeutic process to disappear into the background, and did this for reasons which were rationally justifiable, since they were called for by the technical needs of the treatment that would lead to recovery.

Anyone who is acquainted with this special kind of treatment and can criticize it in the light of this knowledge will not say, if asked *what* the patient *does* during it, that he is cursing his father and wants him to die. He will simply say that the patient is abreacting his infantile emotional complexes. It is the same as in the case of a surgeon: he will say that he is operating on his patient, not that he is inflicting wounds upon him. Inflicting wounds for technical reasons in the course of treatment is quite a different thing from "wounding someone," even though from the purely material point of view the activities are identical.

The moralist habitually proceeds quite differently when he is called upon to judge such kinds of behaviour as emotional transference and abreaction. He makes use of certain ideas which distinguish between the *materially bad* and the *formally bad*. In other cases he distinguishes between a good aim *which is directly attained through* a bad means and an aim which strictly speaking *is not realized by* a bad means, etc. One sometimes gets the impression that by proceeding in this way the moralist bases his judgment on very formal considerations. In general, it might be more satisfactory from the psychological point of view to make the moral value of a particular kind of treatment depend directly on the actual *psychic reality* behind the behaviour, i.e. on its meaning *as* behaviour and not on the material elements which make up its substratum or parts. This, however, is a point of view which is not often adopted in the moral judgment of behaviour. It would in fact give rise to new problems. The chief thing to notice is that *the meaning of the behaviour* must not be confused with the *personal intention.*

We shall here confine our attention to the problem of emotional abreaction in the therapeutic situation. We have shown that a new kind of behaviour is involved here. The moralist cannot therefore be content to pass judgment on it simply by applying canons established *a priori.*

Many patients who feel morally responsible for the expression of their own feelings reveal a strong moral inhibition against the abreaction at the beginning of treatment. They have still not realized that the nature and meaning of their behaviour depend on the therapy of which it is part. They mistake what is taking place in them. This is why it is desirable that the therapist should make the nature and moral value of these emotional reactions quite clear to the patient. The patient will then grasp the exact meaning of the treatment as a whole and eventually assume it in his moral life-attitude. Thus the patient will be able to unify his personal intentions and the inner meaning of the kinds of behaviour which he adopts.

There remains a still more delicate problem, that of the influence which the emotional abreaction produced in the course of treatment may have on the patient's behaviour in his daily life.

Assuming that the therapeutic situation is sufficiently well guaranteed, it is reasonable that the conscious personality should suspend control over anything concerning the abreaction of emotion. But in his ordinary life the patient must re-assume control over his actions. The kinds of behaviour which he desires to adopt as a result of the new attitudes which have appeared in the course of treatment must be judged from the point of view of his personality as a whole. It is clear that tendencies of a more or less unconscious kind will influence him in making this judgment; they will eventually trouble his moral sense. Nevertheless, he will judge his motives *as they present themselves to his consciousness* and according to his intellectual capacity. The therapist has a part to play here. Just as he has endeavoured to give the patient a clear perception of the meaning of the emotional transference that takes place during treatment, so he will now endeavour to enable him to understand the motives that impel him towards certain acts. This task devolves upon the therapist particularly when the acts are important for the patient's future life. The therapist will not proceed authoritatively. He will be content to give the patient a clear idea of the secret or unconscious motives behind his acts, and by so doing he will not be overstepping the limits of his role. He will also abstain from any sort of moral interference, but will occupy himself exclusively with the work of reconstructing his patient's psychic personality as a whole. This is why he must make sure that the patient does not perform any acts of whose dynamic origin he remains ignorant. He will also be concerned with the scale of spiritual values adopted by the patient, even when in the course of treatment he reacts strongly against such moral or religious values. He will realize better than the patient the extent to which these actual defence-reactions are directed against the neurotic forms taken by religion and morality in the patient's development. It is in the treatment of patients who have remained most strongly attached to religious values that one comes across the strongest defence-reactions and the most violent outbursts of hatred against God. It is especially when the patient wishes to do something whose consequences might be irrevocable—get a divorce, for example, or adopt a new conception of life by joining some group or other—that the therapist will have to enlighten him on the real nature of his tendencies. The therapist must not, however, make any positive effort to dissuade the patient, for this would mean going beyond the limits of his role again; but he will do something which usually proves more efficacious, whilst at the same time remaining within his proper limits. By interpreting the patient's feelings and impulses, he may perhaps make it clear to him *that it would be wise to put off any decisive action until the end of the critical period of treatment.* The problem of deciding the *moral* value of acts actually done in such circumstances, i.e. when the patient decides to act in spite of everything, lies beyond our present scope. How far the patient acts under the impulse of unconscious forces is a very difficult question indeed, and one which it is perhaps impossible to answer.[1]

These few reflections should suffice to draw the attention of the psychotherapist to an aspect of analytical therapy which is certainly his concern, i.e. the moral character of certain kinds of behaviour adopted within the general framework of the therapeutic situation. On the other hand, they should reveal the difficulty of the task by which the moralist is faced when he aims to make a moral judgment of human behaviour as it exists in its psychological reality.

[1] For an account of those problems as seen from the purely moral point of view we should like to refer particularly to the important contribution made by Dr. A. Snoeck, S. J., "Moral Reflections on Psychiatric Abreaction," *Theological Studies*, 1952, XIII, pp. 173-189.

PART II

A DYNAMIC

THEORY OF NORMAL PERSONALITY

INTRODUCTION

1. The Study of Personality and General Psychology

The study of human needs and tendencies is one of the most important chapters of psychology, and is of primary importance to the theory and practice of psychotherapy. Although it belongs primarily to *general* psychology—i.e., the study of the processes and functions of normal behaviour—it received surprisingly little attention in this field until the time of Kurt Lewin. Whilst the sensory functions, memory, and the elementary reactions were explored in great detail, the dynamic and emotional life of the normal adult was usually examined only in its physiological aspects, and in connection with its repercussions on the organism.

It is no exaggeration to say that the whole study of personality has, generally speaking, been carried on independently of experimental psychology. Psychologists, investigating the personality or the psychology of the *individual*, in Binet's sense, formed a group apart from the exponents of general psychology. In an interesting article on this question, Michotte observes that the absence of contact between the two groups used to be strikingly evident at international congresses; and he goes on to emphasize the importance of a close union between these two branches of psychology.[1]

It seems obvious that the study of the dynamic aspects of personality should, in principle, be closely connected with the *general* study of behaviour. In this way the science of human personality would gain a great deal from the data of general psychology. However, one of the reasons why this study remains detached from general psychology seems to stem from general psychology itself: from the fact that it has neglected the study of the dynamic side of behaviour because of difficulties of method. This neglect has alienated all the people who have been chiefly interested in "personality." The dynamic aspect of behaviour is in fact, along with the problem of aptitudes, the one which chiefly interests exponents of individual and clinical psychology.

As regards the dynamic aspect of personality, the old *introspective* psychology no doubt produced a number of important works, particularly on *voluntary activity and intentional effort;* but these played very little part in the subsequent development of psychology. This was mainly because the tendency was increasingly towards a psychology of behaviour, and clinical psychology; the field and method of introspective psychology were gradually abandoned. The study of voluntary activity emphasized the psychic dynamism which was connected with cognitive factors, i.e. the knowledge of means and ends; whilst behaviourism and the various systems of depth-psychology concerned themselves primarily with irrational dynamisms, i.e. unconscious psychological needs and drives.

The study of learning and behaviour development also reduced the importance of *cognitive* factors to a minimum. Behaviourism explained the progress *towards the end* which reveals itself in the learning process as a *selection* of reactions performed automatically according to the *physiological effect* of need reduction, or success.

Psychoanalysis, again, made cognitive functions a factor of minor importance; since their main rôle, as we have seen, was simply to prevent the blind libido from breaking against reality.[2]

---

[1] Cf. A. Michotte, "*La psychologie expérimentale et le problème des aptitudes,*" *Mélanges Pierre Janet* (Paris, Ed. d'Artrey 1939), pp. 155-167.
[2] See *supra*, p. 42.

One of the chief objects of this study is, however, to bring out the close connection between the cognitive and the dynamic aspects of behaviour, and to show that *specifically human* needs seem to answer to the upper levels of cognition in man. The rehabilitation of the cognitive functions in the psychology of behaviour and the study of human needs is an urgent necessity if we are to advance beyond the incomplete views of Behaviorism and the doctrine of instincts as formulated by the various depth-psychologies.[1]

The *experimental* study of behaviour has, in fact, until recently been only mildly interested in the dynamic aspect of specifically human behaviour. This gap has, however, been largely compensated for in other branches of psychology. In two fields particularly, important contributions have been made to our knowledge of the emotional side of human behaviour and its motivation; they are pathological psychology, including psychoanalysis and depth-psychology in general, and animal or comparative psychology.

The study of abnormal behaviour on the one hand, and the countless experiments on the motivation of animal behaviour on the other, have been the two richest sources of new psychological data for decades. They have put the general psychology of normal man in the background.

This state of things, which is particularly noticeable in American psychology—and America is the preponderant influence in modern psychology—derives to a certain extent from our contemporary mentality. The modern mind best understands phenomena whose development it can trace from the very beginning; it therefore attempts to explain the psychological processes by *more elementary forms*, i.e. in this case, *animal* forms. Pathological phenomena, moreover, are often looked upon as *regressions*, and thus, when compared with the normal, as more primitive forms of behaviour. These phenomena also supply particularly favourable conditions of study, as the conflicts and tensions of personality manifest themselves in a *more pronounced form*.

[1] A development in this direction can be observed, particularly under the influence of Köhler's ideas on learning by insight, in several branches. See, for the psychology of behaviour, the works of Tolman and especially those of David Krech; and concerning depth-psychology, the recent contribution of Thomas French (cf. above, p. 107).

The fact that behaviour has been studied in its more or less pathological or animal forms, and been interpreted on the basis of that kind of observation, has had a profound influence on the picture which contemporary psychology has formed of human personality.

We shall not enter into any detailed examination of the influence which the study of animal motivation has had on certain systems.[1] This development in animal psychology has had one consequence worth noting, however, and that is that many psychologists will not accept the existence of any fundamental needs in man except those *whose basis is physiological.* Any other needs or aspirations which may be involved in an adult's actions are supposed to arise from organic needs ("tissue needs") by means of some process or other—either learning or conditioning or socialization.

We should like to draw particular attention to the fact that the most influential theories about any systems of psychic forces have been developed on a basis of *psychopathological* facts, i.e. from the study of phenomena and processes which appear when the *mental balance* has been disturbed. A picture of the normal man has then been produced by simply touching up a little the dynamic phenomena revealed in pathological behaviour.

The student of psychology is already so used to this factual situation that *normal* psychology hardly seems to interest him as far as the dynamic structure of the personality is concerned. When he starts studying the dynamic aspects of personality, he takes to psychopathology as a matter of course.

At first the various systems of depth-psychology were mostly closed systems having no contact with general psychology, whose most fundamental principles and data they frequently ignored.

Nevertheless there is no doubt, we repeat, that a theory of the dynamic structure of personality has its place in a *general* psychology of the normal man. It is also certain that any sound ideas that have been introduced by psychoanalysis or the other

---

[1] See, for example, the central idea of "need reduction" in the system developed by Clark Hull, *Principles of Behavior* (New York, Appleton-Century, 1943).

systems must be integrated into the general psychology of human behaviour.

The difficulty lies in the following fact. Psychoanalysis, on the word of Freud himself,[1] is no more than a *fragmentary contribution* to the study of personality. Freud explored this from the special point of view of the *unconscious*. Conscious life—which seems, after all, to have some influence on human behaviour—remained in the background. Increasingly Freud used this partial point of view to develop a dynamic theory of man *as a whole*, and because of this, over and over again, he forgot his own critical appraisal of the limitations of his discoveries.

One example will suffice to show this. Intellectual knowledge and sense knowledge are indubitably important psychological functions in normal life, and play a leading part in human behaviour. Yet, as we have already seen, Freud's ideas concerning functions of this kind belong to the most undeveloped part of his system and are quite without any satisfactory scientific basis.[2] Thus an essential element in behaviour is almost completely ignored. This is all the more regrettable, since *knowledge penetrates so deeply into man's motivation, and since so many of his needs and tendencies may be inextricably involved with the special nature of his cognitive functions.*

The development of a dynamic theory of the *normal* man, therefore, seems to us an urgent necessity in contemporary psychology. Such a theory, whilst taking into account pathological facts, *must be the work of general psychology* and must aim to embrace the behaviour of the normal man *in all his functions and at all the levels of his activity*.

2. Personality from the Point of View of Psychopathology

Two crucial problems regarding the dynamic structure of personality must be faced: first, the problem of its *basic or funda-*

---

[1] Cf. Freud, *"Kurzer Abriss der Psychoanalyse," Gesammelte Werke*, XIII, p. 427: "Sie (die Psychoanalyse) kann also auf jedem Wissengebiet nur Beiträge liefern, welche aus der Psychologie des Ichs zu ergänzen sind."
[2] Cf. *supra*, pp. 41-42.

mental needs; and secondly, the problem of the *tensions and conflicts which appear and develop within it.*

(1) FUNDAMENTAL NEEDS

Let us first briefly summarize the data of the problem, and then recall the solution offered by psychoanalysis. In human personality there is a great variety of drives and needs, and various forms of emotional receptivity corresponding to them. Man needs affection as much as he needs food; he needs some sort of recognition of his personality by others; he has sexual needs; he needs to give meaning to his life and work.

It is an old problem, how to regard this mass of tendencies and needs; and there have been many attempts to reduce it to a few *fundamental tendencies* or "instincts." But *a high proportion of these systems have been developed on logical and finalistic principles rather than psychologically and genetically.* This is so, for instance, in the classification by which the instinct of self-preservation is opposed to the instinct towards the preservation of the species. On the other hand, as we have seen, theories based on comparative or animal psychology admit no fundamental needs except impulses that can be derived from *physiological* bases.

During the last few years, under the influence of depth-psychology, two needs in particular have been stressed as fundamental "forces": the sexual instinct (Freud) and the power instinct (Adler). Psychoanalysis has claimed that the constructive forces in man can in the last analysis be reduced to sexual libido: so that this need is not only the basic drive, but ultimately the *only* one. Thus the dynamic structure has been reduced to its simplest form.

If we look at this idea from the point of view of general psychology, what conclusion do we come to?

The psychoanalytical theory of man's dynamic structure depends fundamentally on two classes of data. On the one hand, Freud believed that he could prove that the sexual instinct plays a decisive part in the conflict that lies at the root of psychic troubles. On the other hand, it was shown that all sorts of activities and motives—including those usually considered the most "elevated"—contain elements of sexual libido. In the light of these discoveries it seemed reasonable to Freud to regard the libido as "the" basic drive. He showed, in fact, with the help of data drawn from sexual psychopathology, that the libido can take on a great *variety of forms*.[1]

There can be no doubt that psychoanalysis and also Adler's *Individual Psychology* have brought to light a great amount of highly interesting data in this field. What we have to consider in this chapter is whether it is true that either the libido or the will to power dominates all psychic activity. It may be that the observation and interpretation of data from the *psychopathological angle* has endowed certain needs with an importance which is not justified when these are examined in the light of *general psychology*.

(2) FUNDAMENTAL NEEDS AND CULTURAL ENVIRONMENT

Let us first consider the significance of the fact that Freud and Adler find, respectively, the sexual instinct and the power instinct at the very beginning of pathogenic conflict.[2]

It would show a wrong idea of the value of clinical results to accept them as important in *psychopathology* but not in the psychology of *normal* man. When the frustration of a certain need seems repeatedly to be the main cause of a breakdown, this can surely be taken as a sign of the importance of this need and its satisfaction in human life *in general*.

It seems quite likely, however, that certain kinds of cultural environment tend to create a critical situation for some human needs, so that these find themselves more frequently exposed to frustration or to states of extreme tension. In such conditions they form a sort of vulnerable zone in psychic life and tend increasingly to attract attention.

This phenomenon seems to be taking place, to some extent, in our own culture, as far as sexual needs and the self-assertive tendency are concerned.

Social research has shown[3] that a transition from one life-con-

---

[1] Cf. *supra*, p. 15.

[2] The fact that in this work we frequently mention Freud and Adler together does not mean that we ignore the differences between their systems. We are here considering the two systems together because both, on the basis of psychological facts, have made a certain need the central force in human behaviour.

[3] See particularly E. H. Stofflet, *A Study of National and Cultural Differences in Criminal Tendency* (Archives of Psychology No. 185, 1931).

ception or form of culture to another, involving entirely *new* standards of value, leads to a critical period for a great number of people, i.e. the transitional generation is specially subject to internal conflicts, as is reflected in the high percentage of suicide cases. This conflict-situation is the result of the tension which develops between the old standards of value that are being abandoned and the new forms which there is a general desire to adopt. People are still attached to old standards; they still *feel* their restraining or commanding influence to such an extent that they cannot follow the new ways of living as they would like to, and so be free of their old obligations, without feeling scruples about it. Thus a transitional or evolutionary period weakens the power to live according to the old rules, whilst at the same time it leads to a certain uneasiness and psychic tension if the individual attempts to free himself from the old standards, so deeply rooted in him.

An evolution involving the substitution of new standards for old ones has been at work in our Western civilization for a long time. But during the last few decades the change has spread to much larger masses of people. As regards our own problem, it has taken place particularly in the field of sexual needs and the desire for pleasure in general. The old standards have been transformed or abolished. Nevertheless, in a great number of people there still remain resistances, psychic inhibitions, which continue to be active even in people who, on the conscious level, have rejected all the old restrictions. Our culture is in fact still profoundly involved in the Christian conception of good and evil, which continues to exert a strong social pressure. In the education of children particularly, the old standards are still applied with all the old rigour, and in forms which for children in contact with the real conditions of life may raise conflicts whose importance can easily be underestimated. For there is often such a gulf between the standards taught and imposed upon them, and the real forms of behaviour with which they are bound to come into contact, that the first contact can give rise to anxieties which cause certain kinds of conflict.

Thus the standards and rules persist, whilst the life-conception which gives these forms of behaviour their meaning and value has for many people disintegrated; and the individual, pulled in two ways at once, loses all psychic stability; the situation gives rise to intimate contradictions and tensions which, in psychologically weaker people, may destroy mental balance. Hence our age is more productive of maladjustments and neurotic troubles than periods of less heterogeneous culture, such as the times of unrestrained paganism or profound Christianity.

To mention one example only, connected with the sexual education of children: the castration complex, to which Freud ascribes such great importance, is found less frequently in surroundings in which sexual initiation occurs early, and particularly where the attitude towards sexual matters is more matter-of-fact than it was in so many families fifty years ago.

Our age is also a period of extreme tension for the second tendency, i.e. the need to assert oneself and gain a recognized place in the eyes of the world. Never before, perhaps, in any civilization, has competition between man and man been so systematically insisted upon as it is in our Western civilization today. From the very first years of his life, the individual's achievements are scored and compared with those of others. At school and university, with examinations and other heavy requirements; in daily life, with its struggle for jobs—on all sides young people are faced with extreme demands. The phenomenon is no less apparent in the efforts made by young women to keep up with males in all kinds of performances in professional life. Young people's faculties are stretched and exploited to breaking-point, and this condition of things imposes on many of the psychically weaker ones demands which go beyond their strength.

In people who do not feel strong enough to deal with demands imposed upon them, a conflict breaks out between their feeling of powerlessness and the "instinctive drive" to assert themselves in spite of everything. This conflict frequently lies behind neurotic troubles.

In these circumstances it is easy to understand that our state of culture becomes a breeding-ground for maladjustments and neuroses, which, moreover, now more than ever, assume *the form of conflicts with either of these needs, sexuality and the need for self-affirmation.* Thus the psychiatrist, in the course of his clinical observations and studies, is continually discovering frustrations and conflicts in these two fields, in patients forced to submit to such conditions of life. No wonder if the psychotherapist comes to attribute to them a preponderant and perhaps excessive part in the dynamic structure of personality.

Attention must, moreover, be drawn to a fact which illustrates how a strong subjective factor may enter into the interpretation of disturbances. Very early in his career, Carl Jung noticed that a case could be explained just as easily in terms of Adlerian psychology as in terms of Freudian psychology. In a number of people the most striking conflicts do in fact concern sexual troubles, when at bottom their trouble involves more general attitudes and weaknesses of the ego. It may happen that sex is simply the field in which the individual's lack of mental balance manifests itself. Thus lack of self-confidence can prevent a person from having normal sexual relations, and this will be the starting point for pathological deviations. The two needs being so intimately united in one single deviation, it is possible to interpret the disturbance as a result of either of the two systems.

In the new cultural situation such as we have been experiencing in recent years, other needs become profoundly frustrated. The fundamental disorder of our civilization—as appears particularly in the literature and philosophy of Existentialism—has accentuated the absurdity of human life. Now more than ever, certain psychotherapists are struck by the number of cases in which the absence of any meaningful philosophy of life seems to be the deepest cause of neurosis.[1] Thus it is possible that the need to find a meaning in life is revealed more clearly today than in former days, when such a need was more easily satisfied.

It follows that the needs which, in a given culture, particularly attract the attention of the psychiatrist do not necessarily give us a complete view of the dynamic structure of personality. In psychotherapy the most frustrated needs always appear most clearly. Therefore we shall have to attempt a more systematic examination of human needs, surveying man as a whole.

[1] See *infra*, pp. 227–230.

(3) INTERNAL TENSION OR "REPRESSION"?

In the second place, we consider that psychoanalysis has envisaged the problem of the *conflict or the state of tension in man* from too exclusively a *psychopathological* point of view. Freud devoted himself above all to the study of the *pathological* development of this conflict. As a psychopathologist, he paid particular attention to the fact that certain needs become thwarted by *foreign* powers which *censor* and *repress* them with pathogenic consequences.

Repression therefore came to be looked upon as the essential process in which *the state of conflict in man ends*. The forces in conflict are said to be the native libido and the *super-ego*, which is rather of "foreign" origin, since its content is made up of external social influences. The conflict is said to be pathogenic in its effects, unless the repressed forces manage *to escape in disguise*.

The condition of *mental balance* is also looked at from a typically pathological point of view. Normal equilibrium is supposed to come about simply because the repressed forces find themselves sufficiently dammed up, or manage to "by-pass" the censorship, hence mental balance means merely that the pathogenic factors have not released their effects.

When we say that Freud particularly emphasized the pathological element in psychic life we do not mean that he showed no interest in the normal and constructive aspects of human activity; on the contrary. But we do say that he looks upon everything normal, and everything worth while in human culture, as a *superstructure* or a fortunate *outlet*, of forces which, if it were not for this subterfuge, would be bound to disturb mental balance. To use Freud's own terms: these things are simply *substitutes* for the satisfaction of *repressed* desires which are alive in every mind from the first years of childhood.[1]

This is a typical example of what we mean by a dynamic theory of personality developed from a *psychopathological* point of view. When personality is *looked at from the point of view*

---

[1] Cf. *supra*, p. 44 (italics mine). See also the important passage quoted on p. 177.

of general or normal psychology, it may appear in a rather different light. Possibly, too, in a normal person the conflict-situation can appear within the dynamic structure in other forms besides that of repression. The professional bias of the psychopathologist often leads Freud to look upon *normal* phenomena as *deviations from the abnormal*. We have already mentioned one example of this in connection with religion. According to Freud, the practice of religion is to be looked upon as an obsessional neurosis, *mitigated by being so common*.[1] This example is typical of his method, which involves taking the *pathological* as a basis and then understanding the *normal* in the light of it. This may result, however, in seeing the normal *abnormally*.

Our aim in the second part of the book will be to give an outline of the *normal* personality, considered in its dynamic aspects. We propose to examine first the *internal tension* that characterizes human behaviour. In Chapter V we shall discuss its *fundamental needs*.

[1] Cf. *supra*, p. 68.

CHAPTER IV

INTERNAL TENSION AND THE CONSTRUCTIVE DEVELOPMENT OF PERSONALITY

1. Realization of the Ideal Self and "Repression"

It is a fact of the first importance that man's psychic dynamism cannot be looked upon as a *single* vector following a definite direction. The dynamic structure of personality is characterized, as we have said, by internal conflicts and tensions. We must first consider this condition of conflict within the personality. And we must consider it not only in its destructive aspects, as these appear in pathological dislocations (which Freud particularly did), but also *in the light of the total meaning which this conflict takes on in the human personality.*

(I) THE SPECIFICALLY HUMAN FORM OF SELF-REALIZATION

We must first notice that what is involved here is a specifically human phenomenon of conflict. The behaviour of animals seems simply to follow the strongest impulse of the moment; there are no real conflicts, except in a certain sense, in artificial circumstances as in the technique of "experimental neuroses." As a rule, animal behaviour is confined to the biological development dictated by the species.

Now, man manifests, besides dynamisms similar to those of animals, one characteristic feature: his dynamism goes beyond the boundaries of a biological species. In human activity there is a drive toward a certain self-transcendence, i.e. a force which tends, by *conscious* intervention and *personal* effort, to go beyond the merely spontaneous developments of the biological process of growth. The *way* in which man frees himself from the automatic development of his being—in other words, what he *does with himself*—is, to a certain extent, a matter of *personal* responsibility.

This process is not a purely subjective phenomenon, accessible only to introspection. On the contrary, it involves the most overt and "public" fact of human *behaviour* as a whole, compared with animal behaviour. For human activity is, in fact, characterized by *constructive development, progress,* which is in utter contrast to the *stagnation* of animal behaviour. Human civilization and culture are a manifest proof of this. But this phenomenon of cultural progress—which is above all a *social* fact—necessarily has its source and concrete realization in the activity of the *individual* man. There is a constructive tendency *active in the individual* which lies behind social and cultural development, though, of course, the *individual* is necessarily in constant contact with his environment and the people who compose it.

In different cultures this "drive" appears in different forms. In certain civilizations progress is directed particularly towards bigger and bigger achievements in the material and social fields; whereas in other cultures it may tend rather towards some form of inner perfection, or it may endeavour to establish a harmony between both these forms of development.[1]

This internal force which lies behind progress is simply the actualization of ever new potentialities in man; and it is intimately bound up with the life of consciousness. A certain ideal image, i.e. an image of what man proposes to make of himself, or what he

[1] The fact of *progress* in human development which we mention here does not by any means mean that human culture follows an ascending curve and never declines. The decadence of civilization is also produced by man's pursuing certain "personal" *ideals;* even in its decline, culture is a different thing from animal stagnation.

wants to aim at, is present to human consciousness. This image is simply a concrete form, developed under the influence of a deep-lying urge, of an ideal of self-realization. This ideal, it is true, is inspired by social and cultural conditions, but to some extent it depends on personal spontaneity.

The individual and social fact of cultural progress is so characteristic of human activity as a whole that it can hardly be ignored. Many philosophers, psychologists and biologists have concerned themselves with it. Nevertheless, the most various and unsatisfactory interpretations have been proposed to explain it.

Often this "drive" is looked upon as a simple organic force, manifested by the living organism in the actualization of its own biological form. Every living organism does indeed to a certain extent manifest activities directed towards a fuller vital development and a wider integration of elements in the environment.[1] Besides this purely biological phenomenon, there is a *specifically human drive* which will provide us with the starting-point for our explanation of *specifically human* behaviour. The general tendency towards self-realization which runs through the whole of man's psycho-physiological organism is undoubtedly a biological reality. We shall have to discuss it later, and we shall recognize it as one of the fundamental dynamisms of behaviour. We must first of all realize, however, that on the human level, this universal "drive" involves new and irreducible forms, because it is at work in a kind of psychic life which can know and desire realities that transcend the limits of the material universe. The fact that the human psyche "opens out" by means of consciousness to a world beyond that of organic impressions, and is thus not simply "affected" by, or "absorbed" into, biological realities, gives to the dynamism of human self-realization an entirely new form of existence.

Thus, not only can man aim at new "personal" forms of development, but he can also to a certain extent *take up an attitude* towards the form of development that he has actually reached. He can

[1] See, amongst others, the work of Monakow and Goldstein. A certain amount of data relating to this idea will be found in Rümke's synoptic study: "*De drang tot volkomenheid,*" *Studies en Voordrachten over Psychiatrie* (Amsterdam, Scheltema and Holkema, 1943), pp. 315-321.

become conscious of himself and of what is going on inside him, —hence the specifically human form of the tendency to self-realization: on the one hand, *the form of life towards which he tends is present in him as a kind of personal ideal;* on the other, he can *take up an attitude towards the present state of his personality and the tendencies which are at work in it.*

Moreover, it is a fact that no matter what the form of personality may be which a man finds present within himself at any given moment, the forces of development will act in *different directions.* There are some especially which will not be in harmony with the concrete ideal which he has at that particular moment. It can even happen that a man will look at things from different points of view and feel inclined to actualize several potential forms of personality within himself at once, i.e. he feels inclined towards forms of behaviour which lie in different directions and are incompatible with each other.

Thus, when a man has considered all that is involved and decides to actualize his "higher" potentialities—whether in the moral, intellectual, social, economic or any other domain—there will still be other forces of development within him—forces presenting an ideal along a less constructive way: an abandonment, for instance, to the impulse of the moment; whereas, on the other hand, in the man who has adopted this abandonment to impulse as his ideal, tendencies of a more constructive nature may be still present.

This characteristic of the human drive to self-realization causes an *active state of conflict* in man, i.e. an opposition and a tension experienced at the very heart of the psychic dynamism. Man does not simply follow the impulse which leads to his personal development. At every moment he finds himself confronted as a *person* with several possible forms of self-realization and with forces acting in different directions.

The sexual instinct is perhaps the most powerful conflict-force which has to be mastered in order to realize a constructive image of personality. Abandonment to sexual tendencies can absorb mental life to such an extent that they can very largely turn it away from any constructive activity which is specifically human. Not active only periodically as in animals, the sexual impulse in man can engross a great part of his activity, dominating his point of view in all his social relationships if there is no resistance to its satisfaction. It will therefore easily be understood that the most *constructive* forms of the human ideal come into conflict with this impulse particularly. Within himself man feels the need to fight against it—as against many others—if he is to realize the constructive ideal emerging within him.

In social life the same opposed forces and the same states of tension are found at work. Every culture, in fact, is the embodiment and expression of one form or other of the constructive ideal of human personality. In his collective as in his individual life, man sets up resistances to whatever is hindering the form of realization he is aiming at. That is why the manifestation of certain needs is excluded from social life, in so far as these are opposed to the realization of the current image of personality. By such social norms collective man defends himself against the forces which create obstacles within him to the ideal realization of his potentialities.

In social life, too, it is clear that the sexual instinct is of all human needs the one which has been most powerfully hemmed in by well-defined rules and standards. Every cultural group, however primitive it may be, defends itself against the onward rush of this instinctive force, because man feels that he is here faced with an instinct which is the most dangerous enemy of the constructive realization of his own personality.

To sum up: An analysis of the normal activity of human personality reveals that the state of conflict which appears in man must be deeply rooted in the specifically human form of psychic life. From the very nature of this conflict it can already be deduced that the aim of psychotherapy will never be simply the mere suppression of this tension, which is in fact a result of the complex of forces that make up the complete human personality.

(2) CONSTRUCTIVE TENSION OR "REPRESSION"?

Looked at from this point of view the problems of psychological *conflict* and *repression* take on a rather new significance.

The "repressive" force is no longer a superstructure of purely social origin inhibiting man's constructive forces, or only allowing them to manifest themselves in a distorted way. The tension in question is *itself* the most positive and the most constructive force in man. It is, as we have shown, the dynamic force which tends, by realizing our *specifically human* potentialities, to transcend the automatic development of the psycho-physiological organism. Its influence is *directly* constructive; contrary to Freudian theory, it stimulates the higher activities, and gives birth to cultural values, *not* by a *transformation* of libidinous forces but by an actualization of *specific* potentialities.

On this point we disagree with Freud entirely. According to Freud, the line of development in human beings is no different from that which can be found in animals.[1] We, on the contrary, have insisted on the opposition between these two forms of development, which is manifest particularly in human culture, as compared with animal stagnation. This objective fact focuses our attention on the difference between the dynamic factors behind the two processes.

According to Freud, the tendency towards self-development and perfection (which exists in only a small number of people) can easily be explained as a consequence of the repression of instincts, "which explain whatever is most valuable in human culture." The repressed instinct never loses its longing for complete satisfaction. This complete satisfaction, says Freud, is realized in the reproduction of the primitive feeling of pleasure which man experienced at the infantile stage of his life. Thus, the tendency towards perfection and progress can be finally reduced to an impulse to *return* to the infantile stage and recover the feeling of pleasure experienced then, and the tendency towards *progress* is in reality a *regressive* force. The effort which man makes to revive the "infantile" feeling never completely succeeds, because resistances and repressive mechanisms raise obstacles to such a return. Therefore, says Freud, *there is nothing left for man to do except to progress along the only line of development left open to him:* the line of culture and spiritual activity.

Man's cultural and spiritual development, therefore, consists for Freud in the escape of the libido along the only line of devel-

[1] Cf. particularly *"Jenseits des Lustprinzips," Gesammelte Werke*, XIII, pp. 44–45.

opment open to it. It is a way taken over by, or created by, the pleasure instinct, because the "way back" to the infantile stage is obstructed by repression and social censorship.[1]

We find ourselves faced with a way of thinking which is very characteristic of Freud. He cannot see anything except the negative side, i.e. the obstacle to the impulse of instinct, in the fact of this extraordinary development of the human spirit. He does not seem to show any awareness of the real nature of the *positive potentialities implied in such a development*.

It is obvious that the line of man's cultural development cannot be explained by saying *that it is the only way of development that remains open to the instincts*. Similarly, concepts like that of *sublimation* have no explanatory value at all in this connection, for they do no more than *express* a hypothetical transposition of the libidinous into the cultural.[2] If every constructive force in man is reduced to libido, what is responsible for this positive transformation of the libido into such marvellous activities as those of the human spirit? It is not even clear where resistance to the libido originates. Social censorship and inhibitions can only

---

[1] In view of the importance of this theory of Freud's we give the following translation of the passage in which it is most clearly expressed: "The development of man up to now does not seem to me to need any explanation differing from that of animal development, and the restless striving towards further perfection which may be observed in a minority of human beings is easily explicable as the result of that repression of instinct upon which what is most valuable in human culture is built. The repressed instinct never ceases to strive after its complete satisfaction, which would consist in repetition of the primary experience of satisfaction; all substitution—or reaction—formations and sublimations avail nothing towards relaxing the continual tension; and out of the excess of the satisfaction demanded over that found is born the driving momentum which allows of no abiding in any situation presented to it, but in the poet's words 'urges ever forward, ever unsubdued' (Mephisto in *Faust*, Act I, Faust's study). The path in the other direction, back to complete satisfaction, is as a rule barred by the resistances that maintain the repressions, and thus there remains nothing for it but to proceed in the other, still unobstructed direction, that of development, without, however, any prospect of being able to bring the process to a conclusion or to attain the goal." Cf. Freud, *"Jenseits des Lustprinzips," Gesammelte Werke*, XIII, pp. 44-45. The English text is taken from the English translation by C. J. M. Hubback, *Beyond the Pleasure Principle* (London and Vienna, The International Psychoanalytical Press, 1922), pp. 52-53.

[2] Cf. *supra*, p. 45.

supply a secondary explanation, for such resistances and transformations must, in the final analysis, come from *positive* forces in the *individual mind*. We have indicated above how social resistance develops from psychic forces in the individual man. This line of specifically human development requires its own potentialities, and also higher possibilities of knowledge which, *as active forces, tend towards their own actualization and unfolding*. The essential aspect of the problem passes completely unnoticed in Freud's theory. If it is admitted that the human line of development as a whole requires no other basis than animal need, the question arises, why are not exactly the same processes of resistance, repression and sublimation found in animals too? They possess a sexual instinct. How is it that their libido does not find a way of escape analogous to that of culture and the human spirit?

(3) "CENSORSHIP" OR PERSONAL IDEAL?

In the second place, it must be emphasized that the thing called "repression" is not the kind of *censorship* mechanism which is *foreign to the intrinsic dynamism of the human personality*. The tendency towards a constructive self-realization is *the most specific* need of the human personality.

It is on the basis of very unconvincing examples that Freud tries to build up his thesis of an extrinsic *censorship*. He believes that the pleasure instinct is more intimately related to the individual than the "repressive" force whose nature tends to be more exogenous. He quotes certain phrases to prove his thesis. Thus, a man says, "I feel inclined to do this or that because it would be pleasurable" but "My conscience says no." This example is supposed to indicate the existence of a "separate power always on the alert," which takes upon itself, against the *I*—i.e. the real individual—the functions of restraint and censorship.[1]

It is clear, however, that his is simply a case of different forms of expression manifesting a *duality* within the personality; in particular, the duality which gives birth to the conflict mentioned previously. The same condition of conflict can be expressed just as well by saying: "*My instinctive tendencies* would like this or that, but *I* will not consent to it."

[1] Cf. "*Neue Folge der Vorlesungen,*" *Gesammelte Werke*, XV, p. 65.

Nevertheless, Freud is quite right to introduce the process of *identification* into the constitution of the "repressive" force, which he calls the *ego-ideal*, or the *super-ego*. Whatever is "higher" in man is realized through a kind of identification, i.e. a process by which the individual makes *his own* whatever he has discovered to be a "value." In our own cultural environment, it is undoubtedly in the personality of his parents that the child most frequently first discovers these values. But the very formation of the ideal, and especially the tendency to *identify himself* with it, originates in the *fundamental tendency to achieve a more complete self-realization*. The child, in fact, in his effort to identify himself with the ideal father, actualizes higher potentialities which exist within himself.

Once again, it is not sufficient to say, as Freud does, that this identification with the ideal comes about as a result of a failure of sexual possession. We have already seen the technical difficulties involved in the application of the Freudian theory in this context.[1] But what above all must not be lost sight of is the fact that this process of identification implies the positive dynamism of self-development. It is this dynamism which creates in man the true ego-ideal, and this ego-ideal is the human personality itself, to the extent that it transcends animal individuality. The contents of this ego-ideal are of course made up of values embodied originally in the parents.

(4) FIXATION OF THE INFANTILE IDEAL OR REAL DEVELOPMENT?

There seems to be no reason for saying, as Freud does, however, that the process of identification and the later stages in the development of personality remain genetically bound up with the ideal images *of infancy*. In the course of his development the individual seems capable of acquiring *new* contents of quite a different nature. A critical analysis of our contents of consciousness shows that besides infantile elements and forms which undoubtedly continue to exercise an influence on the grown man, there are also contents of quite a different origin which transcend the infantile idea of the father. I am thinking particularly, for instance, of the metaphysical knowledge of God, of the absolute

---

[1] See *supra*, p. 19.

character of moral obligation, etc., which cannot be reduced to emotional complexes, nor to dream images, nor to the unconscious.

In this book it is not our object to prove *from a philosophical point of view* that contents and values like the idea of God, moral obligation, etc., transcend the infantile ideal of the father. Only technical philosophy has methods adequate to this task, and it has indeed supplied the proofs. Our aim is purely psychological. For this reason it will suffice to illustrate our thesis by a single example drawn from practice. In the course of being analysed, a young man of about twenty years of age gave us the following associations for the word "God": "A powerful force which shatters me; I cannot escape from it. I have the impression that a man is pushing me forward; he is pushing me in the back with a stick; I must walk. I can see my father; he is punishing me; I cannot escape from his anger, he is spoiling my life. I no longer have this idea of God; I know quite well that God is utterly different, but when I was young I was afraid of God and of my father, without them I could have done what I liked."

On the intellectual level this young man had liberated himself from his father and from his infantile idea of God, but the emotional states experienced so intensely in childhood went on echoing in his psychic life. Nevertheless, his actual idea of God was neither the continuation nor the development of his infantile experience. "If there was only that," he said himself, "I should no longer believe in God." There were, therefore, emotional echoes which went on resounding in him, but besides these there was a mental content within him corresponding to another idea of God. This latter idea had a different origin, although it was not completely separated from the first; it was in fact an *intellectual understanding* of the necessity of a first cause or a final explanation of himself and the world. It was this mental content which had partially replaced or completed the first idea; this new idea of God explained why he still clung to Him at a level of his intellectual life where the first emotional content alone would have been incapable of maintaining this attitude.

Only a philosophical analysis of knowledge can reveal to us the proper value, the exact significance, of these metaphysical notions which develop in man as his intellectual life expands within him.

Such an analysis shows that it is impossible to conceive contents of this kind as mere offshoots of emotional complexes. They imply the activity of psychic functions of quite a different nature, although this activity—like any other human function—cannot be separated from psychic life as a whole. Such metaphysical notions are indeed connected genetically with the emotional background in which they developed, but their specific content implies an activity which cannot be *reduced* to an emotional complex.

It is easy to understand that Freud did not look at psychic contents in the light of any philosophical criticism of knowledge, but that explains why his ideas in this field remain, according to his own words, mere suggestions, to be completed by the further contributions of others.

More generally, we can say that one of the great gaps in the psychoanalytical interpretation of man lies precisely in its underestimating what emerges as "new" in the course of man's individual and social development. Freud regards all this as simply the *manifestation in new forms* of primitive, repressed, unconscious desires.

This way of looking at things not only lacks any foundation in fact, but it prevents psychoanalysis from reaching an impartial view of the *facts* that characterize the development of human personality.[1] Genetic psychology, no less than the philosophical analysis of our contents of knowledge, shows that the ideas of moral and intellectual relationships which the child develops are modified and *change in content* in the course of mental development.[2] This enrichment of the contents of knowledge is bound up with the actual growth of the mental powers, and it is absolutely impossible to look upon them as a manifestation of emotional unconscious attitudes of the infantile stage.

These new ideas and conceptions cause the child to develop new relationships and new attitudes towards social standards and absolute values, at the same time creating a different attitude towards himself and humanity in general.

[1] Cf. on this point Sherif and Cantril, *The Psychology of Ego-involvements* (New York, John Wiley, 1947); especially pp. 481–506.
[2] See especially in this connection the remarkable work of Piaget on the development of the moral and intellectual ideas of children.

It is in the perspective of this spiritual development as a whole that one must see the evolution of the individual's ideals and standards. When this complex process of growth is looked upon as a mere manifestation of the sediment left over from the Oedipus complex, or a simple transposition of infantile contents into new forms, the development of the human personality is reduced to an emotional echo which, though it certainly continues to exist, *is only one component of human development as a whole*.

To sum up: The same tendency towards self-realization animates the child who identifies himself with his father and the man who, from contact with a widening reality, conceives and realizes ever new values and ideas. This constructive force, together with the instinctive impulse which drives man to seek the pleasure of the moment, constitutes *one single* psychic dynamism, which is as complex and as torn within as human personality itself, yet inseparably united to personality. Hence the ego-ideal and the "censorship" of Freudian psychology are not to be looked upon as alien forces which *repress* the forces *proper* to the human individual; they are two dynamic orientations which form a creative tension, and thus together construct the development of the human ideal. Nor is this ego-ideal fixed for ever in infantile forms, for new elements of quite a different origin appear in it throughout the development of the personality.

One further point: the fact that Freud limited the phase of real psychic development to the first six years of life is responsible for the idea that every normative value in man is *external* in origin and has no other function except that of "repressing" the impulses of the vital instincts. During these years of childhood, it is true, every standard and value comes originally from outside and opposes itself as an exogenous force to the impulses of the individual. But the psychic development of man, i.e. the process by which he really becomes a *human person,* consists precisely in the fact that these realities and values answer demands and potentialities which gradually grow up in his psychic life. Without this endogenous phase of development, all these realities would ultimately be eliminated from the adult personality, as happens in the case of many specifically infantile psychic contents. Hence the social imposition of these realities and values is merely a preliminary phase which does not stand on its own and which is to be explained, genetically, by the endogenous development of the human personality. The fact that Freud limited the really active and creative period of human development to these first years of childhood means that he did not take into account anything except this limited, exogenous phase in the development of the ego-ideal. Thus he cannot see any constructive forces in the later development of personality except external censorships and the endogenous impulses which these censorships check. This arrest of the *real* development of personality at the infantile stage is one of the great *psychological* errors of orthodox Freudianism. It is not only contradicted by the facts; even more seriously it makes any adequate theory of personality impossible. The only truth which lies behind it is that some remnants of infantile experience do enter into even the most intimate aspects of later psychic development. This was a discovery of the first importance; it deserved to be explained in closer conformity with the real facts about the structure and growth of human personality.

2. Constructive Development: Integration of Personality

To get any adequate idea of the dynamic structure of the human being, it is essential to realize that the two lines of dynamic development of which we have been speaking are rooted in the *unity* of human personality, and arise from this unity. *To a certain extent, and on their own level, they can be considered as constructive forces,* and for this reason personality cannot develop normally if either of them is "repressed"; on the contrary, a balanced development is achieved rather *by a process of integration, in which the two lines of construction meet to create some form of personal ideal.*

With the development of this integrating process, man is at every moment faced by *a choice.* He has to choose between the satisfaction of certain needs deriving from one or other of his potentialities. Usually, he has to renounce *this* to gain *that;* he has to fight against something in order to win something else. He will not only have to renounce the satisfaction of *organic* needs and impulses, but he may have to draw in the reins on quite a number of so-called "*higher*" aspirations, and refuse to follow ways of development which are too elevated, in order not to destroy the balance of the whole process. *It is by repeatedly consenting to the satisfaction of certain needs, and refusing to satisfy others, that human dynamism develops throughout the greater part of man's life in certain special directions.* Some of the existing potentialities in the personality are used to the full, *others remain unused.* Certain objects are consciously sought and thus lead to new dynamic developments, whilst other desires are rejected. As a result, many potentialities end by *losing a great deal of their dynamic force, whilst others become more powerful.* In other words, *there is a canalization of active needs and potentialities,* as a result of which human behaviour develops in certain directions, to the neglect of others. Thus *some real potentialities gradually disappear or atrophy, because they have not been actively developed—i.e., have not involved any activity in line with the individual's aspirations.*[1]

The question arises, how exactly are we to imagine this process of development through canalization, which we have thus briefly outlined?

The data of general psychology, particularly the results of experiments on the development of behaviour and the canalization of needs, can provide us with the materials for a general theory of the development of personality. This, if it is to be understood concretely, must be understood as a development of dynamic contents and of behaviour in general. *A synthesis of the laws of behaviour with those of the development of personality is a task of the highest importance.* It is this that we shall now attempt to perform.

---

[1] G. Allport seems to have envisaged a similar process in the development of psychic dynamism. Discussing the idea of sublimation, he says in a note that "An individual may, without serious conflict, forego some specific gratification, provided that he finds other sources of equal satisfaction . . . In such instances, the individual simply disregards his unfulfilled desires, letting them atrophy or repressing them without disaster in the interest of an alternative plan of life that satisfies, not these desires only, but satisfies *him* as a whole man." Cf. *Personality* (New York, Henry Holt, 1937), p. 185. It will be seen that the ideas which we shall try to develop *on the basis of the data and theories of the experimental psychology of behaviour,* are similar to these intuitive ideas of Allport's.

(1) THE CANALIZATION OF NEEDS AND THE LAW OF EFFECT

It is the *law of effect*—which we have explained elsewhere[1]—that we shall use as a basis for our theory of the development of personality. Experimental data about the way human personality develops from past experience show that *normal forms of behaviour, and the dynamic forces which lie behind them, tend to develop according to the success achieved;* that is to say, forms of behaviour *which lead to a satisfactory result* are maintained by the organism, whilst the kinds of behaviour that end in failure or a comparatively unsatisfactory result are increasingly eliminated. This, in the most general terms, *is the law of effect,* as it is more or less universally accepted.

This process of development is to be understood as follows:

(a) At the root of any kind of behaviour there lies a dynamic force, a need. The kinds of behaviour which we say end unsatisfactorily are those in which the need does not achieve any abreaction; in other words, in which the purpose is not attained. In this case the dynamic force sets in motion other forms of behaviour.

On the other hand, behaviour that leads to a satisfactory and adequate result constitutes a way of release for the dynamic force, becoming a kind of *canal along which the need flows* and the aim is realized.

The fact that a certain kind of behaviour serves as a sort of "exhaust-pipe" for a state of psychic tension is the very mechanism by which this behaviour gets integrated and subsists in the psychophysiological organism which is man. We have ascertained that when a "response" or a certain kind of behaviour finds itself *incorporated or integrated into a system of psychic tension,* it continues for this very reason to exist in psychic life.

As a result of this process, the behaviour which ends in a satisfactory result is more or less united to the dynamism which

[1] Cf. J. Nuttin, "Respective Effectiveness of Success and Task-tension in Learning," *The British Journal of Psychology* (General Section), 1947, XXXVIII, pp. 49–55. A more detailed and more fully developed account of this idea of the law of effect will be given in a work which is due to appear in 1953 under the title *Tâche, échec et réussite dans le comportement humain* (Publications universitaires de Louvain).

arouses it. It is simply a way created for itself by the need; whilst the dynamic force *is itself moulded, so to speak, by the forms of behaviour through which it manages to find release.* The need, or psychic dynamism, finds its concrete realization in kinds of behaviour which serve it as ways of abreaction. This is proved in the well-known phenomenon of the canalization of needs: dynamic psychic forces which begin by being comparatively unspecified and undifferentiated, are canalized and *made concrete in the specific forms of behaviour which have satisfied them.* By this mechanism, for instance, an undifferentiated need—eating—is specified into a desire for a particular kind of food. *The need manifests itself increasingly in the concrete form of a particular activity—* eating a certain kind of food in a certain place. *It has become a form of dynamic behaviour;* and this is *incorporated* into the dynamic development of the personality. It is precisely this incorporation into a dynamic system which has been shown by experiment to be responsible for the integration of this form of conduct into psychic life. The development of personality is made up of this integration of dynamic forms of behaviour, i.e. these concrete developments taken by the total activity of the psyche in contact with reality.

(b) On the other hand, it sometimes happens that certain forms of behaviour which were formerly able to satisfy the individual no longer produce a satisfactory result—either because he has discovered forms of behaviour whose result in the total situation gives him more satisfaction, or because his needs and tendencies have undergone further development.

An experiment in animal psychology may enable us to understand this more clearly. Craig[1] raised pigeons under special circumstances, in which their instinctive desire to make nests was worked out by picking up little bits of paper, which they used as building-materials. The pieces of paper thus became objects on which the need was successfully directed. Later, the same pigeons were put under different conditions; they were given not only

---

[1] Cf. W. Craig, "Appetites and Aversions as Constituents of Instincts," *Biological Bulletin*, 1918, XXXIV, pp. 91–107. Also, by the same author, "Male Doves Reared in Isolation," *Journal of Animal Behaviour*, 1914, IV, pp. 121–133.

little pieces of paper, but also twigs. The need soon focused itself on the latter, and the abreaction now came through picking up the twigs. The earlier form in which the need had manifested itself, through picking up the pieces of paper, was completely abandoned: the paper no longer had the slightest attraction for them.

This phenomenon can be explained by the fact that the *new kind of behaviour led to greater satisfaction,* so that there was a better abreaction. Thus objects which have been made use of can lose their attractiveness and *certain tendencies and certain kinds of behaviour die out.*

A similar process can be found in the development of personality. Objects on which tendencies or needs have been fixed, and certain kinds of behaviour which make possible the release of these needs, usually lose their active potentiality because at a later stage in the development of the individual new *kinds* of needs appear, or the forms of behaviour no longer satisfy.

Obviously this process is not a repression of the previous needs; these lose their active potentiality either by a change of conditions, *or in the very process of growth, as is shown by the experiment* we have described.

This process of development appears at different stages of human growth. It can appear either spontaneously, as the result of an *inner* development, or because the *environment* raises alternatives to a certain need. Thus thumb-sucking loses its attraction for a child when, under the influence of his surroundings, the sucking need is "liquidated" by the more powerful tendency not to want to be looked upon as a baby. The first need is not "repressed," but *its satisfaction by means of the usual forms of behaviour leads increasingly to less pleasant results,* and for this reason it gradually loses its dynamic potentiality.

Thus, in the same way, auto-erotic satisfaction is usually "liquidated" by the inner development of sexual need at the end of the period of adolescence. Normally, no repression is involved; but because new possibilities appear in the adult, a certain kind of dynamic potentiality dies away and a certain kind of behaviour disappears. This inner development means that other things and other kinds of behaviour—for example, heterosexual contacts—become more satisfying to the whole personality. The auto-erotic acts, which were formerly so powerfully attractive, gradually lose their dynamic "reality" through the canalization or the development of the need into new and more satisfying manifestations.

Similarly, as the personality develops towards its ideal social image, many of the ways in which needs are satisfied become less satisfying, because *such ways no longer bring satisfaction to the whole personality*, whilst other needs and other kinds of satisfaction finally prove more satisfying to the personality as a whole.

It is important to note the difference between the *nonsatisfaction* of a need (sucking, for example) because the individual prefers in his total situation to satisfy another need (to appear "grown-up"), and the mere *frustration* of a need. In the first case, there is a frustration which can be described as *positive;* it does not have the same repercussions on the mind as the purely negative kind.

Thus some dynamic potentialities develop, whilst others lose their "psychic reality." This does not mean, however, as Freud thinks, that the latter are simply repressed and continue to exist as dynamic realities after they have been eliminated from conscious behaviour. They have lost their dynamic value because they no longer correspond to the situation created by the needs of the whole personality. In other words, they are got rid of by a process of *constructive* elimination. This is a result of positive growth, of the canalization of needs along new ways which are better adapted to the total development of personality. We shall later give a detailed account of a case of this kind.

To sum up, we can say that certain forms taken by the satisfaction of needs can gradually lose their dynamic value and be eliminated by one of three different processes. Firstly, there may be a conflict between one kind of satisfaction and the awakening of a new tendency, as in the example of the thumb-sucking child who experiences the new tendency to be "grown-up." Next, there is the appearance of a new stage in the development of the need itself, as in the change from auto-erotic to heterosexual acts. Finally, there may be a development of the whole personality towards its ideal image, as a result of which certain kinds of behaviour become less and less "satisfying" to the personality *as a whole*. We must insist that *this elimination of dynamic forms must not be looked upon as the repression of one force by another, with no change in the dynamic character of the repressed force. On the contrary, such processes of elimination appear in the normal course of the growth of personality, and are explained by the fact that certain forms of need become dynamically unreal, because for the personality as a whole, and for positive reasons, they become less and less satisfying.*

(2) A CASE OF CONSTRUCTIVE DEVELOPMENT (RAYMOND)

We wish now to illustrate, by means of a concrete example, this process of constructive development which leads to the *positive elimination*, not the "repression," of certain dynamic contents.

For several years we were able to follow closely the development of an adolescent boy, without in any way subjecting him to psychotherapeutic treatment. The boy in question, Raymond, from about the age of twelve onwards, showed a very pronounced and rather morbid tendency to spy upon young couples, though he showed no inclination to be with girls of his own age.

Raymond went through a period of normal adolescence. Between the ages of sixteen and eighteen his whole personality developed to a quite remarkable extent. He still had this tendency to spy upon others, but as his social personality developed this trait harmonized less and less with the rest of his personality, hardly expressing itself at all at the level of his social behaviour and only appearing when he was left to himself and adopted a way of thought and behaviour which only existed at the most intimate level of his personality. When brought face to face with himself, he recognized quite clearly that this trait, though abnormal and humiliating, was a *real fact* of his mental make-up. But gradually he came to look upon this picture of a young man spying secretly on others as something absolutely *foreign* to himself. Every time he had given way to the inclination, he was astonished at himself as soon as he became calm. Obviously this form of behaviour is out of harmony with the constructive development as a whole. And, increasingly, it gave less and less satisfaction to his personality as a whole; the fact of satisfying it meant frustrating other dynamic forces which were at the moment more actively at work within him.

It often happened that whilst he was indulging in this spying the

boy *recovered his self-possession.* This means that the social or
ideal form of his *personality*—his personality as he wished to
develop it—grew so powerful that it erupted, so to speak, into
his secret way of behaving and neutralized its appeal. Then, sometimes, he would manage to interrupt his spying deliberately. "It
was as if all of a sudden I became myself again, just as I usually
am," he told me later.

This secret behaviour which had not been integrated into his
constructive personality thus gradually declined. His personality
realized increasingly the social and ideal image developing within
him: he became more and more what he wanted to become. He
confessed that *these secret acts gave him less satisfaction and that
he experienced a feeling of great joy every time he overcame the
need to indulge in them. Thus a refusal to give way to the tendency became more satisfying for his personality as a whole. Yield-
ing meant failure; refusal, success. His failures decreased, and the
need made itself felt less imperiously: this particular form of sexual
dynamism gradually atrophied because of the positive development of the personality in directions in which the need was not
incorporated.*

Two years later, when he was twenty, I had a frank and intimate conversation with Raymond. He remembered all this almost
as though it belonged to the dim and distant past. Latterly, he
said, he "had not even thought about it."

Since then I have noticed that the old tendency still manifests
itself occasionally in this young man, but very rarely, and very
feebly. Usually, he overcomes it easily. Meanwhile he had undergone a normal sexual development; though he has not yet decided
to marry, nor had any other sexual outlets, he has nevertheless
begun to see a great deal of a certain young lady.

Here, therefore, we have a boy who might have become a
sexual pervert, a "peeping Tom," who has nevertheless developed
in such a way that he has practically eliminated from his dynamic
structure this perverse form of erotic need. This elimination was
accomplished in the first place by dismissing into the intimate
sphere (which we shall discuss in a moment) a kind of behaviour
which did not fit in with the constructive image of his personality.
In his personality as a whole, as the young man developed it within

himself, this tendency gradually lost its dynamic power and "psychic reality."

In other words, it does not seem possible to account for this case by any theory of repression or sublimation. No doubt an attempt could be made to do so, assuming the existence of all kinds of hypothetical processes which would have to be described as "unconscious" from lack of proof of their real existence. It is not proved that the tendency in question continues to *exist in its dynamic form*—i.e., as an active energy in the *unconscious* of the young man. The fact that in certain abnormal cases tendencies which have not been satisfied show themselves genuinely active in distorted forms does not mean that we can generalize this process and apply it *a priori* to the kind of development which we have just described. We simply need to see whether there are any other conceptions, based on known laws, which can better explain the line of development as presented to us by the actual facts.

The idea of "repression" does not account for the way in which one form of a tendency is left behind by a constructive development in another direction. The "higher" development of this young man was *not the result of the repressed tendency* manifesting itself in a "sublimated" form; on the contrary, *a dynamic development of a more constructive kind caused the first line of development* (the wish to spy) *to atrophy*. Nor is there any reason to look for the origin of the tendency towards a constructive development in an earlier repression. We have indeed shown that at the very root of the ego-ideal, which—according to Freud—would be the "repressing" force, one must assume the existence of a dynamism which encourages the human being to realize his potentialities in new, constructive ways.[1]

Hence we consider the theory of repression to be distinctly unsatisfactory when it comes to accounting for the constructive development of normal man.

(3) PSYCHIC INTIMACY AND THE UNCONSCIOUS

We have tried to sketch the general process by which certain dynamic forms are developed or eliminated according to the results of their manifestation in behaviour. We must now examine

[1] See *supra*, p. 179.

a second aspect of this process of development: that of the *psychic contents as they actually are lived* in the course of the process.

Instead of falling back on the *unconscious*, into which, according to psychoanalysis, the contents which are not accepted are *repressed*, we shall now try to develop the idea of a *psychic intimacy* to which certain dynamic contents which do not agree with the social or constructive form of the personality are relegated. For a fuller treatment of this subject, we refer the reader to an earlier study of psychic intimacy; here we shall only deal with one aspect of the problem.[1]

It is a fact that in our culture, at least, one can divide the psychic contents into several layers, belonging either to the "intimate" or to the "public" part of personality. As lived at the most intimate level of personal consciousness, personality is not absolutely identical with the personality which lives and unfolds in the realm of public and social life.

The contents belonging to the *intimate* level of psychic life are not a mere amalgam of separate elements but a more or less integrated *whole* that makes up the *image* or the *form* of the personality as lived in the intimacy of the inner life. This form or mode of existence of personality does not absolutely coincide, as we have said, with the image which the processes of *socialization* and *personal construction* have developed in us *through our contact with others*. In so far as it is constructed by the process of socialization and exists at the "public" level of its own psychic life, the social personality, i.e. the ego, is a *"persona"*—etymologically, a mask—but it is also a "person" which *has become "ourselves."* It has the same right to be considered part of the ego as the most intimate form of our personality. This "public" form of our personality appears in our contact with others, but it is also the person *we are* and *know ourselves to be* in our ordinary social life. In the midst of this social life man can, of course, withdraw into the privacy of his own self; or he can discover his intimate personality to some other person in a special private contact. It is also possible for the intimate form of his personality to be badly

---

[1] Cf. J. Nuttin, "Intimacy and Shame in the Dynamic Structure of Personality," *Mooseheart Symposium on Feelings and Emotions*, ed. M. L. Reymert (New York, McGraw-Hill, 1950).

"protected" during his social contacts in general, and thus to threaten at any moment to pierce the "*persona*"—making the man "self-conscious" in his social relationships. The balanced person, however, has developed a "public" form of his personality which holds together perfectly by itself and in which he *is* as much himself as in the most intimate part of his consciousness—he may perhaps feel even more *at home* there, for the intimate part of consciousness can frighten and upset people.

We must first see how, at the very heart of the unity of the human personality, these different forms of the ego are created. The problem of intimacy as a whole is too big to be treated within the limits of this book, and only one aspect of it will concern us here: the relationship of the intimate sphere to psychic *dynamism*.

From his earliest years man feels impulses which, as we have shown, come into conflict with other dynamic forces, or with the image of man that has been crystallized in the customs and standards of his civilization. A child very quickly realizes that a great number of psychic contents and many different kinds of behaviour are not admitted into public life; some may be admitted privately, but there are others which must never be expressed or reveal their existence at all. Thus certain psychic contents, and certain forms of behaviour, become incorporated in a totality of situations (for example, family situations); whilst other contents and other forms of behaviour are generally eliminated from this aspect of life and so become completely alien to it. They no longer even attempt to appear in this aspect of life, because they no longer form part of it—they have not been incorporated into it. Thus there are created in the child areas of psychic life and forms of behaviour which are more or less private or more or less "public," i.e. *forms* of the personality.

Meanwhile, within the child's own psychic life there gradually develops a very delicate, very vulnerable core, the ego itself, a source of *insecurity* and *weakness*, the human being alone with himself. Man does not like displaying this before others, because of the very nature of social contact and his desire to preserve his individuality and prove his own value.

Around this vulnerable, spontaneous core, and deriving from

it, a form of being and behaviour develops as a result of the process of socialization and the positive impulses to realize an ideal of personality. This form of being and behaviour is better adapted to "publicity" because the elements of which it is composed are to a great extent borrowed from the cultural environment.

Personality, if it is to reach a balanced development, here finds itself faced with a difficult task, for a dangerous tension can arise between this intimate form and the *"persona"* which develops and makes a "public appearance." As the psychic forces themselves should be integrated—in the way described above—so there should gradually develop an integration of the psychic contents which make up the different images of the personality.

This process of integration involves several phases, or at least several aspects. The first phase develops at the level of the intimate sphere itself, and consists essentially in the intimate acceptance of self. That is to say, the self must accept positively all the personal characteristics, potentialities, insufficiencies and impossibilities which it discovers and experiences in the most intimate depth of its own nature. This acceptance does not mean that man bows to his intimate personality as before an accomplished fact, but that he accepts the task of becoming himself and of constructing for himself a life and a personality from the data *which he finds within himself*.[1] It is well known that a great number of psychic disturbances arise for this very reason, that the person has not managed to reconcile himself with the *given facts* of his personality. He wishes to be other than he is, and he refuses to construct anything positive with the material at his disposal. He wastes his energy in revolt—against himself, against society, or against "fate."

The second phase in the integration develops at the level of the *socialization* of personality. This aspect of the process consists in knowing how to *take possession of* the totality of *forms* and *possibilities of existence* offered or imposed by the cultural environment in which one is called upon to live. There are many people who develop a negative attitude of opposition towards the social modes in which their life should take its form, and so fail to adapt themselves to them. Thus their personality becomes closed

[1] See on this point our remarks on Rogers' "acceptance," above, pp. 98ff.

in upon itself, and once again psychic dynamism wastes itself in sterile or destructive irritation, for they come to look upon all the forms and institutions of society as hostile forces preventing the flowering of their own personality.

Further, in the harmonious integration of personality there must be a third essential phase, consisting in a reduction of the antagonism between the intimate sphere and the social structures of personality.

In the course of this stage or aspect of integration, the two spheres succeed in growing together into the unity of a *social ego*, in which the *intimate* part is no longer a frustrated ego and the *social* part no longer a "mask" but a form of expression—always, it is true, incomplete—of the integrated realistic ideal of the personality.

What this really implies is that the internal tension which characterizes man's psychic dynamism is progressively dissolved by the *canalization of needs* mentioned above. The two aspects of the constructive development of personality are here united. The various needs which do not fit in with the line of development which the person has chosen for himself go on existing for a considerable length of time, but this existence goes on in the background of the constructive personality. Not being considered as useful material in the construction of the ego, they are nevertheless not *denied;* the normal man in fact accepts them as *realities,* but realities whose potentialities he does not intend to develop.

Not being included in the active development of personality as it builds itself up and expresses itself consciously, *these contents in the background or in the intimate sphere of personality are precisely those forms of need of which we have already said that they no longer manage to satisfy the personality as a whole, as regards its active and dominant form.* Hence some of them—precisely through not being in line with any active development—gradually atrophy. In other words, *because the total personality gradually expresses itself more and more in a constructive and explicit form, the tension between the two spheres—the intimate and the social—decreases; the intimate contents which have not been integrated into the constructive image become less and less real as active components in behaviour.*

It will be noticed that we have here restricted the term *"intimate contents"* to those psychic contents which do not fit in with the explicit constructive image which the person is tending to realize within himself. This ideal or image of the personality can of course itself be *intimate* in a different sense. A person may not wish to acknowledge publicly the line of development which he has chosen for himself privately. This meaning of the word "intimate" does not concern us here. It is simply an added complexity or "duplicity" in the structure of psychic dynamism—unless of course it is simply the normal amount of *discretion* and *reserve* which a man exercises in everything that concerns his own personality. It is sufficient here to point out that intimate contents of this kind are, *from the very fact of being inserted into the active development of the personality*, active in their dynamic potentialities. Therefore they cannot die. In short, it is not from being *intimate* that contents lose their dynamic character, but from not being included in the canalized development of tendencies and needs. But any tendency which belongs to a line of development *opposed* to what man wishes to realize within himself is, in a certain sense, relegated to the background. These contents usually constitute one of the elements of the intimate sphere, and it is in this sense that we use the word "intimate" here. The more positive contents of the intimate sphere—including, amongst others, the "personal" forms of the self-imposed ideal are treated elsewhere (cf. the study mentioned above). The intimate contents of which we speak here become less and less active as man advances along his chosen line of development. Thus at the *beginning* of the situation of conflict the content which has not been integrated can be a very active and dynamic element in the intimate sphere. It can threaten at any moment to penetrate the image of personality which has been built up, as frequently happens in the case of youths not yet fully developed. But as the development proceeds these contents become "vaguer," almost foreign elements, so that a man is surprised that they could formerly have been such moving *forces* in his life.

It should be added that the needs or dynamic contents which man thus relegates to the background of his personality can be the so-called "higher" potentialites just as easily as "instinctive" impulses.

(4) A CASE OF THE "INTIMATE CONSCIOUS" (ALMA)

What we wish particularly to emphasize, in introducing the idea of *intimacy* into our description of the conflict which characterizes the development of personality, is that psychoanalysis has been too prone to describe as *unconscious*, contents which in reality have simply been relegated to the background in the development of personality and therefore find themselves incorporated into a different image of the personality from that which is "lived" actively and revealed on the level of every-day personal relationships.

Instead of getting involved in theory, we shall try to give our idea concrete shape by means of an example which will involve actual facts of experience.

During a consultation, a girl of sixteen described a scene which had taken place recently in her own life. She had been lying in bed with a girl friend and suddenly, for no apparent reason, burst into tears. She trembled as she recalled the incident. When she was questioned, the girl, Alma, replied that she really did not know why she had cried: "Really, I can't say. I don't know why I should have cried."

Later in the interview the question of her relationship with her parents came up. The conversation had already reached a more intimate level; the question of her future and her vocation in life had been discussed quite freely and openly. Then once again, the conversation went off to the scene in which there had been that outburst of tears. To the question, Why had she cried?—asked quite simply, as though for the first time—she replied that it was the conflict with her mother, about her future and her vocation, which was upsetting her and had made her burst into tears: there had been an argument on the very morning of the day on which she had cried. This was all said quite spontaneously and sincerely, like the first time: the young girl seemed not to remember her first reply.

Towards the end of the consultation, there came to light conflicts of an even more intimate nature. It was now no longer a case of conflict between the girl and her mother but a tension at the very core of her own mind. It appeared that the girl had given up the idea of marriage because of higher aims; her constructive ideal in the development of her personality was towards virginity, and works of social charity. At the same time, she was beginning to develop maternal tendencies, which she had not positively fought against—she considered them noble and fine—but they were "not for her": she had not incorporated them into her personality, which she wished to develop in the direction of her own positive ideal. She was not therefore fighting against her maternal drive *as such;* on the contrary, she was a very cheerful and balanced kind of girl; but in her personality, *as she lived it explicitly in her behaviour,* this drive had no place. She did not include it in her plans for the future; it did not "exist" consciously at this level of her psychic life. It certainly did exist—and the girl did not deny it—when, with her gaze turned inwards, she expressed her personality not only according to the line of its constructive development, but face to face with her most intimate self—i.e., with all the data, all the psychic material, which "existed" in the most intimate depths of her being.

When she had descended to this most intimate level, the girl "realized" what was tormenting her. Her friend, who had been lying beside her when she cried, was the incarnation of her maternal longings—this friend had told her that she had the same longings—and she had also become the object of Alma's need for erotic affection. The true nature of the conflict inside Alma became clearer and clearer. Once again the conversation approached the subject of that scene of tearful crisis. The girl repeated what had happened, but this time emphasizing her relationship with her friend. To the spontaneous question, Why had she cried? she said quite simply, but with great feeling: "It was because I no longer knew what I should do. I was so unhappy that night because I didn't know whether I ought to get married or not."

On the "public" and social level of her constructive personality the girl had not experienced this conflict consciously. During the first stage of the interview, in which she had described what had happened in her life of social relationships, she had replied quite sincerely that she did not know why she had cried. Must we say that she had *repressed* the conflict between the new phase of active erotic needs and her sense of her vocation in life? That the repressed conflict and tendencies no longer existed, except in her unconscious? In our opinion the facts suggest another conception approximating more closely to the reality and complex structure of personality.

To relegate these tendencies and this conflict to the unconscious is to fall back on a *rather crude* solution which does little justice to the subtlety of the modes of existence of these contents in the human mind. It is truer to the facts to say that certain contents, of which one is perfectly conscious at a sufficiently intimate level of the personality, *fail to get incorporated* into a certain way in which one is oneself—in this case the social form of personality. This form, it is true, is not to be looked upon as absolutely isolated and self-enclosed. The "intimate" contents exist as a more or less vague substratum in the "public" personality, but not being perfectly at home there they do not *enter* so spontaneously into the behaviour of this form of personality; they are, so to speak, less easily available to the individual. Thus the effective relationship between a certain form of behaviour and these "alien" elements is not easy to see in this form of personality. But as soon as a person sees his own intimate personality completely, other contents come into the foreground, outlined more clearly, and he *finds it easier to see the relationship* between them and the form of behaviour in question.

It would not be true to say that the interview itself *made conscious* the unconscious contents and conflict. The girl admitted that she had often thought about these things, and she was conscious of nothing that she had not already discovered by herself. At the most, she simply saw more clearly into the *relationship* between certain facts whose significance and implications she had previously not been so clear about.

For this reason, we think that many psychic contents which have been too easily described as unconscious—to fit in with certain plausible schemes of thought, which have not, however, kept sufficiently close to the facts—can more justly be considered as *belonging to a more intimate form of the conscious personality*. It is in this intimacy—in the special sense we have given to it—and because these contents do not participate in the main dynamism of the constructive personality, that certain tendencies can be dissolved and become atrophied according to the mechanism already explained. In the case which we have just described, the intimate contents kept all their dynamic tension. After a few years, if the girl succeeded in developing positively along the line of personality which she had set up for herself, this tension would probably decrease. Since we are speaking here not of a *particular form* taken by a fundamental need, but of the fundamental need itself, its appeal will be felt for a long time on the intimate levels of the personality.

Nor must it be forgotten that it is not sufficient in such cases of internal tension to obey the conflicting tendency (in this case, to marry) if one wishes to break the tension; for then the other need, the one which is actually satisfied and integrated into the constructive line of development of the personality, sets up a conflict. The facts show that it may be no easier for a man to renounce the constructive ideal which he has set up for himself than to combat the forces which are attempting to turn him away from it. We are here face to face with the inner conflict inherent in the very dynamism of human psychic life, whose normally constructive part we have already described.[1]

In connection with this problem of psychic intimacy and the unconscious, the reader will remember the case described above of the invalid girl who ended by admitting that she was trying to get a personal satisfaction out of her illness.[2] At the deepest level of her intimate psychic life she "felt" that her illness flattered her self-love. Her lack of *sincerity* and *simplicity*, however, prevented her from recognizing this real intimate feeling at the level of her social and ideal personality. Here again, the thing that was necessary to reveal the intimate content was not for this girl to "become aware" of a "repressed" content, but for her to adopt a spirit of absolute sincerity towards herself and enter into the most intimate form of her own personality.

To become "oneself" in this way, right to the very depths of one's own intimate personality, can call for an extraordinary effort of sincerity and simplicity from certain people. Because they do not want to recognize or even "look at" certain intimate feelings,

[1] See *supra*, pp. 171ff.
[2] Cf. pp. 131ff.

the distance and the tension between the intimate form and the ideal form of the personality increase. This *distance causes the ideal form of the personality to develop a certain kind of psychic hypocrisy*—not moral; psychic—often met with in certain categories of "virtuous" people whose psychological integration has lagged behind their virtue.

It is quite likely that some psychologists will be inclined to look upon what we have described as *intimacy*—that which has *not been integrated into the constructive form of the personality*—as "repression" and the "unconscious." If this is so, we still maintain that it is a great help not to use vague, crude terms like "repression" and "unconscious" for processes which can be described and analysed more subtly. We believe that the analysis of psychic intimacy, and of the relationship (often quite subtle) between the constructive form of personality and the intimate sphere, can help us towards a clearer conception of certain kinds of tensions which exist within personality. We do not mean to deny the existence of the process of repression or the notion of the unconscious; but we do believe that other processes of a more delicate nature play a considerable part in the formation of the normal personality. A few slight deformations of normal psychic life—such as the *hypocrisy* we have just mentioned—can in our opinion be more satisfactorily expressed in terms of the relationship between psychic intimacy and the ideal personality, and with reference to a process of integration, than in the monotonous scheme of repression, the unconscious, and some form or other of sublimation.

(5) NORMAL PROCESSES OF DEVELOPMENT AND PATHOLOGICAL DEVIATION

The process which we have just described explains only one form taken by the development of personality, the *normal* or ideal form. We shall carefully avoid the exaggerations and hasty generalizations of the psychologists we have been criticizing and not make this the only process that exists!

In personalities that are very loosely integrated, the dynamic tension implicit in the development of personality frequently takes on more striking forms. Such people have not, in fact, managed to achieve the canalization and the successful renunciation which are a sign of constructive development. The drive towards self-realization—which can be seen at work in the individual and, in a crystallized form, in the standards of social life—is not for them the beginning of any constructive development; it is simply for them a power of inhibition and a source of frustration.

When this is the case, the complex dynamism of personality is *not canalized* in the direction which the individual has chosen for himself or positively accepted from society; there is simply an *obstruction* in the way of the manifestation of certain needs, and no positive construction at all. In such cases a certain kind of frustrated need can be carried to the length of paroxysm by the process of frustration rather than lose its dynamic power. This can cause in the individual obsessional returns towards the object which has been refused him; aggressive attitudes; fixations. The theory which we have expounded does not by any means underestimate the importance of any side of this kind of *pathological* development. What we have tried to show is that there is also a *directly* constructive process in the development of the psychic dynamism of the *normal* man.

It is one of Freud's great achievements to have investigated the destructive aspects of the process of motivation so closely and unmasked them under certain constructive appearances. But this discovery of the psycho-pathological form of the process is itself simply one more "contribution" to our knowledge of the development of personality, and it needs to be "completed," particularly as regards the general normal psychology of personality.

To realize the complex reality of the development of personality, it should be remembered that the two lines of development, the normal and the pathological, are not simply alternatives. In the development of the individual, the integration of personality as we have described it is never completely achieved; at any given moment there will be some potentialities whose integration is not desired, and these will remain to a certain extent *dynamically active*. Thus, for example, certain forms of the tendency towards self-assertion which have been consciously eliminated from the constructive development of the personality can have lost a considerable part of their dynamic reality whilst nevertheless continuing to manifest themselves under more subtle and less obvious appearances—not, let it be said, by any kind of "sublimation," but more subtly, through psychic hypocrisy and duplicity; a compromise between the ideal form of the personality and certain kinds of "intimate" impulse.

Thus it may be that there is never a single conflict between the constructive development of the personality and the impulses fighting against it which becomes completely resolved. As the individual successfully overcomes one conflict, other mechanisms may be active *in a sort of parallel fashion,* and have a rather disturbing effect. This admixture of the "normal" and the "pathological" is very frequent—one might say, *normal;* precisely because the conflict is very rarely resolved constructively at all the stages of its development. There are always, at some stage or other in the development, half-hearted solutions, compromises, camouflaged defeats.

It is for this reason that even in the best-integrated personalities there are often to be found attenuated forms of emotional complexes, and all kinds of remnants of conflicts that have not been absolutely resolved. It might even be true to say that not a single person exists whose process of psychic *growth* has developed without *out*-growths and deviations.

It must also be remembered that from personal aspiration or the educative action of the environment many people erect an ideal of personality which does not allow sufficiently for the *total reality* of human nature. This may come about because these systems or ideals refuse to recognize the spiritual element in man, just as easily as from a denial of the organic and instinctive. It is here that one frequently finds the fundamental cause of pathological elements which have begun to interfere with the balanced development of the personality. The *realism* of the constructive ideal of the personality depends not only on its efficiency in life, but on mental honesty: it requires a certain sincerity and simplicity towards *all the data* of human personality, things which are not always present in those who imagine themselves as the representatives of a high spiritual tradition. Nevertheless, we repeat, the relationship between the constructive form of the personality and psychic intimacy is an active process which deserves all our attention, and it is neither adequately expressed nor adequately explained by the crude theory of repression and the unconscious. There are many psychic "deformities" which have their origin in normal people in too tenuous a relationship between these two spheres of the human personality.

There is thus, as we hope to have shown, a "normal" and directly constructive development of the personality which combats the mechanisms tending towards deviation and disaggregation.

CHAPTER V

BASIC NEEDS

1. The Three Levels of Psychic Life

The second problem which we must deal with concerns the basic needs that give dynamic life its content and direction. The question is, Can this dynamic life, which breaks up into a mass of needs and tendencies, be ultimately reduced, as Freud thought, to one positive force?

We have already shown that the specifically human form of the tendency towards progress or self-realization implies that specific potentialities and functions exist in man which cannot be looked upon as mere forms of escape for the libido. If we now attempt to discuss the problem of fundamental needs from the point of view of general psychology, *we must take into account certain fundamental facts provided by the analysis of psychic life as a whole.*

Our brief analysis of the cognitive aspect of psychic life has already shown that our activity and contents of consciousness exist at various levels. Some of these contents are closely bound up with the facts of sensible experience, whilst others cannot be defined according to any material process and imply higher and even spiritual activities. On the other hand, we can find even in our most general and *abstract* ideas, traces and clear signs of *sense* knowledge. This does not justify us, however, in *reducing* intellectual knowledge to sense knowledge pure and simple, even though the intellectual and the sensible are so closely bound up with one another.

We record these simple facts, drawn from a philosophical analysis of human knowledge to show that, on examination, the human mind as a whole reveals an essential diversity at the innermost heart of psychic functions, and that it is therefore dangerous to attempt to reduce the number of levels on which our psychic life unfolds. There is a risk, in fact, of losing sight of everything *specific* in the intellectual knowledge of man by treating human knowledge as nothing more than an *elaboration* of sense data. It is a mistake which one often sees made: one aspect or another of some psychic activity is examined, and *all the other aspects* are got rid of by a vague formula which says that they are simply an extension, or a complication, or an elaboration of what has already been examined.

We also know that human needs and tendencies are intimately bound up with the contents of consciousness. In fact the *cognitive and conative functions are simply two aspects or manifestations of* a psychic activity *which is functionally one.*[1] We can therefore *expect a correspondence between the specific forms and levels of knowledge and the forms of tendencies and needs.*

From the methodological point of view the general ideas we have mentioned, regarding the different levels of activity, are important for the solution of our problems. A general theory of the reducibility or irreducibility of needs does not follow directly from the facts themselves, it is simply a hypothesis built up on the basis of a certain *interpretation of factual data*. These "factual data" include, for instance, the fact that elements of different needs are sometimes involved with each other. For example, it is a fact that *erotic* elements are often discovered in religious delusions. But

---

[1] The intimate connection between cognitive and conative aspects of psychic activity is increasingly attracting the attention of experimental psychologists. The work of Tolman and Krech (formerly Krechevsky) is important in this connection. Cf. also the account of "motivation" in Krech and Crutchfield, *Theory and Problems of Social Psychology* (New York, McGraw-Hill, 1948). Cf. Chap. 2, "The Dynamics of Behaviour," pp. 29–75.

this can be interpreted in several ways, and one's own interpretation is based on *more general ideas about the structure of the mind as a whole*. Hence it is important to be explicit about the general ideas which lie behind one's explanations and theories—ideas which are always more or less philosophical in nature, and which should, therefore, rest on serious and technical philosophical foundations rather than on the sketchy "general ideas" which men of science like to develop in a rather inappropriate fashion.

It is not our intention to go into detail about the philosophical problem of man's psychic activity. We shall simply try to indicate from a study of the observable facts the different levels or "layers" which are to be distinguished in our psychic life in general. This general structure of the mind must necessarily be of importance in connection with the dynamic aspects of psychic life, i.e. our needs.

In our opinion, three main levels of activity should be distinguished in the human mind; that is to say, an analysis of any *concrete* psychic act ordinarily reveals three different kinds of elements, each with its own irreducible properties, each implying different functions and each obeying irreducible laws.

Some psychic activities and contents of consciousness are very closely linked with physiological states of the organism; they are, so to speak, simply the reverse side of a psycho-physiological condition or process of the complex human organism. Thirst, for instance, can be looked upon as the psychic aspect of an organic condition. We can describe these processes and phenomena as a whole as constituting the *psycho-physiological* level of our psychic life.

Then again, some psychic events or behaviour patterns are bound up with the fact that we find ourselves *in a world* which we *understand* and which we develop *by giving it a meaning:* the world of people and things around us. We may call this the level of our *life of relationships* on the "social" or "worldly" level. Here the word *social* means primarily that this aspect of psychic life involves essentially a *lived relationship* between ourselves and the world of people. The most *private* spheres of our life or relationship with the world are found at this "psycho-social" level. For even the intimate situations which could be described as non-social take somehow into account the presence or absence of other "persons." When a person feels "alone," "others" are implied in this intimate experience in the sense that they are experienced as absent. In this wider sense we can describe this level of the life of relationship as "psycho-social."

Many kinds of behaviour and many drives are connected with this level of psychic life. Thus, the need for social recognition or esteem—and the kind of behaviour corresponding to these needs —is directly connected with the fact that man *assimilates his environment not only at the biochemical and physiological level but also as a "meaningful situation."* This form of psychic life is fundamentally different from the psycho-physiological level as such, and implies other functions and *potentialities* in man. Indeed, the experience of the environment as a *meaningful situation* is quite a different thing from the biochemical experience of the same environment in the process of metabolism. And the *experience of meaning,* as such, has no physiological equivalent.

Finally, we discover in our psychic life contents and activities which in the light of deeper analysis are found to transcend the limits of immediate *facts* and the material process. Such are the problem of man's destiny and his existence; the affirmation of absolute *being* or *value* which he makes about certain realities; the experience of moral obligation; the problems concerning the value of his knowledge, etc.,—all these psychic contents imply that in some way or other my psychic life transcends the limits of my being "affected" *hic et nunc* by a certain stimulus, a process which is materially "enclosed" and determined in itself. It is the task of theoretical and philosophical psychology to discover the nature and implications of such activities. Here we will simply content ourselves with affirming the existence of this level, and remind the reader of the theoretical and philosophical arguments in favour of the irreducibility of certain aspects and components of these activities to mere material fact. We may call this layer of psychic life the *spiritual level.* But we must take care not to ignore the forms of psychic dynamism which may ultimately be discovered to correspond to this spiritual level. The aim of this enquiry into psychic activity in general is indeed to help us not to lose sight of a single aspect of the complex, dynamic life of man.

Psychological analysis shows, further, that these different levels of activity are *inextricably mingled* in any concrete human act—for instance, in seeing a book or feeling thirsty or unhappy. With the release of the nervous stimulus and the whole *psycho-physio-logical* process, there is not simply a "sensation" of pain, etc., but a grasp of a *meaningful situation*. A man will realize, for example, that something is going badly, or that as a result of illness he will not be able to realize a certain project. There is furthermore the metaphysical content of the conscious "I" finding itself face to face with itself or an "object" or an external situation. In the concrete experience, the "I" is a subject which in the psychic act itself or in reflecting on this act *becomes conscious* of a "given" situation and thus *transcends* the mere fact of being "affected."

In the light of these general considerations we can now attempt to discover the fundamental needs which manifest themselves *as the dynamic aspects of man's complex psychic life*.

The age-old wisdom of man and his systems of practical moral-ity and asceticism, so rich in psychological intuitions, agree with the systems of dynamic and depth-psychology with regard to the fact that man's erotic and self-assertive tendencies are very power-ful needs. This general agreement is a fact of the highest impor-tance.

There is also increasing agreement that it is not necessary to exalt either of these needs at the expense of the other, but that each is important. Jung said as much in his very earliest works, and tried to adopt a point of view which would embrace the sys-tems of both Freud and Alder.[1] Some of the latest developments in psychoanalysis, as we have seen, similarly adopt Adlerian ten-dencies and ideas into their systems, without simply reducing the self-assertive instinct to a narcissistic form of libido, as Freud did.[2]

We can, therefore, begin from the following position. We can consider the two needs in question as being both important *com-ponents* in the dynamic structure of the personality. We can also

---

[1] Cf. C. G. Jung, "Über die Psychologie des Unbewussten" (fünfte Auflage von das 'Unbewusste im normalen und kranken Seelenleben,' 1916). Zürich, Rascher, 1943.

[2] Cf. pp. 81ff.

adopt as a principle of development the idea that the *fundamental* needs of man probably enter into all the complex aspects of his life and eventually manifest themselves in *specific* forms at every level of his psychic life. For we have just seen that human activity develops at different *irreducible* levels: i.e., certain forms of activity imply potentialities and functions essentially different from those of other forms of activity. Note, however, that these principles can only serve as guides to facilitate the observation of the complex and varied *facts* which may be presented to us. *The facts alone*, and not assumed principles, can allow us to admit the existence of any particular need in the fundamental structure of personality dynamics.

2. The Drive to Vital Development and the Need for Biological Contact

To begin at the purely biological level: it is known that the organism differs from its surroundings by a relatively constant pattern of biochemical properties. These constant properties constitute what has been known since the time of Claude Bernard as its *internal environment*. The amount of sugar, calcium, salt, protein, oxygen and water, etc., in the blood remains, within well-defined limits, fairly constant. The temperature of the blood, too, and of the internal environment in general, varies very slightly. But the external environment in which the organism moves, and with which it is constantly interacting, possesses chemical and thermal characteristics which vary considerably. The organism manages to preserve its own characteristics in the midst of this changing environment and in a constant relationship with it. It maintains, so to speak, its biological individuality.

This stability of the internal environment of the organism, now known as homoeostasis,[1] is not a mere fact of existence; it is an

---

[1] Cf. W. B. Cannon, *The Wisdom of the Body* (New York, Norton, 1932). On the subject of the problem of biological regulation and the connected questions of an organizing life-force, the penetrating account by W. Koehler, *The Place of Value in a World of Facts* (New York, Liveright, 1938)—cf. pp. 279–328—should especially be read. This important book also contains several chapters directly concerned with the problem of the dynamic explanation of human *facts*. See particularly the chapter

absolute *necessity* for the continuance of organic life. When the environment is *normal*, the organism maintains the balance of its own internal environment as the result of a complex of processes. These processes constitute what is known as the *adaptation* of the organism to its environment. As soon as this balance is disturbed by extraordinary changes in the chemical composition or the temperature of the environment, a co-ordinated system of processes is released within the organism. These processes, which are known as *regulations* and which involve the nervous system, the endocrine glands, the heart, the lungs, the kidneys, etc., re-establish the balance of the internal environment. When these regulative processes fail to preserve this homoeostasis, the organism dies.

It follows that on the biological level the organism has a certain kind of active *individuality* which it must maintain in its interaction with the changing environment or else disappear as a living organism; and that "in order to" maintain its individuality, i.e. preserve its homoeostasis and thus protect its life, it has to put forth an intense amount of activity in which various organic functions are *co-ordinated*.

It is not necessary to assume any unscientific finalism or vitalism to transpose these facts of experimental biology into *dynamic* terms and say that there must be an *active direction*, or a *directed force*, behind these regulative processes—without, of course, imagining that this "force" can explain the appearance of these processes, but in the sense which Claude Bernard means when he says that this force *directs* phenomena which it does not produce, whilst the physical agents *produce* phenomena *which they do not direct*.

In this sense homoeostasis, or the "tendency" of the organism to preserve the stability of its internal environment, seems to be the primary dynamic force in a living being at the biological level of its existence. The regulative processes which we have mentioned are not, however, the only forms of activity which help to ensure or assist towards the internal stability and life of the organism; for a break in the biological equilibrium often sets

---

"Facts and Forces," for the problem of causation and requiredness. *Ibid.*, pp. 329–368.

up reactions in the organism which are still more complex. These are known as *behaviour*.

We must take it to be an admitted fact that there is a difference between biological regulation and psychic behaviour. To prove this would demand a whole treatise on general psychology. Moreover, in order to concentrate on our one fundamental aim, we must limit ourselves here to the behaviour of one kind of psychophysiological organism of the human person. Now, changes in the surrounding temperature, for example, not only set up physiological processes of self-regulation in man, they also involve all kinds of reactions of the person as such, i.e. behaviour tending towards the same effect: adapting the organism to its environment and recovering homeostatic equilibrium. These behaviour-patterns can range from a simple move from a sunny spot into the shade to the complex organization of the building industry in modern society.

The important thing to realize here is that a break in the biological equilibrium of the organism does not involve merely a biochemical state and set up merely chemical and physiological reactions, but also exists, in the *psycho*-physiological organism of man, *as an experienced, concrete sensation*, producing meaningful kinds of reactions that emanate from *man* as a vital unity and are called *behaviour*.

The processes by which the human, psycho-physiological organism *experiences* and *lives* its organic states are characteristic of man, distinct from physiological processes, and called *psychic*. They include sensations, perception, imagination, memory and even intelligence. All these, in their own way, help to develop the organic state, the individual's "situation," and collaborate in the building up of a co-ordinated "response" to this "situation." Thus changes in temperature, when they are psychically experienced and assimilated—i.e., when heat and cold are felt and ultimately *understood as part of the human situation and condition*—set in motion complex activities such as intentional movement or the development of the air-conditioning industry.

It is well known that at the lower levels of the animal scale, the same biological states set up behaviour with the same meaning and aims. Thus it has been shown in rats that if, as a result of the removal of the thyroid and the pituitary, the regulative processes fail to preserve constant physiological temperature, certain kinds of behaviour begin to develop whose nature is designed to preserve the thermic homoeostasis. The rats, in fact, begin to collect bits of paper and use them to build nests "in order to" protect themselves.[1]

It has thus been established that the preservation of the stability of the internal environment, i.e. the preservation of organic individuality and organic life, does not only set up physiological processes, but is a root force behind human and animal *behaviour*.

On the psychological level the break in organic equilibrium is experienced as a state of uneasiness. It is an *experienced need*, which sometimes creates a state of anxiety and random movement until the behaviour reaches a satisfactory result. This need to re-establish the state of organic equilibrium, i.e. the need to return to the experienced condition of functional well-being, appears in several forms, hunger, thirst, etc., *organically conditioned* according to the particular kind of disturbance threatening the preservation and progress of vital development. What characterizes all these different needs and behaviour-patterns is the fact that they are all *directed*, more or less consciously, towards the state of functional well-being, i.e. towards the *preservation and development* of biological life. This purposiveness makes a *dynamic unity* out of the various intentional and meaningful behaviour-patterns. These behaviour-patterns should not be considered merely as predetermined physiological processes; *their physiological or neuromuscular scheme may vary indefinitely* but they are characterized either by the *dynamism* which sets them in motion, or by *the result to be obtained*. Moving towards a shady place, for instance, is not a scheme of muscular reaction, but any physiological *scheme* that ends in the desired result. The particular reaction, therefore, can only be defined "globally" in the light of the meaning which comes from its dynamic orientation. This meaningful orientation is finally the need for the well-being, the preservation and unfolding of organic life. That is why this well-being, preservation and

[1] Cf. C. P. Richter, "Total Self-Regulatory Functions in Animals and Human Beings," *Harvey Lecture Series*, 1942, XXXVIII, pp. 63–103.

unfolding is not simply a *unity of effect*, extrinsic to the manifold processes which result in it; it is a *dynamic unity*, which on the psychic level creates the actual behaviour-pattern as a unity of intentional and meaningful reactions. Thus the grouping together of the manifold behaviour-patterns tending towards the same effect, which we call *manifestations of the need for organic preservation and development*, is not a logical or finalistic unification, it is a *behavioural unity*, since it is the dynamic unity of this need which makes up these behaviour-patterns as such, i.e. as significant unities reacting to a concretely experienced situation.

As soon as this development is interfered with, the organic situation is experienced as a state of distress, which the whole organism makes every effort to get out of. It is in this negative form—i.e., of nonsatisfaction—that these dynamic forces usually appear most clearly. Nevertheless, it is quite evident that this experience of an unsatisfied need is simply an expression of a positive orientation towards the preservation and unfolding of life itself. Sometimes this unfolding, this normal functioning of the organism, can be experienced positively as a state of physical well-being, or as an aspiration uniting all the powers of a strong, healthy organism.

Note, finally, that this drive towards the development of life is simply the "strong" form of the drive towards *self-preservation*. And the *defence* behaviour-patterns, in their turn, with their corresponding dynamic psychic forces, are simply special forms—relative to the given conditions of the environment—in which the dynamic force of *self-preservation* manifests itself.

If we continue our study of human life on its biological and psycho-physiological levels, we find ourselves faced with a second fact. Self-preservation and self-development imply for every living creature *close contact, i.e. mutual exchanges, with the surrounding biological sphere*. Life in fact *is* this continual exchange, this assimilation and reaction of the living creature to its environment.

Hence the human organism too is integrated into the biological sphere. Several ways of access implied in the actual physiological constitution of the organism make these contacts and exchanges between man and the biological sphere possible. For the organism, living, self-preservation and self-development mean, on the biological level, being actively involved in such continual contents and exchanges by means of all the physiological and biochemical ways of access at its disposal.

The whole activity of the organism is *directed* towards the realization of these contacts and exchanges, which it "needs." It needs food, air, light, movement, etc. These are the kinds of contact by means of which the organism "lives." Organic life *is* biological "openness" to the environment; vital activity *is* a dynamic orientation towards biochemical contacts and exchanges.

Once again, the lack of such contacts—a lack which in the first place involves purely physiological reactions—is also experienced on the psychic level of human life. Lack of food and air, etc., causes certain *needs to be felt* and hence produces different kinds of *behaviour* more or less adapted to these needs. These behaviour-patterns manifest themselves here too as active tendencies towards the satisfaction of the frustrated need. There are many animal and human forms of behaviour which have their ultimate source in some form of this need for contact and exchange with the physical environment.

The need for physical contact manifests itself and is experienced by man in a variety of forms, corresponding to the different physiological conditions behind them. In this sense hunger is a different need from thirst, for instance. But—once again—the *dynamic unity* which lies at the root of these different needs and behaviour-patterns—and which is the actual vital activity itself—is the active "openness" of the organism, the search for contact and vital exchange with an element that tallies with a certain way out on to the biological sphere.

The third and final fact which we must emphasize is that this need for vital contact and exchange is very intimately bound up with the dynamic force of organic self-preservation and unfolding which we have already mentioned. It is *in* and *through* biological *contact* that the organism *preserves* itself and *develops*. This fact is too obvious to need insisting upon here, but we shall have occasion to return to it when we discuss the needs which lie at the other levels of our psychic life.

It is, however, necessary to examine one special form of this need for contact on the psycho-physiological level of human existence: the need for *sexual contact*. Besides the physiological conditions and functions which, when experienced psychically, impel the organism to seek food and air, etc., other biological conditions drive it to make specific kinds of total contact with the actual bodies of its fellow-creatures. The biological organism is not only a "mouth," "open" to certain elements in the biochemical sphere, it is also an appeal for total contact with certain bodily forms in the social sphere (i.e., one's fellow-creatures). Here too, special physiological, chemical and physical factors condition the sexual need; nevertheless, as psychically experienced and as manifested in behaviour, the sexual need is one aspect of this need to enter into contact with "others." It is this need which spontaneously impels the individual to physical intimacy, and to total contacts with others which are as varied as are the chemical exchanges in the biological sphere.

Hence the human organism, this core of life which preserves its own individuality in the face of everything that surrounds it, is not self-centred; its life is a call to others; and the intensity of its life is to be measured by this very activity, its contacts and exchanges with the elements and organisms surrounding it. Cut off from these contacts—either by lack of "contributions" or by an organic shrinking of its ways of access, i.e. its vital functions—the organism experiences all the agony of *suffocation*. There exists, therefore, on the biological and psycho-physiological levels of human existence, and under a multitude of specific forms which have been physiologically conditioned, a need as fundamental as the need for vital development and which is indeed intrinsically bound up with that need—the need for exchanges and contact.

In the exercise of this vital contact the organism experiences a sensation, varying in intensity, of pleasure. This sensation too is psycho-physiologically conditioned and differentiated. It seems to be inseparably bound up with the proper functioning of the organism itself. This sensation of pleasure increases the dynamic power which drives the organism to satisfy its needs. Thus the impulse arises to satisfy a need—either from the pleasure expe-

rienced or expected in satisfying it, or from the displeasure and
tension created by its frustration.

"INSTINCTS" AND "HUMAN" NEEDS

One final remark is necessary, to show the psycho-physiological
needs of man in their proper mode of existence and activity.

The mode in which these "biological" needs exist in man and
the way in which they influence conduct are both *specifically
human*. It must not be forgotten that the various manifestations
of the "drive" to self-development and biological contact are
integrated in man with a psychic life possessing cognitive and
conative functions which are specifically human. This leads to
modifications in the concrete mechanism by which the psycho-
physiological needs influence and govern human behaviour. Thus,
for instance, the need for food does not only drive a human being
to appease his hunger or go in search of prey; it is experienced by
him as a total being, i.e. a being who in his specifically human
knowledge transcends the limits of the momentary experience of
hunger and the instinctive mechanisms by which animals see
ahead and store up food. Man certainly experiences hunger as a
state of displeasure, but he also "understands" it as a *"significant"
situation* and even as a *condition of life*, governing his whole
existence. For this reason, this need can produce in him activities
which are considerably wider and of considerably greater import
than those engendered by the immediate or instinctive satisfaction
of hunger. In man this human need becomes the source of an
intellectual organizing activity, of which the economic structure
of our society is only one manifestation. Moreover, his *emotional
life*, which is connected with the satisfaction and frustration of
his needs, is considerably affected by it. There are very few emotions in man directly connected with hunger, at least in the
normal conditions of an organized civilization, but on the other
hand a great deal of unrest and suffering is created in man by the
threats which come to him from the economic situation. This is
why it is so important to remember that in man *all* these so-called
"instinctive" or biological needs act *in a specifically human fashion*,
as regards both the kinds of behaviour in which they are mani-

fested, and the emotional and dynamic potentialities and repercussions which correspond to them. What we have said about hunger can be repeated *mutatis mutandis* for the sexual need, the need for self-protection, self-defence, etc.

3. The Development of the Personality and the Need for Psycho-Social Contact

Man is not only integrated into the biological sphere; he is also, as we have already suggested, a being who understands his position amongst the men and objects surrounding him. At every moment of his life he is building up and nourishing his personality *in* and *through* contact with others. At this level of his psychic life he also endeavours to maintain himself and develop. He does not wish to *disappear socially*. If he feels completely ignored or neglected—i.e., someone who "doesn't count"—he experiences this as a *loss to his personal and social existence*. In fact, the man who at the psycho-social level of his existence fails to preserve himself, fails to "be someone," fails to assert himself or develop his nature according to his own "scheme of life," can be compared to the mollusc whose regulative processes do not succeed in preserving the stability of its internal environment. When, by the process known as osmosis, water penetrates the organism of the mollusc, it is said to "dilute" its internal environment to such an extent that the creature can no longer be distinguished from the surrounding environment. In the same way, the man who does not manage to "be somebody" at the psycho-social level of his existence, "disappears." The psychic organism defends itself against this "social death," developing all its resources, just as it releases them to safeguard its individuality and biological life. Man needs to take "his" place in some group or other and maintain himself and develop there. In his own eyes especially he needs an inner "consistency" which gives "value" to his own particular psycho-social existence.

The strength of this aspect of the psychic dynamism is not so obvious in the man who has already succeeded in taking his place in the psycho-social sphere, or who is striving to gain it in a spirit of absolute self-confidence. But as soon as a man *fears* that his effort to be "himself amongst others" is being defeated, or if he begins to doubt whether he will be able to maintain himself and develop, because he is losing confidence in himself, then a state of extreme tension develops and a break of the normal equilibrium may follow. We can easily see how much psychic energy lies behind this "drive" if we imagine for a moment how much effort and hard work are required, for instance, of any young man who is being educated for a *career* designed precisely to make him "someone" in the world.

On the other hand, it is clear that besides this drive to develop his own psychic individuality, man experiences and manifests a *need for others*. Apart from any external dependence on his fellow-men, he feels an internal need of contact, exchange, communication, support, sympathy, self-giving. This need for psychic contact and exchange, under forms which may be more or less passive or more or less active, lies at the very root of man's psycho-social life.

Again, the energy of this dynamic force is not at first sight so evident in the person who is comfortably installed socially, because in this case the need is normally satisfied. But it is just this fact of being socially settled, this interpenetration of personal psychic life with that of others, that forms the framework of that unstable edifice, the individual isolated personality.

The most primitive and fundamental feeling of this personality seems to be a feeling of insecurity, uneasiness and misery at being lonely. Nothing is so disturbing, so "stifling" to psychic life, as the experience of feeling derelict and alone; it seems to correspond to the condition of the organism cut off from all contact with the surrounding air.[1]

We must not, of course, confuse this psychic loneliness with material separation. There are many people living far from their kind who nevertheless remain in close psychological contact with them; whilst others feel alone even when they are with their nearest and dearest. The misanthropist and the anti-social individual undoubtedly live in contact with others; but they experience this contact negatively.

---

[1] As regards this fundamental feeling of misery in psychic loneliness, see particularly Karen Horney, *The Neurotic Personality of Our Time* (New York, Norton, 1937).

On the psycho-social level the need for contact manifests itself in many different active or passive forms, in love, friendship, sympathy, respect, domination and submission, etc.; above all, in the form in which it unites with the need for development, i.e. in the tendency to develop the personality by means of an intense interaction, a giving of self, a utilization of one's own talents—in one word, in that overflowing psycho-social activity by means of which man develops his capacities in a continual exchange with others and finds an intense delight in doing so.

These forms of the need for contact are so clear that there is no need to say anything more about them. It suffices that we have realized the power and universality of these tendencies and of the part they play in our lives.

We must repeat that at both the psycho-social and the biological level of our psychic life the two needs are inseparably connected. Thus the child, for example, needs support and affection (contact) whilst at the same time he wants to "be somebody" amongst others (self-preservation and development); but it is only *by feeling that he is loved and surrounded by affection* that he can acquire *confidence in himself*, feel himself to be "someone" and *preserve* and *develop* himself psychologically.

The opposite is also true; being oneself and having confidence in oneself are *indispensable conditions* for being able to make contact with others. It is necessary to possess a minimum of self-confidence —i.e., to be oneself—in order to be able to come out of oneself and enrich oneself by a psychic contact in which one both gives and takes. The man lacking inner consistency becomes closed to others, i.e. though he experiences a very strong need for support and contact, he does not possess the vital strength by means of which the mind can open to the contact and interaction that make up life. He is like the debilitated organism which, as the need for contact with the biological sphere becomes more imperative, becomes less and less capable of realizing the interaction which should restore its strength. Adler has shown very clearly that "lack of personality" and self-confidence are obstacles to psychical contact and can even make impossible the self-giving which is demanded by love.

Thus, just as the organism maintains itself in existence and develops by contact, through assimilation and reaction, so man develops and unfolds his social and psychic personality through a variety of active and passive forms of contact with others. It is by feeling himself to be loved or esteemed, backed up or recognized by others, and especially through the *active, self-forgetting gift of self*, that he achieves his aim. The remarkable thing about this development of the psycho-social personality is that man maintains himself and develops better, the *less* he concentrates *directly* on himself and the more he opens himself to others. This is clear in the case of the timid or self-preoccupied person who turns out a social "failure" *for the very reason that he concentrates exclusively on himself.*

It is by giving himself to what is *objectively valuable*, i.e. by not being directly concerned with himself, that man really *develops*. The person who concentrates on himself, remains self-enclosed, fails to expand psychically. This is a law of psychic development. We must add that it is by the same gift of self to something objective that the personality develops *egoistically* too. Seneca's words can be understood in this psychological sense: *"Alteri vivas oportet, si vis tibi vivere."* Nevertheless, it is only through an *altruistic* gift of self that the personality can develop *fully*.

EGOISTIC CONTACT AND ALTRUISTIC CONTACT (LOVE)

In those last sentences we have touched on an essential point in the development of personality. The tendency to self-development and psycho-social contact exists in double form, and we must now endeavour to make this additional complexity more explicit. This is important both for the understanding of certain deviations, or rather "strictures," of personality, and for a clear idea of the ideal development which we have in mind.

We must first explain more fully what is meant by the gift of the self to *what is objective*.

In psychology, the "drive" to self-preservation is often regarded as an egoistic tendency, under the impulse of which the individual *relates* everything with which *he comes into contact to himself* and utilizes everything to the advantage of his own ego. Besides this egoistic tendency to self-preservation there is an opposite tendency towards an "altruistic gift" of self through which man liberates himself from himself.

So far, we may have given the impression that we are only concerned with the egoistic tendency, and intend to ignore the profoundly human tendency towards this altruistic self-giving which plays such a considerable part in social conduct. This is not so; and we intend now to explain our interpretation of the drive to self-preservation and contact with others.

We have already said that the drive to self-preservation in its narrow sense is simply one form, and even the "lowliest," of the need for self-development and self-realization. The development or realization of all its potentialities, in a given line of development, is the "strong" or "vital" form by which the individual core maintains itself.

It seems to be a fundamental law of life that man maintains his own existence better and develops more fully the less he concentrates directly on himself and the more he directs his attention on to the "object": the most efficient and efficacious way of developing through one's actions is to be not immediately occupied with oneself, in order to be able to give oneself completely, *psychologically*, to "others." Remember the example of the shy person, who in social life concentrates upon himself and for this reason never reaches more than a low stage of self-development in society.

This ability to concentrate on some activity to the complete forgetfulness of self is what we mean by the "psychic gift of self" to the object.

The basis of this law of psychic life seems to be found in the very nature of life itself. On the biological level, as we have shown, it is only *by opening* as wide as possible *to that which is other than itself*, and by feeding on this source, that life expands; in the same way, the individual who is psychologically centred upon himself grows vacant and stony.

This principle, which is valid on both the biological and the social levels, applies equally to the *moral* development of the personality.

So far we have considered the "gift of self" from a purely *psychological* point of view. In this sense, it consists in not concentrating one's "attention" directly on oneself when involved in any activity, as does the self-conscious person, but in concentrating wholly on the object of the activity. From the *moral* point of view, this *"psychic* gift" to the object may remain purely *egocentric* or egoistic. The activity to which a man gives himself psychically can, as regards its *direct object*, be entirely directed towards himself; whilst the man whom shyness prevents from freeing himself psychically from himself can have the most altruistic intentions.

To the concentration on oneself or on the object at the psychic level corresponds the concentration on oneself or the gift of oneself to another on the *moral* level.

The general law of which we have been speaking is valid too for the moral development of personality. The gift of self at the moral level does not necessarily imply a *psychic* concentration on the object of the activity; it means rather that one gives oneself to someone else in one's *aim* or *intention*. Note, however, that a *psychic* orientation towards the object is the "normal" substratum for the moral gift of self. The man who has the best of "altruistic" intentions, but fails to liberate himself psychically from himself, does not possess a healthy natural basis from which the "moral sense" of altruism or charity can reach a full and perfect flowering. Again, it is by this "moral" gift of oneself to someone else that one's whole person maintains and develops its own personality in the best and "richest" way. For what we have called a "gift" means in fact, above all, *being actively open* to others and *widely receptive* to them. This *openness* and *receptivity* are simply means of being oneself and becoming oneself, not within the narrow limits of the isolated individual ego but according to the expanded potentialities of an ego *integrated with the world of men and the absolute*. And this is the only "complete" ego; the other is truncated. It is fundamentally false to consider "others" as a limitation of the ego. Contact with "others" leads to an *enrichment* of the ego when it is not made "on the defensive." It is this psychological attitude of "defence"—the attitude of the "weak" ego *afraid* for its own existence—that "projects" the object of its *fear* (i.e., attack) upon others. This means that "others" are looked upon as a threat to the ego, because of the ego's own feeling of insecurity and inner weakness. The philosophy which sees the "object" and "others" as primarily *limitations* of the ego is a result of this psychological attitude of the "weak" and aggressive ego transposed into metaphysics. The philosophy of Fichte and especially some modern systems of existentialism supply us with striking examples of this "weak" psychological attitude towards the personality of others.[1]

The drive towards self-development and self-preservation, therefore, does not mean a concentration of the "little individual ego"; it is the essential need of the whole personality tending to realize its own active integration with the world. This drive can, however, appear in two forms. There is firstly the "debilitated," "shy" form; as it occurs in the man who lacks the strength to realize himself fully, who *dare not* or *cannot* open out to others and thus come out of his isolation. In this case, the person maintains himself and develops very imperfectly—on the social or the moral, or the biological planes. There is, on the other hand, the "rich" form of self-preservation and development, which consists in *being open* to others as to a source of riches in the same three spheres. This "openness" is the channel by which man "gives himself" and by which he "receives," i.e. his channel of self-realization. It is *life itself*.

The "drive" of the human personality towards the preservation and development of its own being should thus, in our opinion, be conceived in a much wider sense than is often the case. When seen as a whole, it is by no means an "egoistic" tendency. It is a need which man cannot deny without annihilating himself. His perfection depends on the extent to which he can develop through being actively involved in the world of men and the absolute.

There is here a paradox arising from the fact that words like

[1] The "enlarging" influence of love and sympathy, as against the retracting influence of a direct concentration on self, has been described in a remarkable fashion by Dr. E. De Greeff in his work *Les instincts de défense et de sympathie* (Paris, Presses Universitaires de France, 1947). The reader will have noticed that the aim of this work is to show that "defence" and "sympathy" can be looked upon, not as *two instincts*, but as two ways in which the need for development and contact manifest themselves in man.

The influence of these two emotional orientations on man's attitude to God and faith has been brought out by W. Smet in his essay *"Liefde en Godsgeloof"* ("Love and Faith in God"), Louvain, 1949 (unpublished).

"self-renunciation" and "abnegation" are often used to signify a renunciation from concentration on the little isolated ego. But, as we have just seen, personality unfolds most fully when it succeeds in going out from itself and in "giving itself" to "others." Self-renunciation, in this sense, is therefore the "vital" form of self-development of which we have been speaking.

We believe that even from the *psychological* point of view it is only through the *moral* gift of self that man reaches the full development of his personality. There is no doubt that the man who is psychologically and biologically open can reach a very high degree of development, but it will often be found that his moral egocentricism contracts his psychic "openness." His moral concentration on himself prevents him from seeing others, from understanding them, from "receiving" them *in their full reality*. Reality, indeed, is only discovered through "respect" and *respect*, which is the moral basis of the knowledge of the "real," implies a certain moral detachment from self, i.e. that the ego shall not be the only point of reference in every action. The morally egocentric person deforms others by approaching them entirely from the point of view that everything exists "for me." This same psychological attitude, transposed to the philosophic plane, causes others to be looked upon as limitations and obstacles to the ego.

On the other hand, the kind of personality which gives itself to others in a way that is morally admirable but has not reached a state of psychic self-detachment does not, as we have said above, possess the psychological basis on which a thoroughly sound moral personality can be established. Nor does this condition allow personality to reach a harmonious state of development. For the moral personality is often in this case something which has been added on afterwards and which, like a plaster, hardly hides the deformities underneath. It is for this reason that in some people the moral qualities, or virtues, often seem to have something "unnatural" about them, something which betrays the absence of a healthy psychic basis.

Thus the "moral" aspect of the unfolding of personality—in the sense in which we have employed this term—seems to be essential both as a component and as a condition of psychic development. The psychic aspect, in its turn, is the substratum which alone can support a balanced moral development.

ACTIVE AND PASSIVE FORMS OF THE NEED FOR CONTACT

The need for contact, which manifests itself at all levels of our biological and psychic existence, can find expression in forms which may be more or less *active* or more or less *passive*—in the tendency to dominate, in the active gift of self, or in the need for submissiveness, sympathy, support, protection. The need for "others" is as imperative in the leader and the "strong" man as in the weak person who needs support. The one feels unhappy as soon as he is left without anyone on whom to shower his orders or his protection; the other needs advice or orders or encouragement to keep him going. Usually, however, the two poles of this "active-passive" opposition appear in the same person. Most "strong" people reveal in some respect or other, at some moment or other, or when faced with somebody or other, tendencies towards passive contact. The opposite is true for those whose part is usually passive. The woman, who needs support, protects those who "maintain" her and surrounds them with care; whilst the "strong" dominant male has moments when he requires love and protection. Both forms of contact are variants of the need for "others," a need which constitutes both the weakness and the strength of every human being.

4. The Need for "Existential" Support and Universal Integration

Man is therefore a vital centre maintaining the "internal environment" of his life and organism by means of regulative mechanisms and adaptations in his behaviour; that form of psychic life which consciously finds itself amongst creatures like itself and desires to unfold as a "person" amongst them; a being who in his interaction with the world, assimilates biochemical agents and develops "significant" situations; *furthermore, he opens out upon the whole of reality, in which he feels himself to "exist."* Man is a being who knows himself to be situated in *that which is.* In other words, man lives his own life in the world, in such a way that he is neither exhausted nor absorbed by that which *affects* him. This undeniable cardinal fact must be realized, that man is a being who asks himself questions *about his very existence*. Contact with the "world" causes biochemical reactions in him; this is a fact, examined in all its detail by natural science; but this same contact with the "world" rouses the problems of existence in him—this is another fact, which we see no reason for science—in this case, psychology—to remain silent about.

It is because, and in so far as, he is not completely absorbed in his social and biological environment, in so far as he truly *is* and truly lives his existence, that, as we shall show, man experiences the need to maintain his existence and develop himself in existence, and the further need to "illuminate" his existence. This need for development in the consciousness of existence takes diverse forms. For some, it means developing complicated philosophical ideas— in the affirmation of immortality or in theories of the purest materialism. But all, by trying to realize what they are, or what they imagine themselves to be—i.e., by growing fully conscious of their own existence—will be obeying the *need to be more completely themselves*. "*Non omnis moriar*" is one expression of this need for self-preservation and self-development; but a philosopher who considers that his personality will disappear for ever into matter is being no less obedient to the need to realize the meaning of existence, i.e. to be more completely oneself by understanding as a *conscious* being what one is.

It is more pertinent here, however, to examine the expressions of this need in its more ordinary manifestations in the ordinary, everyday man. In the first place, we discover this need of self-preservation and self-development extending beyond the limits of biological and social "fact," in certain universal *religious tendencies* of mankind; a need sometimes expressed in the saying that man wants to "save his soul." Now, from the psychological point of view, "saving one's soul" means primarily maintaining oneself in existence as a personality integrated with the absolute.

It is true that in our civilization *this religious form* of the desire for self-preservation and self-development according to an absolute order of values has been transformed for many people into aspirations of a more or less philosophical kind. But the man who sees his life as a link in the chain of evolution or the development of matter is trying, no less than the person who aims to save his soul, to maintain himself and develop through the same kind of integration into an absolute order.

Again, at a certain moment in the individual's existence or in the development of human culture, this general need for self-preservation and self-development can appear in a much more pronounced fashion at the psycho-social level than at the absolute level, so that it will be difficult to recognize the need in its absolute form. A man of thirty, for example, experiences this need much more intensely in its social form than as a desire to make sure of his eternal salvation. The opposite can be true of the man who retires from social life. Thus Liebman, in his famous *Peace of Mind*, was able to say that modern man is concerned about success in the same way as the man of the Middle Ages was preoccupied with his eternal salvation.[1] It would be a mistake to imagine that the social need is a temporary or artificial one, but it is true that the philosophical ideas which man develops about human existence in general can change *the forms* in which the corresponding dynamism *appears*.

In this particular field of philosophy, and of intellectual life in general, the same need is again apparent in the natural tendency profoundly rooted in man, to believe in the immortality of his soul, or in some sort of persistence of life after death—in the form, for instance, of survival through his descendants or his work. This tendency is also obviously bound up with the fact that through knowledge man *transcends* what is *actually* given and experienced.

It is not our intention here to analyse in detail all these manifestations of the need for preservation and self-development. There are characteristic forms of this need in Chinese and Egyptian civilization. It appears in the joy of the grandfather who holds on to life by growing attached to his grandson; it can be found in the zeal of the master who educates his disciples to prolong the life of his own ideas and discoveries.

[1] Joshua Liebman, *Peace of Mind* (New York, Simon and Schuster, 1946). See also Werner Wolff, *Values and Personality* (Grune and Stratton, 1950): ". . . the cause of neurosis . . . is man's experience of having lost his connection with the universe."

Many and manifold are the concrete manifestations of the need, felt universally by man, to preserve and develop himself on the specifically human level to which he has been raised by his transcendent spirit. The force which drives man to exploit the earth and incessantly enlarge his fields of knowledge and technique comes partly at least from the need he feels to develop the intellectual aspect of his personality. It is not only the scientific research-worker, the engineer, the technician, who experiences this need; the adolescent can exhibit it in a pronounced degree. In the same way, the man who adopts as his supreme law of conduct fidelity to himself, to his own past and his own principles, and remains consistently himself, is manifesting a form of the need to maintain and develop the moral personality.

It must be remembered that at this spiritual level the ways by which man tends to maintain and develop his personality are not physiologically conditioned, as is the case for his biological development. At the spiritual level man tends to maintain and develop himself in a certain direction according to his own plan for his personal life or according to the ideals set before him by society; hence the great variety of forms in which this need can appear in different people and in different civilizations. The concrete form of the need depends upon either a cognitive element or a theory of life.

On this spiritual and transcendent level of our human existence the need for *contact* manifests itself in specific forms. Before any biological or bodily interaction, and even before communion of any other kind with his fellow-men, man needs a more universal sort of communication and support and integration; he needs *to be able to know and feel himself integrated into an absolute order of existence*. Perhaps never before in human history has there been such intense experience of *absolute* despair and loneliness, such a feeling of utter dereliction, such lack of all transcendental contact, as there is today.

At a time like ours, when the various attachments to past and future, to the earth and the family—when the thousand and one things to which existence attaches itself, and which give existence its meaning and value—have been dissolved, man feels utterly "uprooted." The need to find some absolute meaning in life, i.e. the need to become integrated with existence, makes itself felt more and more imperiously. But this need has gone on being frustrated: man has continued to see before him nothing but the horror and emptiness of his isolation and the absurdity of his existence. It is a situation which brings out more clearly than ever the *reality* of man's "spiritual" needs—and it is amazing to find so many contemporary psychologies incapable of seeing this and giving all their attention to mere "tissue needs" instead.

Here one is faced with a concrete manifestation of a fundamental need of human existence itself: a need for contact with the whole order of reality, the only kind of contact which can give meaning to life. It is this frustrated need which gives rise, at this moment of the world's history, to the metaphysical misery and despair apparent not only in the philosophy and literature of existentialism but as the background to a great deal of the insecurity and psychic troubles of today.

We mention these cultural facts simply to give tangible reality to the need in question. The *positive* forms of higher needs are usually less tangible than the states of derangement caused by their frustration, and it is through these negative manifestations that there becomes evident a form of need which can easily pass unperceived in the man whose conception of the world makes up a harmonious whole.

To mention a few more positive manifestations of the need for contact at the spiritual level of our existence: religion—a phenomenon so universal that, though it can be *replaced* by other forms of transcendent contact, it can rarely be *extinguished*—provides one of the most striking manifestations of the need for a kind of interaction and contact which goes beyond physical and social facts. It can be expressed in the *feminine* form of a "request" for support from the absolute, or in a more masculine kind of desire to be *at peace* with one's conscience or with God. Not to be at peace with one's conscience or with God means in fact to experience the rupture of a transcendent order of absolute values.[1]

[1] In some people the need to be at peace with God or their own conscience may also be the manifestation of a desire for a stainless egoistic perfection. Such people do not want to be debtors to anybody; they want to manage their own affairs to perfection. They transpose to the absolute level of their relationship with God the mentality of a petty accountant.

In the *intellectual and philosophical* domains, as we have said, there is the need *to give a meaning to existence*, i.e. the need to know oneself integrated meaningfully into an absolute order of existence. This is the vital force behind our spiritual existence itself, forcing us out of our absolute isolation. Just as the organism is stifled and asphyxiated when it is isolated from its biological sphere, so a spiritual being becomes absurd to itself when it does not open out and enter into significant contact with the whole of reality.

The power of this spiritual impulse appears most clearly, we have said, when it remains *unsatisfied*. Besides certain currents in contemporary culture to which we have already alluded, psychopathology too directs our attention towards this human need. A great number of people who on the surface seem very sure of themselves are subject to neurotic disturbances whose roots must be looked for in their failure to integrate themselves into a wider reality, i.e. their failure to give a meaning to life. The Social Security Board of the United States of America recently expressed concern at the increasing number of neurotics in that country. On the other hand, the immense enthusiasm recently aroused there in the hearts and souls of millions of readers by Liebman's book, *Peace of Mind*, reveals something of *what is* missing in these "restless" people, and *what* lies at the root of their distress. To these millions of readers, all seeking interior peace, Liebman says that it is their "insecurity and forlornness," from lack of any metaphysical basis to their lives, which makes it impossible for them to surmount their existential misery unless they have faith in the "worthwhileness" and therefore the *meaning* of life. The only thing that can re-establish the disturbed equilibrium is "the confidence that God will *not cast us aside* but will *use each of us as a piece of priceless mosaic in the design of His universe.*" The

---

They want to "win" what God has promised to give them. Thus they try not to get beaten, to affirm themselves, or protect themselves. This attitude of mind towards God and religion has been described most suggestively by Mauriac in his novel *La Pharisienne* (Paris, Grasset, 1941); American edition, *Woman of the Pharisees* (New York, Henry Holt, 1950). This reveals once again the way several tendencies are *involved* in one single human activity. We shall have to return to this point, *ex professo*, in a later paragraph.

echo aroused by these words in the souls of millions of readers gives the psychologist some idea of the "reality" of the need for universal contact and integration, the need to know and feel oneself as a precious stone in the universal mosaic of the absolute divine plan. The moment this need is frustrated, it begins to raise its voice above all the noise of *business relationships* and *sex appeal,* creating in the human soul a silence and emptiness that no external disturbance can fill.[1]

In all these forms of aspiration we see the needs for self-development and contact which we have already discovered on the psycho-physiological and psycho-social levels of human existence. Here specific forms of these needs arise because human existence is conscious of itself and conscious of being involved in a whole order of reality, and we see the dynamism of the spiritual ego which in its *knowledge* and its *aspirations* transcends its spatial and temporal limitations. This spiritual ego too experiences the tendency to *develop its existence* and *feel itself in contact* with its spiritual environment.

SUICIDE AND THE DESIRE FOR SELF-DESTRUCTION

Before we end this account we must pause for a moment to examine a phenomenon which at first sight is at the opposite extreme from this tendency to preserve and develop oneself in existence. We mean suicide and the more or less pathological desire for self-destruction. Let us examine a few typical cases.

A woman patient, treated by Rogers, who entertained thoughts of suicide, said, "I just don't want to live." What is the exact meaning and significance of this desire? The context shows it quite clearly. The same patient said, "I cannot be the kind of a person I want to be. . . . There is such a wide, wide gap between my ideal and what I am . . . and either I accept the fact that I am absolutely worthless, or I fight whatever it is that holds me in this terrible conflict."[2] In the light of this confession we can understand the origin and significance of the desire to stop living. This woman

---

[1] See also Fulton J. Sheen, *Peace of Soul* (New York, McGraw-Hill, 1949).

[2] Cf. C. R. Rogers, "The Attitude and Orientation of the Counselor," *Journal of Consulting Psychology,* 1949, XIII, p. 93.

wanted desperately *to be something*, something *more* than she actually was. This need to be something more, i.e. to realize her *ideal*, seemed impossible to her; there was a "gap" between her and it. It was the impossibility of satisfying this need to be more than she was that created the unbearable state of tension from which only death could deliver her. For as long as she lived, the desire and the tension would persist.

In our opinion this is an absolutely typical case. The man who commits suicide, or who wants "to stop living," is either someone who is tired of the fruitless combat that has to be waged in the effort to maintain himself at some level or other of his existence, or else it is someone who has lost all integrating contact with the world, and whose life for this reason no longer has any *meaning*. As long as man exists, the need for *meaning* and the need for self-preservation are at work in him; and when he despairs of being able to satisfy them he longs to be delivered from the unbearable tension which they create in him. Only death can deliver him from them: he commits suicide, not, generally speaking, because he wants to destroy himself, but because he can no longer endure the form of existence in which he *means nothing* and *is nothing*—i.e., because he can no longer bear "to be nothing." Thus suicide confirms rather than destroys our thesis that it is impossible for man to despair absolutely of being something or meaning something, either on the psycho-social or the absolute level.[1] The desire for nirvana, on the other hand, seems to be simply the desire to have done with all the imperfect and incomplete forms of existence; it is the desire to enjoy a more stable, more perfect existence, to participate in absolute being.

In certain pathological cases another form of the desire for self-destruction appears, in the form of a desire to choose always that which is most painful, that which does most harm or most wrong; in a word, the desire for whatever is most destructive for the individual himself. This is a very mysterious tendency, and it has attracted the attention of a great many psychologists.

---

[1] We are aware that there are many other forms in which the tendency towards suicide manifests itself. Suicide as sacrifice, as protest and heroism, implies even more clearly than the case mentioned above the tendency to self-development.

It appears in a variety of forms; Freud found it necessary to make it a separate fundamental instinct in man. We cannot discuss now in detail the vast problem raised by these curious manifestations of personality dynamics but wish to draw attention to one aspect of the question only. We have known several cases of people who found themselves irresistibly impelled to do harm to themselves, to make life impossible for themselves, to make others believe that they were utterly useless; committing all manner of lies and acts of savagery, trying to ruin their future, their relationships, etc.

In the course of examination we have often discovered that, fundamentally, such people desperately desire the opposite of the thing towards which they feel themselves to be irresistibly attracted. But they are afraid that they will never be able to realize what they really want; afraid that the opposite of what they want will turn out to be true. They are afraid that people will scorn them, that their future is bound to go wrong, that some misfortune will overtake them, etc. The fear of never being able to get what they want, or that something which they long to avoid will fall upon them, creates a state of uncertainty and psychic tension of a kind to drive them distracted. The object of their fear is constantly coming before them—they are afraid that this object, which they so much want to avoid, will overtake them, and this fascinates them. They are obsessed by the thing to be avoided; above all, they are tormented incessantly by *uncertainty*.

It is in this condition, and to put an end to the unbearable tension, that they long to *escape from the state of uncertainty*. The object which they fear, and which obsesses them, attracts them irresistibly. At the root of this attraction is the idea that only by giving way to it can they escape from uncertainty. By choosing the worst they are no longer subject to either the fear or the uncertainty: "Once you throw yourself in, it's all over."

There was a young man who wanted to be a brilliant lawyer and who was highly esteemed by everybody, but he was convinced that he would never become the lawyer he wanted to be. He was afraid that some day or other everybody would discover all the wrong things he thought he had done in his life. For this reason he lived in a state of uncertainty about his future. To put an end to it, when he was with people on whom his whole future depended, he felt impelled to do all sorts of shocking things. In this way his position was made quite clear: he felt free from his fears and hesitancies. It will be obvious that we are only giving a bare outline of this case. In the concrete reality of the situation, his desire to ruin his career makes sense only in a dramatic context, which is to be understood in another, equally dramatic context, suggested by the words, "He was afraid that some day or other everybody would discover all the wrong things he thought he had done in his life." It will be seen that what we have described as the longing to escape from uncertainty is the cardinal point in this psychological situation, and underlies his desire to do himself harm.

Such is the mechanism of the so-called desire for self-destruction, in some cases at least. It is simply a sign of desperation, and in it, under such distorted appearances, can still be seen the desire for self-preservation and self-development, or for giving a meaning to one's life.

We do not by any means wish to make this explanation into a general rule, but it is without doubt one of the mechanisms that produces in certain people the need for self-destruction.

5. The Fundamental Origin of Needs

The question arises whether the impulse towards self-development and the need for contact, as we have described them in their various forms, supply us with that which is most *fundamental* in man's psychic dynamism.

We are inclined to say that they do, because these needs seem *to be rooted in the two essential aspects of human existence*. As we said at the beginning, it is quite clear that in the last analysis the needs of a being have their source in *that* which it is, i.e. in the individual's essential situation, both in itself and in its connections with everything that surrounds it.

In philosophy it would be easy to base this thesis on the essentially dynamic character of finite being, which means that everything that exists is dynamic, because and in so far as it exists. But we shall endeavour to keep as near to concrete facts as possible, distinguishing in the human condition and the human situation the two following aspects.

In the first place, man is an individual centre of life. As we have already said, he forms a kind of core of biological life, which by a system of regulation and adaptation maintains the individuality of its internal environment in the face of the changing environment outside. He is, at the same time, a psychic and social individual, opening out upon and living in the "world." Then, he is a spiritual existence, i.e. an existence which is conscious of itself as distinct from the whole of reality. Man is therefore a being who has a certain internal unity, existing *in himself* and conscious, at least implicitly, of his own individuality; he is what is known as *a person.*

In the second place, this being who exists in himself is not sufficient unto himself. Man, indeed, is not self-sufficient at any level of his existence. *Biologically* he is continually being "fed" by things from the biological realm. At the *psycho-social* level, the contents and activity of his personality develop through psychic contacts and exchanges which go on all the time between himself and the *world* and his fellow-men. His cognitive life in its entirety is born and develops from contact with worldly and social situations. His emotional life is connected by a thousand and one threads with the emotional lives of others. As a psychic individual man only develops *in* and *through* contact with the significant situations of his daily life. Finally, on the level of *pure existence* man is aware that he does not exist by himself—i.e., cannot find in his own existence any ultimate basis for the fact that he *exists.* He finds himself more or less consciously *integrated* with and supported by the order of reality; and it is by *participating in Being itself* that his personal existence is created.

Thus man is a core of life, continually being fed by contact with the biological, psycho-social and metaphysical spheres of reality. His psycho-physiological organism, both in its biological and psychic activities and in its very existence, is intrinsically bound up and involved with that which is not himself.

It is in the framework of this fundamental constitution of man that the essential needs penetrating the whole of his psychophysiological organism must be understood. As he is a core of individual life, the impulse towards self-preservation, self-protection, self-defence, self-realization, self-development, animates him in every field of his activity, and at all the levels at which life manifests itself in him. Here we come across a fact of the first importance: every form of life reveals specific activities, deriving from a fundamental urge which, up to a certain point, tends to safeguard this life, either in the "weak" form of *defence*, or in a more "vital" form of *development* and increasing integration.

As a core of life, *formed and fed by contact with the "non-ego,"* man manifests *a need for others* which appears in various forms corresponding to the various aspects of his complex life. On the biological and psycho-physiological levels these forms of exchange and contact are governed and conditioned by "ways of access" which join the organism with the biological sphere. On the psycho-social and spiritual levels this need for contact manifests itself likewise in specific ways through which the psyche "opens out" on to reality. The *specific nature* of the needs, and the specific nature of their forms of manifestation, must therefore be connected with the psychological and psychic conditions of the human organism and must also be able to be explained by the conditions of the *development* of the organism and its behaviour. These conditions, in fact, account for the concrete forms under which the needs appear in a certain individual. It is the task of physiological and psychological research to show the factors which condition needs and influence their development. But it seems to us important, nevertheless, to synthesize our view of the fundamental needs as a whole, and in their deepest significance, in order to avoid making hypotheses and generalizations which take account of only one element in the complex structure of human dynamism. This sort of "bias" is in fact one of the great dangers in studying man's dynamic structure.

It is such a synthesis that we have endeavoured to make.

To sum up: Man *is*, and "feels" himself (implicitly, perhaps, but fundamentally) to be both a *self-subsistent being*—hence the drive to self-preservation and self-development—and *a being essentially linked to others*—hence the "natural" need to seek contact with everything that maintains and continually "feeds" his existence. This complex double tendency—towards self-development and towards contact with others—which enters to some extent into the whole of human activity, can therefore be considered the *dynamic expression, on the psychic level, of what man is.* Hence follows the intimate fusion of these two needs (in the fact that it is *in* and *through contact* with "others" that man *maintains* and *develops* himself): since they are simply manifestations of two complementary aspects of his single being: he is *a being in himself who nevertheless derives from, and depends intrinsically upon, others.*

6. The Interpenetration of "Higher" and "Lower" Needs

From this point of view, we repeat, it is easier to understand the reciprocal implications of the need for exchange and contact on the one hand, and the drive to self-preservation and self-development on the other. It should be clear by now that it is precisely *through* being bound up with "others" and *in* contact with "others" that man maintains and develops himself.

Various aspects of these implications have been emphasized by depth-psychology. On the psycho-social level, Adler has insisted that the will to power only reaches a happy issue when it is connected with the social urge.[1] Freud himself, in his theory of narcissism, has not only connected but even identified sexuality with the various manifestations of the tendency to self-preservation.[2]

Moreover it is essential for the understanding of our thesis not to imagine, because these drives appear in different forms at different levels of our psychic life, *that they are separate forces.* All these forms and levels interpenetrate each other very deeply in that complex unity of life, the human personality.

In our own civilization, for instance, the biological tendency to protect and develop life overlaps the need to assert oneself in social life. In other words, man tries to provide for his material and vital needs by trying to obtain a good social position. It is easy to imagine the power that resides in these twin currents of human energy when one thinks of the continuous and tenacious activity engendered in man by the need for "a good job." To prepare himself for a "career," for instance, that will guarantee

[1] See Appendix, pp. 263ff.
[2] See *supra*, pp. 57–58.

him a position in society and give him *enough to live on*, he accepts long years of work and study.

The tendency to maintain the spiritual ego is intimately bound up with this social "impulse." Man feels a spontaneous need to *go on existing amongst his fellow-men* either through his posterity or through his work.

There is no need to demonstrate how the desire for sexual contact, the need for *psychic* support, for active and passive protection, are intimately bound up with each other in normal love, and also in certain forms of sympathy, in ascendance and submission, in some manifestations of intellectual adherence and hero-worship. Even the need for divine support is often mixed up with erotic needs for affection and love, especially when these needs do not find sufficient satisfaction at the social level, or when, as is often the case in the first stages of adolescence, the differentiation of these needs has not advanced very far.

When we consider things in this light we see more clearly how needs existing on the "lower" levels enter into those which are more cultural or spiritual. The discovery of this interpenetration marked an important stage in the development of psychoanalytical theory. Nevertheless, when looking for an explanation of the important facts which depth-psychology has revealed in this field, it is by no means necessary, as we have shown, to deny the specific nature of each of these needs and derive them from a common source. In the same single activity "lower" forms of need are found mixed up with "higher" ones, because they are both manifestations of the same fundamental dynamism traversing the various levels of human psychic life.

Contrariwise, we also find traces of "higher" aspirations and activities in the satisfaction of biological needs. The way in which human beings normally satisfy hunger or sexual desire bears the impress of spirit and the gift of self.

A little while ago a psychologist describing his own personal experience, said to me, "I have often noticed that the physical pleasure and satisfaction of marriage are infinitely more intense and 'rich' when I am conscious of the human and spiritual bonds which unite me to my wife—when I realize what the *person* with whom I am united *means* to me; whereas when these relations are experienced at a more purely instinctive and sexual level the pleasure is not so intense or so lasting." Thus spiritual elements do not simply form a *social framework surrounding* or *added on to* the normal satisfaction of instinctive needs; they can be real *components* in a specifically human experience of the instinctive self.

Hence we must not expect any human manifestation to be absolutely "uncontaminated" by contact with "lower" needs. But on the other hand, we shall rarely find activities which do not reveal some trace of man's higher aspirations and potentialities, even if they only appear in distorted or destructive ways. Our only concern, from the scientific point of view, is to respect the specific character of each need and then attempt to analyse it as it appears in the inextricable mingling of needs that characterizes the human psyche. This idea of respect for the irreducible character and function of every form of need and activity is opposed to Freud's theory, which, on account of such an interpenetration, was too prone to neglect certain components and reduce the whole activity to *one single element*.[1]

(1) PSYCHOLOGICAL SYSTEM OR LOGICAL SYSTEM?

The interpenetration of these various forms of need suggests a further point. The question was whether the system of needs which we have described really corresponds to a *psychic* reality or whether it merely represents, as is all too frequently the case, a *logical schema*. Is there really a *psychological unity behind the various forms* of the drive to self-preservation and the need for contact, as we have described them? Is there any real reason for reducing the different tendencies described under the heading of the "need for contact" to such a single need?

Can the manifold dynamic forces which we have gathered together under this heading be considered manifestations of a real *need for self-preservation and self-development*, or is the connection merely a *logical* one based on a conceptual similarity?

It is precisely the interpenetration of these different needs which

---

[1] The reasons for this irreducibility were given above, where we showed that man's spiritual activities *imply specific potentialities*; see, amongst others, pp. 180f. Here we see what positive grounds there are for explaining this interpenetration by other means than that of the *reduction* of "higher" to "lower" *via* sublimation, etc.

shows their *psychological* connection; just as an analysis of the specific elements contained in them gives proof of their essential irreducibility.[1]

Thus there is a real psychological bond between the child's tendency to respect its father, to look to him for support, to identify itself with him, and the human need for God as manifested in religion. The two phenomena are irreducible forms, existing at different psychic levels, of a complex need for protection and contact, a need which, as we have shown, arises fundamentally from man's dependence on the "non-ego."

(2) THE TENDENCY TOWARDS PROGRESS AND THE NEED FOR DEVELOPMENT

A final question remains to be answered. What connection is there between the specifically human drive towards progress, which we discussed earlier,[2] and the fundamental tendency towards self-development which penetrates every level of human life?

When we were discussing the specifically human drive towards progress, we emphasized only one aspect of the need for self-realization; the fact that as a result of his transcendental knowledge and his self-awareness man tends towards some ideal image or other, and therefore experiences more or less consciously a conflict or tension between his actual condition and this ideal of personality which he wishes to realize. It is because of this psychic tension that man tends at every moment to go beyond what is actually given; and this process is the dynamic starting-point behind both individual and social progress, both being to a certain extent a *personal* achievement and not simply an effect of the biological forces of animal development generally.

This specifically human character of psychic dynamism enters into every need. An ideal of self-realization, fuller than that which has been reached at any particular stage, enters into most human activities whilst life is on the ascent.

We can say, therefore, that man's dynamic development involves not only two lines of fundamental needs but also a more or less conscious effort towards ideal forms of self-realization,

---

[1] A further proof will be found above, pp. 213–214.
[2] Pp. 171ff.

developed by each human being personally and causing a certain tension in the development of his personality. These two dynamic lines seem to be intrinsic to man himself as a centre of individual life integrated with everything that exists.

We must add that this drive to self-realization by means of contact with others seems to follow the curve described by human growth, its rise and decline being connected with the development of man's biological, social, and spiritual life. The various curves do not, of course, follow parallel courses: the active need for self-realization can still be rising in an ascending curve, on the spiritual level, when the biological curve is declining towards death.

7. Fundamental Needs and Actual Motives

Psychoanalysis introduced into psychology the tendency to look for the "motives" of any act in the dynamic contents of the individual's *past*. This is the *genetic* or "historical" line of inquiry into the study of motivation. Thus the psychoanalyst will explain an adult's revolutionary activity against a King or President by means of the Oedipus complex—i.e., as an aggressive attitude which as a child he developed against his father. There are now many psychologists who object to this "historical" line of inquiry. They prefer to explain behaviour by means of the actual dynamic forces themselves, i.e. as a result of what is given and experienced in the actual "field" of the situation. (See, e.g., Lewin's *field theory*.)

This objection against the genetic line of inquiry is usually accompanied by a more general objection against the attempt to derive any need from a more fundamental dynamism from which it is supposed to have developed. A young man may become a sailor because he wishes to earn a lot of money that way, but he may come to like being at sea for other reasons too. Then the actual motive behind his remaining at sea can no longer be derived, from the *functional* point of view, from the original desire to earn money.[1]

[1] See Allport's theory of functional autonomy of motives in G. Allport, *Personality* (New York, Henry Holt, 1937), Chapter VII.

The reaction against these genetic theories, and against the reduction of any particular motive to instincts supposedly more fundamental, seems perfectly justified. Thus MacLeod is quite right when he says, for instance, that by this method an actual situation is often explained by means of forces which no longer exist. He is particularly right in emphasizing that *continuity* in dynamic development does not necessarily imply an identity between the essential elements in any motive at two different stages of its development.[1] Yet it would be pushing things too far, to try to separate any *actual motive* from a *more fundamental need*. Reference to a general need does not always mean reference to a stage in development that has been passed once and for all; still less, that only a logical abstraction is involved. There are in our opinion a great number of cases in which a particular motive is simply a concrete form, taken in certain circumstances and as a result of a process of learning, by a more general need which has continued to exist in this form. To be more precise, *the general or fundamental need acts as one of the components of the concrete motive as it appears here and now*. In the course of psychic development a variety of elements and components— cognitive elements, conflicting tendencies and affections, concrete circumstances, etc.—mingle to form an organic whole, and this is the concrete form taken by the actual motive. A fundamental need is never more than *one component* amongst many, in the concrete reality of the motive that leads to action.

All that we have said about fundamental needs must be understood in the light of this. It is the exact opposite of our meaning, to try to *reduce* the multiplicity of motives and concrete needs to the two dynamic forces which we have found to exist on the various levels of our psychic life. But these two dynamic forces are active and real, and enter into the constitution of the concrete motives of actual conduct.

A few examples may show more clearly what we mean. A girl (Mia) used to think up all kinds of tricks in the effort to become acquainted with a young man: this was obviously the motive behind most of her actions. But *this actual concrete motive*

[1] MacLeod, "The Phenomenological Approach to Social Psychology," *Psychological Review*, 1947, LIV, pp. 193–210. See pp. 177–178.

was a very complex dynamic reality; complex, not only in its origin and history, but also in its *reality* and *its actual dynamic constitution.* In it, as active components under various guises, we find the two fundamental needs of which we have been speaking. The girl's desire arose partly—as she confessed— from the desire not to be less successful with young men than her friends who were already engaged or married. It was an essential aspect of the *need for self-assertion or self-development at the psychosocial level* for this girl to be esteemed and sought after by young men. There was one special circumstance which increased Mia's hurry to find a young man. For a long time she had been afraid that God would punish her for certain sins which she had committed; and this punishment, she thought, might mean not being able to get married. This fear tormented her. If she managed to find a young man, she would be certain that God was not angry with her; and when she thought that she might really be forsaken or chastized by God, her life lost all its meaning. There was a third component in her longing to get herself a young man: an erotic and sexual need, especially the need for tenderness, to receive tokens of affection. Then a new element had recently been added: she had not been getting on well with her mother since her elder sister had left home, and she too was anxious to leave. All these elements—and a great many more—entered into the dynamic unity which appeared simply as a longing for a young man, a desire that "caused" a dozen different behaviour-patterns each day.

All these elements were active components in the girl's actual longing. Instead of saying that the fundamental needs to which we have referred are simply abstract entities compared with the actual concrete longing, it is truer to say the exact opposite: mere "longing for a young man" is no more than a vague abstract formula unless it is filled out with the different concrete dynamic contents which *actually lie behind it.*

The point we wish to emphasize is that there is a risk of the study of motives becoming superficial and even "verbal" when they are isolated from their real fundamental dynamic content. The same desire can possess very different dynamic contents and elements. Secondly, an essential characteristic of all human motivation is, as we have shown more than once, its *complexity*. To neglect this complexity is yet another way of making the dynamic study of human conduct *superficial*. Besides the purely historical and genetic explanations, and besides the hasty *reduction* of the *whole* motive to one single fundamental force, there is another possibility.

This point, however, has to be made quite clear: the connection of an actual motive to fundamental needs does by no means amount to its genetic explanation. This does not seem to have been sufficiently realized by many psychologists. We agree with Allport that the actual motivation of the adult cannot be considered simply as a derivation of *infantile* desires; therefore adult motivation may be considered as functionally independent of *infantile* drives: nevertheless, this does not mean that the actual motive is dynamically independent and without any functional connection with *fundamental* needs. In our opinion infantile *and* adult desires are concrete manifestations of fundamental needs which take different aspects according to the differences in the relationships of infants and adults to their "world."

Let us elucidate our point of view by an example. According to psychoanalysis, the adult continues to carry in him the longing after the *infantile state* of being "secure" and protected by the warm sphere of motherly care. In our opinion, however, the fact that infantile elements are found to exist in the *adult* longing for security does not justify the explanation that this adult need is a derivation of infantile needs in man. The longing for security and for affectionate contact may be a "fundamental" need in the sense that it exists at any level of interaction between the human personality and his "world." This need manifests itself in childhood under certain aspects proper to the infantile state, i.e. in the attitude towards the parents. The man-woman relationship in adulthood arouses *other*, and functionally independent, expressions of the same need. Still other forms come about at the adult stage and may belong to the spiritual level of relationship between man and his "world"; they may reveal themselves as a desire to be "secure" in God. It is not necessary to consider these latter forms of the need as simple derivations from the infantile longing in order to explain the presence of infantile elements in them. The desire for protection in the *normal* adult is by no means longing for the infantile state; it is the need of the mature personality for "integration" and "nourishing" contact—a need rooted in the very way of being of man. Of course, later forms of this fundamentally human need may reveal analogies with the way it first appeared in the child. This does not prove that the dynamics of the need itself derive from the infantile state of being.[1]

This is a very important feature of the Freudian doctrine against which Allport very rightly reacted. But a sound theory of fundamental or basic needs does not explain human motivation genetically. *Fundamental* is not identical with *genetically coming first*. What is fundamental or basic in personality dynamics can only be discovered by examining the basic forms of relationship between man and his world, and by pointing out the profound resemblances in the dynamic orientations of the behaviour-patterns at the various stages of development. Fundamental needs are to be conceived as the specific forms of basic relationships which, at the different levels of interaction with the "world," seem to be necessary for the functional well-being of personality as a psychophysiological whole.

8. Inadequate Theories

Finally, we must draw attention to two essential omissions which, in our opinion, prevent many systems from giving a satisfactory account of man's psychic dynamism.

(1) HUMAN DYNAMISM AND THE THEORY OF EQUILIBRIUM

Man's psychic dynamism is often looked upon as a tendency towards equilibrium and rest. The destruction of the equilibrium causes tension and activity, and the aim of this activity is to re-establish the equilibrium. The break in the equilibrium gives rise to a condition of displeasure, and the activity is set in motion by the force which tends to re-establish the equilibrium and thus

---

[1] Yet it is certain that emotional and behavioural patterns *may* keep their genuinely infantile character and continue to exist as such in personalities who have not developed in a normal way, or whose development has been impeded. Still, once more, these *abnormal* conditions cannot serve as measures for the development of the normal personality.

put an end to the disagreeable state of tension. Man therefore tends essentially towards a state of repose and dynamic equilibrium.[1]

There is a great deal of truth in this idea; we mentioned it in our discussion of the biological level of psychic dynamism. Indeed, it is because a great number of dynamic theories of personality are based entirely on biology that the idea of a tendency towards equilibrium is so popular. On the other hand, as soon as human dynamism is considered in its entirety, one is struck by another aspect of the question. The human personality does not simply endeavour to reduce the tension created by a loss of organic equilibrium; the most striking fact about it is that it contains a *constructive* impulse which tends towards new realizations, and thus destroys the state of rest or equilibrium as soon as it has been reached. There is not merely an automatic break of biological equilibrium; but the constructive force which we mentioned earlier is always suggesting new ideals of human development. It is not, therefore, the mechanism behind the reduction of tension or need which should be our main concern; for the chief characteristic of the human mind is its inability to resign itself to "rest" and its active potentiality for "personal" construction and self-realization, as we have already explained.[2] To neglect this *constructive* aspect of human personality and see no more than a force tending to reduce an organic need or bring a disagreeable state of existence to an end, is to ignore the most specific element in the dynamic development of human personality. In several fields of his activity man does not tend directly towards pleasure or the avoidance of displeasure; he *desires to realize something.* The kind of pleasure which he experiences is frequently *that of having fulfilled his intention;* and his dissatisfaction—which may upset his whole mental balance—comes from not having realized the aim or plan which he had set himself. It is only by taking into account this double activity—constructive "realization" and the reduction of needs—that human dynamism can be understood in its entirety.

[1] Cf., amongst others, P. Symonds, *Dynamic Psychology* (New York, Appleton-Century, 1949).
[2] See pp. 171ff.

(2) HIGHER NEEDS AND SOCIALIZATION

There is a second and equally serious shortcoming which often prevents a satisfactory view of human personality: this concerns the insufficiency of the processes referred to in order to explain the existence of so-called "higher" needs. It is often considered sufficient to refer to the processes of *socialization* and *learning*. It is said that the fundamental needs must be rooted in the physiological bases of the organism (tissue needs), and the "higher" needs developed in the course of human existence are simply products of socialization, or of learning under the influence of social and cultural factors. This idea is very similar to the Freudian theory, according to which the super-ego, which *originates in society*, transforms the organic needs (in this case of libido) into "sublimated" forms. In both cases, *social* influences are supposed to transform organic needs into "higher" aspirations.

We have already pointed out the insufficiency, the superficiality, of this "explanation." Here we merely wish to emphasize the fact that this attitude has prevented a number of systems from developing satisfactory theories of human dynamism. To reach a full view of the forces or motives behind human behaviour it is essential to include the *new* and *irreducible* elements involved *in human culture and the process of human socialization*. Social influence can never be given as the ultimate explanation because it is in the human mind itself that the origin or basis of cultural and social construction must be looked for.

It should be noted that the problem of the reducibility of human needs to organic needs, either by means of socialization or sublimation, is not a question for positive psychology, any more than the problem of the reducibility of vital phenomena to chemical phenomena is a question of experimental biology. Positive psychology has to demonstrate in ever greater detail the action of organic and social factors on the origin and development of *every* human need. But the question of the reducibility or irreducibility of the *whole* of our human activity to any *single one of its levels* is a *theoretical* problem which every psychologist solves either avowedly or unavowedly with the help of a more or less consciously held philosophy.

Thus the philosophic problem of man is inevitably involved in any *general theory* of human dynamism, because our theories about the moving-forces in man depend on our ideas as to what he *is*.

In this book we have endeavoured to keep as close as possible to *objective fact*. But it must be realized that here, as in any other theory of the dynamic life of human personality, our ideas are not entirely founded on fact but partly on *implications* drawn from fact.

FINAL CONSIDERATIONS

---

1. The Place of Psychoanalysis in the Development of Contemporary Psychology

There are many people who still equate modern psychology with psychoanalysis. There are others for whom psychoanalysis is not a scientific system at all; they therefore either refuse to take it seriously or simply oppose it. Thus for both parties psychoanalysis exists in splendid isolation, apart from the rest of modern psychology.

These two points of view are quite out-of-date, as regards both the development of psychology in general and the development of psychoanalysis itself.

A. The contribution made by psychoanalysis to our idea of psychic life has been so important that its influence on the development of the whole of psychology will one day be obvious to everybody.

This influence has been exerted chiefly through clinical psychology. We have, we hope, shown that psychoanalytical ideas have entered deeply into clinical psychology, which in its turn has taken such an important place in psychological activity as a whole that its problems and lines of development now exercise a strong influence on psychological research in general.

The influence of clinical psychology on experimental psychology, and especially on the so-called psychology of behaviour, appears in various ways. Psychologists studying behaviour—Watson, Thorndike, for example—used to pay little attention to the dynamic factors in human personality, whereas at the present day concepts such as those of *need, satisfaction, frustration* are given a place of central importance even in the schools of Behaviorist psychology—as appears in the work of Clark Hull.[1]

It is the great merit of clinical psychology in general and psychoanalysis in particular to have brought into prominence the dynamic factors in behaviour.

It is under the influence of clinical psychology too that the idea of *personality* has recovered its true meaning in American psychology. Instead of being used simply to describe the individual as a meeting-place where various connections and forms of habit joined together, it now once again implies a dynamic and purposive unity, whence all human behaviour arises. From such a dynamic core behaviour draws both its meaning and its psychological unity.

The highly promising development of modern experimental psychology is characterized by the fact that human behaviour is increasingly being studied *in its real complexity as an interlocking structure of external form and internal meaning.* It is no longer the old "laboratory psychology," which was frequently so remote from man's real psychic existence. Scientific psychology is taking a firmer grasp on psychic life.

This development we owe in part to the *rediscovery of the dynamic element in personality as the source of behaviour and psychic life as a whole;* and for this we have clinical psychology to thank. It is also attributable in part *to social psychology,* and especially to *the increasing adoption of the social point of view in the study of behaviour.* Man's psychic life *takes place in society* as a *dynamic development* of his personality; it is not a complex of reactions to laboratory stimuli. It is *this social behaviour* which

[1] See Hull's last work, *Principles of Behavior* (New York, Appleton-Century, 1943) and *A Behavior System* (1953).

is coming more and more to be studied by experimental psychology. Even the specialized study of the various functions which make up behaviour—such as perception, memory, etc.—are feeling the influence of this global point of view of behaviour as a psychic unity. History will show that both social psychology and psychoanalysis have had an important influence in this direction by emphasizing the human personality as a dynamic unity.

B. Furthermore, psychoanalysis itself, as a result of its contact with the various experimental systems, is moving towards a new phase of development. We have shown how its ideas and theories are submitted to experimental research or revised in the light of experiment. Moreover, research into social and cultural psychology has forced Freudian ideas out of the narrow confines of the analyst's consulting room and made them relate to human situations and relationships in other kinds of environment: we mean the various kinds of research which we mentioned in our discussion of Freudian theory as working hypotheses—for instance, all the work on the Oedipus complex, the castration complex, sublimation, short and non-directive therapy.

This does not mean that orthodox psychoanalysis and the Freudian conception of man now exert only a tiny influence on contemporary analytical practice. In many cases the opposite is true. There are many schools of psychoanalysis in existence today which are more pan-sexualist and more dogmatic than Freud himself ever was, and in a far more superficial way. But in this book we have always had in mind "living" psychoanalysis, i.e. those developments which are not linked with Freudian teaching as a dogmatic doctrine but which simply regard it as an ordinary scientific system. This point of view is based on the belief that Freudism must as far as possible be integrated with psychology as a whole. And this contact with psychological research in general must lead it to a continual revising and perfecting of its own positions, as every living science does.

To sum up, the *rapprochement* between social psychology and clinical psychology, on the one hand, and experimental psychology, on the other, is the most promising line of development in contemporary psychology. Experimental psychology in general thus becomes a study of the totality of human behaviour and comes closer to real life, whilst clinical and social psychology go beyond their former empiricism and take on a more experimental character.

Implicit in all we have said is the belief that we should take up a constructive and not a negative critical attitude towards psychoanalysis, regarding it as an "open" system and not as the old "orthodoxy" which is gradually disappearing from the field of positive science.

11. Psychoanalysis and Psychology of the Total Personality

Our basic conception of man as a whole is always a philosophic attitude which, as such, does not enter *directly* into our positive study of behaviour and the dynamic structure behind it. Nevertheless, this conception of man determines the direction of one's positive psychological research and theory. This is a point we have mentioned in connection with Freud's own theories. Finding a complexity of elements in human behaviour, Freud *reduced* them all to one of them. It was in this way that Freudian "philosophy" turned psychoanalysis into a partial theory of human personality. Our own attitude throughout this book is opposed to this kind of reduction; it therefore may be called a *non-reductive conception of man*.[1] In this sense, our "philosophic" leanings—without entering into practical research—should make us capable of looking at man more comprehensively, and prevent us from doing violence to the complexity of the facts.

When, in this spirit of absolute respect for all the facts, we consider the data supplied by psychoanalysis, we discover that it has brought to light an aspect of man's psychic life whose *positive effects* had not been sufficiently noticed in traditional ways of thought.

Psychoanalysis thus presents us with a partial image of man

[1] In the French edition of this book, our *non-reductive* conception of man was called "conception *spiritualiste* de l'homme." In English, however, the term "spiritualistic" has a quite different meaning. By "spiritualiste" we only mean a personality theory in which the *specific human* components of behaviour are not systematically reduced to the so-called "lower" levels of activity. (Author's note.)

contrasting with the traditional picture, which ascribed far too large a rôle to the rational "*faculties*." Psychoanalysis has gone a long way towards helping us to realize the importance of the "lower" components in the sources of human behaviour. It has thus prepared the way for a psychology which will transcend these two partial conceptions and synthesize them in a more comprehensive picture of the whole man. Psychoanalysis itself, however, has not been able to produce this picture; on the contrary, it has entirely overlooked the hierarchical structure of psychic life by *reducing* all levels of activity to one of them. Nevertheless, it is not by rejecting psychoanalytical doctrine, but by making up for its deficiencies in a positive way with the help of general psychology, that we shall manage to create this fuller picture of human personality.

The second way in which contemporary psychology has come closer to the concrete reality of psychic life is through its deeper study of the interpenetration of the instinctive and the spiritual in human motivation. As regards the functions of knowledge, the substratum of *sense experience* lying beneath *intellectual* knowledge has already been subjected to deeper investigation. It has recently been emphasized in the experimental work of Professor Michotte, who shows in particular that the most fundamental ideas in our understanding, as for example, the concepts of *reality* and *causality*, do not only appear on the level of intellectual and metaphysical thought, but that the *perceptual forms* of these contents of knowledge already appear as immediate facts at pre-reflective levels of knowledge. The *concept* has its "preformation" in the content, *immediately given*, of our perceptive consciousness.[1]

The same thing is true of human *motivation*, which is never purely rational and spiritual.

In this very involved field of human needs and dynamics we must also reach a concrete view of the substructures which underlie our intellectual motives. This task can only be undertaken, not

[1] Cf. A. Michotte, "*La préfiguration de notre conception spontanée du monde physique dans les données sensorielles*" (summary). Proceedings of the 12th International Congress of Psychology, Edinburgh, 1948 (published in 1950). See, by the same author, "*La perception de la causalité*" (Louvain, Editions de l'Institut Supérieur de Philosophie, 1946).

by traditional psychology, which adopts an attitude of self-sufficiency and systematic denial of psychoanalysis, but by a general psychology of behaviour which is not afraid of supplementing its ideas and data about man by the manifold elements based on depth-psychology. In this way psychology will develop towards a fuller and more concrete conception of the complex unity of human personality.

III. A Theory of Normal Personality

Our chief aim throughout this book has been to sketch a dynamic theory of personality in which the different aspects of man's complex life are integrated into a harmonious whole. In the conviction that no theory of personality can be founded on exclusively pathological bases or in neglect of general experimental psychology, we have tried to envisage human motivation in a wider psychological perspective. The fundamental needs of man and the internal tension which characterizes psychic dynamism have thus appeared in a new light.

As a result of our study of the *internal conflict* in the psychic life of the normal man, the process of *repression* and the idea of of the *unconscious* have had their field of influence reduced. In their place we have tried to sketch a process of *constructive development of the personality*.

Furthermore, the reduction of psychic forces to one single dynamic element has appeared as theoretically an impoverishment, a result of faulty methods and hasty theories. It is essential to see that the whole complexity of human life is involved in the study of human motivation. Nothing is explained by appealing to processes or influences—the influence of culture or the process of socialization—which are themselves only explained by recourse to higher potentialities in the psychic life of the individual man.

Faced with the Freudian reduction of every constructive force in man to the libido, we have tried to emphasize, on the one hand, the irreducible complexity and, on the other, the inextricable interpenetration of the dynamic life of man. The system of fundamental needs which we have sketched shows clearly these two essential aspects of human "motivation." Progress in the study of personality will not be found in further attempts at *reduction*, but by an increasingly precise analysis of the many *components* which make up the unity and complexity of human life.

Instead of the theory of "instincts," we have suggested that *human needs* enter into the complexity of human life at all its different levels. Both as a spiritual being and as a biochemical organism man has needs. These different forms of need are involved with each other to form complex "motives" that release and govern human behaviour. They can do this "spontaneously," if the need is itself an active orientation, a heightened sensibility of the individual as a whole, towards certain "values." They can also do it when the whole personality becomes conscious of the state of need and develops it into an intentional act: in this case the need directs behaviour through the "personal" or "voluntary" attitude adopted by the spiritual ego towards a value. Thus, man endeavours to eat, and to give meaning to his life—either "spontaneously" or by virtue of a conscious "personal" attitude; in reality he is always involved in a process which is a combination of these two kinds of behaviour.

APPENDIX

BIBLIOGRAPHY

INDEXES

ADLER'S INDIVIDUAL PSYCHOLOGY

---

1. Introduction

In 1902 Alfred Adler, then a young psychiatrist, became closely acquainted with Freud, who had already laid the theoretical foundations of psychoanalysis and was on the point of founding a study circle. Adler, like many more of Freud's brilliant followers —Jung, Rank, Stekel—was for many years a member of this circle, of which he became secretary. Freud used to refer to him flatteringly as "the eagle" (der Adler). Adler, however, was never the kind of psychoanalyst to be led. He was particularly sceptical of Freud's general theory of sexuality, and up to 1911 was the centre of the small opposition group which existed at the very heart of psychoanalysis. In that year he openly broke with Freud.

In the next year, 1912, Adler published his book Über den nervösen Charakter, in which were the foundations of his own doctrine. This came to be known as "Individual Psychology" (Individualpsychologie).

In 1907 Adler had published an important study—Studie über die Minderwertigkeit von Organen—which was a sort of prelude to the major work of 1912

Adler's "Individual Psychology"—which must be clearly distinguished from "individual psychology" in Binet's sense—grew increasingly popular. Soon, books were appearing about it; it had its own magazine, *Zeitschrift für Individualpsychologie;* and many actual centres were founded in the great cities of Europe.

Adler's theoretical position, compared with Freud's, may be summed up as follows. He agrees with Freud in affirming the existence of unconscious forces which direct man's psychic life and can upset it. But the fundamental tendency is not, in his view, libido, or sexuality. It lies in the effort made by the whole person to assert himself: a drive towards the affirmation of his personality, a tendency to self-preservation, or a will to power (*Wille zur Macht*), in the Nietzschean sense of the term. A social democrat, Adler was more interested than Freud in the social aspect of man, and he realized that Freud's neglect of the social aspect meant an essential loss to his work.

Adler's originality—like Freud's—does not consist simply in his having discovered in the tendency towards self-assertion—as Freud did in the libido—essential dynamic forces in man. Ordinary psychology had already recognized this fact. The new element lay in the discovery of the many secret ways in which a tendency can enter into the whole field of human conduct and dominate it.

Before we give a brief description of the characteristic ideas of Individual Psychology, a few preliminary remarks are necessary.

1. Individual psychologists have not remained absolutely faithful to Adler's ideas any more than the psychoanalysts remained faithful to Freud, and their principles and definitions vary considerably. In our account of Individual Psychology we shall not therefore aim simply to reproduce the ideas of Adler himself, but to make a personal summary of what seems to us to be most valuable and useful in the system as a whole.

2. Individual Psychology has endeavoured to make its system scientific, relying as far as it possibly can on biology. It reckons to be able to base most of its fundamental suppositions on biology. But these are frequently so steeped in finalism and therefore so little in harmony with the spirit of modern biology that they remind us more of the phantasies of Lamarck than the ideas of modern science. This connection with biology—clearest, perhaps,

in the work of Erwin Wexberg, who made Individual Psychology into a complete system—has done more harm to the system than good. We shall not, however, be discussing this point.

3. We must finally draw attention to the fact that Adler is a far from systematic writer, and that his work is often deceptive because of its lack of logic and scientific basis. His books make it clear why it is that movements such as Individual Psychology have had difficulty in finding acceptance in scientific psychological circles.[1] Nevertheless, under its unscientific appearance it conceals a fund of interesting and important ideas, which we shall endeavour to describe as systematically as possible.

II. The Finalist Explanation

We must first endeavour to make clear the individual psychologist's way of thinking. Its fundamental characteristic is a finalism pushed to its most extreme conclusions. It considers the organism—in this case the psycho-physiological organism of man —as an indivisible unity, i.e. an *individual* (hence the term Individual Psychology). Within this individual everything is dominated and governed by the *immanent aim* of the organism itself, which is the preservation of its own existence. Adler endeavours to trace this effort towards self-preservation right through the whole life and conduct of man.

According to Individual Psychology, everything that is produced in man can be looked upon in two ways. The first can trace the *causal* explanation of each process and event, showing *how* the process unfolds, or the conditions under which the event appears; or one can seek out the *sense*, the meaning, of this process. This meaning only becomes clear when one adopts another point of view, that of *finality*.

It is only primarily by considering any event in the light of its utility for the organism or the *whole person* that we can *understand* it. The understanding of personality consists, therefore, in

---

[1] Adler never succeeded, for example, in obtaining a chair at the University of Vienna. His system was dismissed by the Council as being without scientific value; whilst Freud found increasing acceptance in the same circle.

realizing in all its manifestations the concrete aim pursued by the person.

In man this finality appears on three different planes. Adler distinguishes between biological finality, rational finality and what he calls "personal" finality. The human being is a psycho-physiological being, and so we discover finality both on the biological and the psychic planes. But the finality which exists on the psychic plane is not simply conscious or *rational*, though it exists on this plane too as a complex of aims consciously pursued; it is also situated at a deeper unconscious level, and this, for Individual Psychology, is the more important of the two. This is the "personal" finality just mentioned.

Biological finality and *rational finality* need no further explanation; but to grasp the importance of *personal* finality we must remember what personality is. For depth-psychology, personality is not the same thing as the conscious ego. At a deeper level than the conscious ego lies the *"Selbst"* or self, the deepest core of the whole (psycho-physiological) personality. The conscious ego is only a small part appearing at a superficial level of psychic life.

Finality is the fundamental law of this deepest personality. This finality is not the rational finality of the conscious ego, nor the purely biological finality of the bodily organism. It exists at a deeper level than these and constitutes the absolute foundation of human personality. It is a *"personal" finality*.

The whole method of Individual Psychology is dominated by this fundamental idea *that personal finality ultimately dominates and determines everything that happens in man*. The rational finality of the conscious ego is subordinate to it, and biological finality may, in Adler's expression, be deviated (*"umfinalisiert"*) by it. By this, Adler means that biological functions may develop a new final meaning as a result of an effort towards a *personal* object. Thus an organic reaction—tears or illness, for example—may acquire, in addition to its finality in the biological order, a new final meaning in the light of the object *aimed at by the person.* One may recall, for instance, our example of the man living in community, who felt he should be the exception to the rule because he was ill. In this example, the organic illness was subordinate to the personal finality according to which the man endeavoured to assert himself by concentrating the attention and care of other people on himself.[1]

The general method of Individual Psychology will therefore be based on an *analysis of finality*, which aims to understand the sense or meaning of conduct and character by considering them in the light of personal finality.

III. The Tendency to Self-assertion and the Feeling of Community (Gemeinschaftsgefühl)

Let us now take a closer look at the contents of this system. How does Individual Psychology account for the development of human behaviour?

Fundamental to the whole personality, we have said, there exists an immanent finality: the preservation of self.

It is not only the biological organism and the conscious ego which tend thus to preserve themselves, but also and above all, the *Selbst*, the profound core of personality which is governed by this same law.

On the other hand, every child lives his early years under circumstances which impress upon him very strongly the fact of his *dependence on others*. For much longer than any animal he is dependent upon his parents and incapable of pursuing his own life in the complex society developed by man. Even when his spiritual faculties and conscious ego begin to develop, he experiences all kinds of desires which are quite unrealizable. There are many things which the child sees and longs for which he cannot have—no doubt by crying he often gets what he wants, but even this method doesn't always come off!

At the same time he discovers that the adults, whom he is gradually managing to make out around him, enjoy a much better state of affairs than his own. They simply have to stretch out their gigantic arms, and there within their grasp are all the things which he reaches for in paroxysms of desire, but in vain. Thus he comes to experience his dependence and powerlessness as a state

[1] See above, pp. 133–134.

of *inferiority* compared to theirs. He is their *inferior;* they are his *superiors.*

In reaction, there is born in his unconscious depths a drive towards superiority. The child finds himself in the *predicament* of either having to assert his individuality, or being psychically drowned in the mass of "superior" beings. This is the foundation, the universal source, of the drive *to assert one's personality, to assert oneself:* under the influence of the feeling of inferiority, the fundamental need—that of *self-preservation*—is changed and converted into an *impulse of self-assertion,* a "will to power." The child wants to be superior because it feels inferior; it wants to protect and ensure its own place on the psychic level because it feels itself to be menaced. In the language of Individual Psychology, the child *seeks compensation for its inferiority feeling.*

Such is the first aspect of the dynamism of psychic life. There is, however, another aspect. Man is not only an *individual;* he is also, from mere biological necessity, a *communal being;* and for this reason there exists in him, besides the feeling of personality, an innate feeling of community.

This community feeling must be understood in the widest sense. It is the faculty of not existing "for oneself" alone, but of being able *to go out of oneself* and give oneself to something, or submit to reality. It is therefore to be found at the root of objective thought, altruism, the feeling of responsibility—in short, everything in man that has an objective value.

In the early stages of life this community feeling is very slight. In the child, egocentricism is the predominant force—which, too, is a result of biological necessity: the child has not yet anything to give, and therefore must first of all live parasitically and demand everything for himself.

This community feeling, present in its full power in the adult man, is an ideal towards which the child has to evolve. The ideal development of the personality lies at the end of the development of the community feeling—i.e., this development has to start from the egocentric feeling of personality and open out increasingly into a more social sense of personality. The feeling of personality and the drive to assert oneself naturally cannot be avoided; in fact, they are the foundation of the personality. But the chief problem raised by human development is *whether the individual can assert himself at the community level*, i.e. where social demands are made on him which are objectively valuable, or whether he will remain self-enclosed in his egocentricity. If the latter process takes place, the individual will assert himself for his own sake alone, at an imaginary level of unreality, responding to illusory demands or even falling into pathological aberrations.

And here we come to the crucial and also the most difficult stage in the development of the personality—difficult, because a certain self-confidence is needed from the very beginning, to go out from oneself for the first time on to the communal plane of effective realization. It is only the person with a certain amount of self-confidence who will have the *Mut zur Hingabe*, the courage to "give himself." A lack of such courage, a lack of self-confidence, lies at the root of all disturbances of psychic development.

Such are the two dynamic aspects of man, and the two directions along which he can develop. We shall now investigate what it is that determines the particular line of development which a man follows, i.e. the way in which he realizes his own tendency to assert himself.

iv. Environment and Psychic Development

According to Adler it is not so much heredity as factors of environment, circumstance, concrete experiences, personal history (especially childhood), which are decisive in a man's life. It is therefore the concrete circumstances in which an individual has lived his life that provide the material for understanding the development of his psychic life.

It is in a context of personal experiences that the fundamental tendency of self-assertion *takes a strictly personal form*. This personal form involves a *plan of life*, an individual *style of life*. These are simply the personal form of the tendency towards self-preservation and self-assertion; the dynamic unconscious source of every form of individual behaviour. Man's later conduct will be fashioned according to this plan and style of life.

1. INFERIORITY FEELING AND COMPENSATION

It is impossible for reasons of space to go into detail here concerning the specific influence of every single one of the innumerable concrete circumstances of life, from which Individual Psychology has managed with a considerable amount of success to deduce a wide variety of traits typical of personality.

We shall content ourselves with pointing out as typical, those categories of circumstances whose influence is especially important. The first category consists of all kinds of bodily deficiencies and infirmities, which *to the extent that they are experienced psychologically* can have a special influence on the feeling of inferiority.

Adler attaches equal importance to the difference between the sexes, as experienced psychologically. A boy, for instance, he says, discovers very early in life, from things his parents say and from the way they behave, that he is superior to girls. Thus, for example, he is always hearing things like: "A little boy doesn't cry"; "You're behaving like a girl"; "A little boy shouldn't be afraid of pain"; "A little boy ought to be able to do that," and so on. Thus the words "man" and "boy" become the equivalent of "strong" or "superior," whilst "girl" and "woman" take on the meaning of "weak" or "inferior."

This reinforces the little girl's feeling of inferiority, for which she may try to find compensation in the wish to be a man. This Adler calls the *masculine protest*. Or a woman may try to assert herself by means of her very weakness, i.e. get herself helped and "allow" others to surround her with attentions. Hence—the two types of woman: the "strong" masculine woman; the "weak" feminine woman. The masculine protest and the "feminine" type of behaviour are both equally effective as a means to the attainment of the desired end. A woman can succeed by either of these means in asserting herself and making herself a centre of interest. Adler sees in the masculine protest the basis of the movement for the emancipation of women.

In the boy, on the other hand, the idea of masculine superiority sometimes gives rise to a masculine ideal which is so high that it is far beyond his capacity. For instance, when he is a child, he will often find that he is unable to stop crying, however much he may be told that a *proper* little boy shouldn't cry; and he thus goes through the further experience of realizing that he cannot behave like a *proper* little boy. Later on he may be called upon to do all kinds of things which lie beyond his capacity. In the moral domain he may be highly esteemed by his teachers and parents, whilst he feels himself inside to be a great sinner. Such "model" little boys suffer enormously from the contrast, real or imagined (through excessive scrupulosity, for instance), between what others think of them and what they themselves in their innermost hearts imagine themselves to be. It also happens that fathers may project an ideal which they have been unable to realize themselves on to their sons, and thus ask the boy to follow a path which does not suit him, attributing to him qualities which he does not possess. Circumstances like this can in extreme cases have very serious consequences: the boy is led either to distrust himself or to lead a *double life:* he feels in his innermost being incapable of realizing the image imposed on him by social life. A situation of this kind can provoke in a child or a young man high states of tension, which may be the beginning of abnormal forms of behaviour.

Individual Psychology even sees in these situations in which man distrusts his masculinity the explanation of many sexual aberrations and perversities. Thus Adler gives a totally different explanation of most sexual aberrations from that given by psychoanalysts. According to Individual Psychology, the "Don Juan" type of man, for instance, is the type of person who unconsciously but fundamentally doubts his own masculinity, and for this reason seeks compensation in a never-ending series of amorous conquests and extravaganzas. Unconsciously he is continually trying to persuade himself that he has the masculine power to conquer the female. There are, on the other hand, people who evade *effective* "conquest," and here we meet the sexual pervert. In the feeling of inferiority and the unconscious fear of failing in amorous affairs an explanation is to be found, for instance, of certain kinds of homosexuality.[1]

[1] By way of example we can describe briefly a case which we had the opportunity to analyse in detail; the case of a young man with a tendency to seduce boys and youths. In his imagination he would see girls present

There are other circumstances which have an influence on this inferiority feeling; for example, *the family circumstances in which the individual develops*. The fact of being an only child, or being the eldest or the youngest, or again, of being one of many—all these circumstances influence psychic development, as Individual Psychology endeavours to show. The social and economic situation of the family, the kind of education, etc., likewise affect character.

2. SUCCESS AND FAILURE

The more the original feeling of inferiority develops, under the influence of events of this kind, into unconscious forms of an inferiority *complex*, the more the conscious and unconscious drive towards compensation is reinforced; for the individual who feels inferior tries in some way or other to find compensation for his feeling. This is the fundamental law of self-preservation on the psychic plane.

When a child tries to realize some demand in order to affirm his personality, either he *succeeds*, or at least gets an encouraging result, or else he *fails*, and his failure can be so extreme that he thereupon loses all confidence in himself.

Individual Psychology gives copious illustration of this process, using events which though apparently insignificant exercise a decisive influence during the early years of childhood.

It can happen, for example, that people may encourage a child to walk, or to realize some other childish achievement of a similar kind, in such a way that the child easily overcomes his first failures and is soon able to go on his way with full confidence in himself.

---

during his activities with these boys. His greatest pleasure was to "see" the girls humiliated by these homosexual relationships. The most exciting thing for him was to show the girls *that he did not need them*. As a child he had frequently been "let down" and humiliated by girls and begun to hate them for this reason. Later, his greatest pleasure was to hurt other girls, imagining that he was thus revenging himself on one particular girl who had most deeply humiliated him. Furthermore, he was considered "girlish" by the boys he knew because of his rather feminine appearance. He bitterly regretted not looking more manly and later began to doubt whether he would ever be able to behave "like a man." All this—fear of failure, and hatred—drove him away from girls and towards homosexuality.

It can also happen, however, that a mistake or failure on the child's part will cause the adults, and particularly the mother, so much anxiety, that the failure is given far too much emphasis: the mother's anxiety prevents the child from overcoming his difficulties, and his courage and intrepidity are thereupon considerably weakened.

We therefore find ourselves faced with two possibilities, two lines of development, which are determined by concrete experiences of all kinds that take place during the first years of childhood. The first line leads to a healthy development through effective achievement and the feeling of community. The individual then succeeds in asserting himself on the social plane *by the sort of realizations that have an objective value*. The second line, on the other hand, leads to an avoidance of real life or social life. This is the cause behind all kinds of psychic disturbances and conflicts. The fundamental tendency of the human psyche to become a centre of interest then has to make use of *unconscious détours* in its efforts to attain its object in the end and in spite of everything; the normal inferiority feeling becomes an *inferiority complex*, and this has a strong unconscious influence on the whole of the individual's behaviour.

v. The Mechanism of Psychic Disturbances

1. OVERCOMPENSATION

What we have just said will help us to understand the mechanism behind conflicts and disturbances which arise from the inferiority complex. The individual is caught in an impasse. His inferiority feeling increases with every failure, and by this very fact his need for compensation—and for compensations which are ever greater —becomes more and more of a necessity. The more the individual feels inferior, the more he needs to effect extraordinary achievements to assert himself in his own eyes. This is the process of *overcompensation*.

On the other hand, repeated failures take away his self-confidence and the courage necessary to realize those achievements. Thus, the fear of failure makes him less and less capable of doing whatever may be required of him on the social plane, and whilst he needs to realize extraordinary things to recover his equilibrium and fulfil his dreams of greatness, he becomes incapable of the effort needed for doing the least thing.

A transposition on to the plane of unreality then takes place— i.e., into the sphere of phantasy, the non-social, the more or less pathological. What the depths of the personality cannot realize on the level of *effective* realization, it attempts to find *by means of détours*. In extreme cases such détours lead to symptoms of neurosis and in less abnormal circumstances to the various kinds of "queer" conduct engaged in by the "difficult" characters whom most of us have learnt to put up with in others.

Two examples will help to clarify this process. Adler describes the case of a student brought up very ambitiously by his father and who asserted himself at school by always being top of the form. This was the boy's ambition—always to be first. The father noticed that during adolescence his son began to behave queerly in all sorts of ways, especially that he avoided company and kept more and more to himself. Nevertheless, he went on studying hard and remained top of the form. His queer characteristics developed to such an extent that finally he avoided any sort of human company whatsoever. The father then went to a psychiatrist. During the private conversation with the doctor, it appeared that the boy thought that his ears were far too small and that he was far too ugly to appear in company. The doctor then pointed out that there was absolutely no truth in these ideas at all, but then the boy remarked on the ugliness of his teeth, his hair, etc. There was absolutely no truth in this either.

Psychological analysis revealed a further fact. The boy was convinced that he could not be just like others; he had to prove his own worth, especially in his studies. To do this he was ready to risk everything. But a rival had appeared on the scene, and his usual hard work and keenness no longer seemed likely to assure him his first place. The boy, feeling his position threatened, had begun to distrust himself.

He had increasingly eliminated from his life all the things unconnected with work, and avoided all contacts with his equals, so that he could devote his whole time to his work. The depths of his personality, in fact, demanded these renunciations, so that he should achieve his object.

That this kind of behaviour was unreasonable, *the boy's consciousness could never have accepted as true.* The depths of the personality exerted their influence on the unconscious in such a way that the boy was unaware of the real cause of his conduct. By this unconscious route the personal finality was quietly achieving its object. Meanwhile, the boy had developed an utterly different reason to explain and justify his behaviour at the level of conscious motivation.

Another kind of case is far more common. A woman of nearly fifty was always complaining about the enormous burden imposed on her by having to look after the house. The whole thing weighed on her—and she was, in actual fact, weighed down by a variety of jobs. However, she would always refuse any offers to lighten her load, maintaining that nobody else could possibly do her job for her, and that she could not afford to neglect any of the things she was doing.

The fundamental point of the problem was this. As a result of the inferiority feeling, which is often stronger in a woman than in a man, a woman is often very unsure of herself and of the place she occupies in the minds of the people surrounding her.

An aging woman especially feels her position threatened, either as regards her relationship with her husband, or in connection with the maintenance of her house. By complaining about her work, this woman was *unconsciously* trying to achieve this object: she was trying to get the important and *irreplaceable* rôle she fulfilled at home recognized. She had the impression that others did not sufficiently appreciate her work, and this was the reason that she rejected so energetically any offer of making her task lighter. Only repeated gratitude for the things she did, and the irreplaceable part she played, could satisfy her.

2. THE CAMOUFLAGE OF FAILURE

The two examples we have quoted show one type of "détour" by means of which the individual maintains his position; in these cases the individual risks everything so that he may remain in the position he has reached. But there exists another way, by means of which the individual uses one pretext or another *to cover his retreat and retire from effective combat.*

Thus, for example, there was a university student who was regularly hindered in his studies and prevented from taking his examinations because of headaches. He was a very capable youth, and he suffered a great deal from the situation, which was endangering his career. A doctor tried all sorts of treatment, but unsuccessfully. During his school days this boy had always been first in his class. In the last year, at the New Year, one of his classmates had beaten him, and it was then that the headaches had begun. These prevented him from taking the examinations at the end of the year. Individual Psychology would explain this case in the following way: it would not deny that the headaches could have a certain objective foundation, but it would say *that the personal finality is exploiting or at least utilizing the weakness of some organ in order to attain its fundamental object.* The détour used in this case by the student is the opposite of that used in our previous example. It is a means of *escape from combat;* the headaches serve as a cover for retreat.

But how does the boy manage to save his prestige and satisfy his tendency towards self-assertion? Here is the unconscious reasoning, if it can be called such, behind the process. If the boy agrees to enter into competition with his classmates, he may lose his first place. In this case there will be a fear of failure. If he loses his first place he will be defeated in his own eyes and in the eyes of others. There is one way out which allows him to avoid this situation and to preserve his prestige without running any risk of failure. This way out is by way of circumstances which have nothing to do with his own will or his personal capacities—an illness, for example, will prevent him from achieving *what he could have achieved if the illness had not existed.* He thus preserves the illusion—and everybody else agrees with him—that he *would* undoubtedly *have been* first if his headaches had not prevented him from realizing what he was capable of.

In a number of people the fear of failure plays a great part in the development of their character and their general attitude towards life. Thus, for example, children (or adults) will make it a great point of honour to accomplish all that they have to do in the way of work or study with a great air of *nonchalance*. They want to avoid giving others the impression that they *are* really *trying hard* at anything. They are never really doing their best, and seem to take nothing with absolute seriousness, but are careless about everything, making jokes and mocking.

Very often these are people who fundamentally can neither give themselves absolutely to anything nor do their very best, because unconsciously they are not sure of being able to achieve anything: they are afraid of failing or of making less progress than others. The best way of never experiencing a real failure is *never to give oneself completely to any task*. Unconsciously, they so arrange things that their failure will be attributed by others not to their lack of ability but to their indifference. People must be heard to say, "If he wanted to he could easily have done it." Thus fear of failure makes lives less fruitful, and even sterile. This situation means that the person becomes incapable, both because of his character and because of his attitude of mind, of being absolutely involved in anything and applying himself to it wholeheartedly.[1]

---

[1] This attitude not only lies behind a great number of scholastic failures but also beyond many moral lapses, too. For instance, we have known many cases of youths failing to overcome the habit of masturbation on account of this sort of psychological attitude. Faced with this habit, and the sense of moral defeat that went with it, they had unconsciously adopted a defensive attitude towards it, a hypocritical defence of their own personality by means of a movement of "unconcern." So that this habit and these moral lapses should not be experienced as real failures, they had "pretended" not to care about them—i.e., during their adolescence they had not succeeded in dissociating themselves from them; they took no account of them in their estimation of their own personality: the acts did not involve their self-concept. This attitude prevented them from becoming involved "personally" to the depths of their being in the struggle against the habit. So long as they thus defended themselves psychologically against their failures by an attitude of "unconcern" they were incapable of fighting effectively against the habit. They were unable to "begin," because that would assume that their personality was totally engaged in the struggle—and if this had been so, the moral lapses would have become real personal failures for them. As long as they "kept themselves out of it," their self-concept remained intact. This is an example of the many *defence-mechanisms of the ego*: the mechanism in question having its origin in a fear of failure and hence in the weakness of the ego. It saps positive activity and makes any *real* expansion of the personality impossible, so as to protect it in an "idealized" imaginary world.

There is another category of people who try to assert themselves in a negative way by criticizing everything done by others, while they content themselves with saying how it should have been done.

vi. Psychotherapy and the Rôle of the Unconscious

It is important to realize the essential part played by the *unconscious* in all these cases. The *conscious* ego could not, in fact, accept such "détours" and retreat from life as a means of attaining its aim. These détours can only become efficacious in the personality to the extent that the *conscious* person is unaware of what is really going on.

Thus the essential principle in the *therapeutic method* is for the psychologist to try to *get the patient to understand* the secret psychic processes and *give him courage and self-confidence*, so that he may exist and develop in a normal way.

In the examples we have quoted we have tried to remain as close as possible to normal life. But the same processes appear in more marked pathological conditions. Individual Psychology maintains that symptoms such as attacks of melancholia, fainting fits, asthma, stammering, and neurotic troubles of all kinds, are essentially *effective means used* by the depths of the personality to reach its fundamental aim by leaving the level of social reality. As a result of such morbid phenomena the patient manages to concentrate all the attention of the family circle upon herself. Everybody is concerned about her.[1] Whilst in other circumstances the same morbid symptoms can constitute an excellent pretext for avoiding competition with others, so that there will not be any danger of being beaten.

All this goes to show that Individual Psychology, the psychology of the "will to power," is principally the psychology of the man who feels *inferior and powerless:* the man who cannot face up to life. Adler's system shows us, behind the mask of the strong, powerful male, the profound picture of a timid, hesitant child.

We remember, in this connection, a passage in the *Confession de Minuit* by Duhamel, in which the author, in the person of Salavin,

[1] See the example quoted, p. 132.

presents the picture of the poverty-stricken child hiding behind the mask of a man. When, tired of struggling with life, Salavin comes back home one evening, he feels on his face the whole weight of the social mask. Driven by an unexpressed desire to recover his true countenance, he goes to see his old mother. For her he is still the little child who needs her love. Salavin confesses, "If I was a general and had lost a great battle, I would go to my mother, and my mother would say to me, 'Don't cry. It isn't as serious as all that. I will give you a piece of chocolate.' And the strange thing is," adds Salavin, "that that bit of chocolate possesses all the virtues which the poor woman gives it. That bit of chocolate would console me."

This passage shows us one of the fundamental characteristics of Individual Psychology. It is the psychology of the powerless child hidden behind the mask of the general.

We shall not endeavour to criticize the Adlerian psychology here. As we have summarized it, it undeniably presents us with a large part of the truth, and it is of great help in psychotherapy. As for the notion of the *unconscious* to which Adler refers, our remarks in Chapter IV apply equally to his theory. The confession of the woman patient reported earlier confirms our belief that many of the contents called *unconscious* by depth-psychology are simply elements found on the most intimate level of psychic life, elements which have not been integrated into the social forms of the personality.

We have also shown that the poverty-stricken child who exists in the depths of every man is not simply a survivor from infancy. We touch here upon a *fundamental need for protective contact*, which enters into the whole man at all levels of his psychic life, and which is rooted in the actual metaphysical structure of his personality.

SUGGESTIONS FOR BIBLIOGRAPHY

These few bibliographical notes aim to give the reader some idea of the vast amount of literature that exists about depth-psychology and the psychological study of the human personality. From this literature, which varies greatly in quality and value, we have made a fairly narrow selection of important works. Even as regards psychoanalysis, our suggestions hardly go beyond the limits of a mere guide to reading. Our aim has been to give those wishing to specialize in this field a preliminary idea of the literature that exists, as an introduction towards a fuller study.

It is highly desirable for the reader to study these works in the original. For this reason, in each case we give the name of the original publication before that of the translation.

1. Psychoanalysis

(a) FREUD

Readers who wish to begin their study of psychoanalysis through Freud's own work will do well to read first:

FREUD, S., *Selbstdarstellung* (1925).[1] *Gesammelte Werke chronologisch geordnet* (London, Imago Publishing Co.), Vol. XIV,

[1] After the title of the book we give the date of the first edition.

pp. 31–96. A separate edition of this small book has appeared: *Selbstdarstellung* (London, Imago Publishing Co., 1946). In translation: *An Autobiographical Study*, trs. James Strachey (London, Hogarth Press, 1935).

Next, the two courses of lectures should be read:

FREUD, S., *Vorlesungen zur Einführung in die Psychoanalyse* (1916). *Gesammelte Werke*, XI. In translation: *Introductory Lectures on Psychoanalysis*, trs. Joan Rivière (London, George Allen & Unwin, 1922).

—— *Neue Folge der Vorlesungen zur Einführung in die Psycho-analyse* (1932). *Gesammelte Werke*, XV. In translation: *New Introductory Lectures on Psycho-Analysis*, trs. W. J. H. Sprott (London, Hogarth Press, 1933).

After these "introductions," the following books, which are essential to an understanding of Freud, may be more profitably studied:

FREUD, S., *Die Traumdeutung* (1899). *Gesammelte Werke, II* and *III*. In translation: *Interpretation of Dreams* (London, George Allen & Unwin). (A new translation of this work, by James Strachey, is in preparation.)

—— *Drei Abhandlungen zur Sexualtheorie* (1905). *Gesammelte Werke*, V, pp. 27–145. In translation: *Three Essays on the Theory of Sexuality*, trs. James Strachey (London, Imago Publishing Co., 1949).

—— *Jenseits des Lustprinzips* (1920). *Gesammelte Werke*, XIII, pp. 1–169. In translation: *Beyond the Pleasure Principle*, trs. James Strachey (London, Hogarth Press, 1950).

The "Introductory Lectures on Psychoanalysis" already mentioned contain an adequate treatment of the analysis of "slips of memory," etc. Readers specially interested in this field, which is the aspect of psychoanalysis most easily grasped, should consult:

FREUD, S., *Zur Psychopathologie des Alltagslebens* (*Über Vergessen, Versprechen, Vergreifen, Aberglaube und Irrtum*) (1904). *Gesammelte Werke*, IV. In translation: *The Psychopathology of Everyday Life* (London, Ernest Benn).

In this context should also be mentioned:

FREUD, S., *Der Witz und seine Beziehung zum Unbewussten* (1905). *Gesammelte Werke*, VI. In translation: *Wit and Its Relation to the Unconscious,* trs. Prof. A. A. Brill (London, Routledge and Kegan Paul). (This book is out-of-print.)

As regards the other special fields of human activity which psychoanalysis has endeavoured to interpret in the light of its own theories, we give the following principal categories:

1. Religion: Freud's ideas on this subject will be found in the following three essays:

FREUD, S., *Totem und Tabu* (1912). *Gesammelte Werke,* IX. In translation: *Totem and Taboo,* trs. James Strachey (London, Routledge and Kegan Paul).

—— *Das Unbehagen in der Kultur* (1930). *Gesammelte Werke,* XIV, pp. 419–506. In translation: *Civilization and Its Discontents,* trs. Joan Rivière (London, Hogarth Press, 1930).

—— *Die Zukunft einer Illusion* (1927). *Gesammelte Werke,* XIV, pp. 320–380. In translation: *The Future of an Illusion,* trs. W. D. Robson-Scott (London, Hogarth Press, 1928).

See also, for the Jewish religion, the last book published during Freud's lifetime: *Moses, sein Volk und die monotheistische Religion. Gesammelte Werke,* XVI. In translation: *Moses and Monotheism,* trs. Katherine Jones (London, Hogarth Press, 1939).

2. Art: For the psychoanalysis of art, see, amongst others:

FREUD, S., *Eine Kindheitserinnerung des Leonardo da Vinci* (1910). *Gesammelte Werke,* VIII, pp. 127–211. In translation: *Leonardo da Vinci,* trs. Prof. A. A. Brill (London, Routledge and Kegan Paul).

—— *Der Moses der Michelangelo* (1914). *Gesammelte Werke,* X, pp. 172–201.

The contributions of Otto Rank are also essential to a proper understanding of this field. The following should be consulted:

RANK, O., *Der Künstler und andere Beiträge zur Psychoanalyse des dichterischen Schaffens* (Vienna, Internationaler Psychoanalytischer Verlag, 1925⁴).

Also worth studying are:

BAUDOUIN, C., *Psychanalyse de l'art* (Paris, Alcan, 1929).

3. Culture: For the psychoanalytical study of culture in general, see especially the magazine *Imago* (see below); also the works of Otto Rank, e.g.:

RANK, O., *Psychoanalytische Beiträge zur Mythenforschung* (Vienna, Internationaler Psychoanalytischer Verlag, 2nd ed., 1922).

From amongst the great number of publications which have appeared in *Imago* two are specially worth mentioning:

"Philosophisches Heft," *Imago*, 1923, IX (Heft 3).
"Ethnologisches Heft," *Imago*, 1924, X (Heft 2–3).

Among the most recent works in the whole field:

ROHEIM, GEZA, *Psychoanalysis and Anthropology* (New York, International Universities Press).

A great part of the work of Carl Jung is, of course, devoted to the investigation of unconscious psychological factors in the manifestations of human culture. See, below, the bibliography of JUNG.

In this connection, mention should be made of an important psychoanalytical study of certain democratic and totalitarian tendencies in our *present civilization*, written by a non-Freudian psychoanalyst:

FROMM, E., *Escape from Freedom* (New York, Farrar & Rinehart, 1941).

4. Method: For a more concrete idea of Freud's method and way of working, certain detailed accounts of actual analyses must be read. We suggest the two following:

FREUD, S., *Bruchstück einer Hysterie-Analyse* (1905). *Gesammelte Werke*, V, pp. 161–286.
—— *Analyse der Phobie eines Fünfjährigen Knaben* (1909). *Gesammelte Werke*, VII, pp. 241–377.

5. Technique: For Freud's technique, treated rather more *ex professo*, see the essays:

FREUD, S., *Ratschläge für den Arzt bei der psychoanalytischen Behandlung* (1912). *Gesammelte Werke*, VIII, pp. 376–387.
—— *Zur Einleitung der Behandlung* (1913). *Gesammelte Werke*, VIII, pp. 454–478. (The original edition of this work appeared under the title: *"Weitere Ratschläge zur Technik der Psychoanalyse,"* in the *Internationale Zeitschrift für ärztliche Psychoanalyse*, 1913–15, I, II, III.

—— *Die Frage der Laienanalyse* (*Unterredungen mit einem Un-parteiischen*) (1926). *Gesammelte Werke*, XIV, pp. 207–296.

The contributions of several of Freud's followers are also important for the study of psychoanalytical technique; amongst others, those of S. Ferenczi. See especially:

FERENCZI, S., *Further Contributions to the Theory and Technique of Psychoanalysis* (London, Institute of Psychoanalysis and Hogarth Press, 1926).

Also the handbook by one of Ferenczi's pupils:

LORAND, S., *Technique of Psychoanalytic Therapy* (New York, International Universities Press, 1946).

For the technique (and theory) of short therapy, see the important book:

ALEXANDER, F. and FRENCH, T., *Psychoanalytic Therapy* (New York, The Ronald Press, 1946).

6. History: For the history of psychoanalysis the following are interesting:

FREUD, S., *Zur Geschichte der psychoanalytischen Bewegung* (1914). *Gesammelte Werke*, X, pp. 43–113. In translation: *History of the Psychoanalytic Movement*. See *Basic Writings of Sigmund Freud*.

7. Freud the Man: The following are of interest:

SACHS, H., *Freud, Master and Friend* (London, Imago Publishing Co., 1945).

REIK, THEODOR, *From Thirty Years with Freud* (New York, International Universities Press).

Certain writers have tried to psychoanalyse Freud himself, and the complexes which lie behind his system and attitude of mind, e.g.:

MAYLAN, *Freuds Tragischer Komplex, Eine Analyse der Psychoanalyse* (München, 1929).

PUNER, HELEN, *Freud, His Life and Mind* (London, Grey Walls Press, 1949).

As regards the large edition of Freud's Complete Works, we mentioned in our Preface the most recent and most complete edition of the original texts: *Gesammelte Werke chronologisch geordet*, 1940–

1952. It comprises seventeen volumes; an eighteenth will contain the indexes. There is already a full alphabetical index at the end of each volume.

The first complete edition of Freud's works appeared under the title: *Sigmund Freud, Gesammelte Schrifte*, published in eleven volumes (1925–1928) under the direction of Freud himself, by the Internationaler Psychoanalytischer Verlag (Vienna). A twelfth volume was added in 1934; it contains the publications of 1928–1933 and two *Nachträge*.

As we said at the beginning, Freud's works should, whenever possible, be read in the original; the many translations often do not give an exact rendering of the precise shades of meaning in his thought.

There is, however, a good translation of all the important works into English, in the series: *Sigmund Freud, Selected Writings* (New York, The International Psychoanalytical Library), of which the fifth and final volume appeared recently (1950). Freud's papers are translated in the five-volume publication: *Collected Papers* (London, The International Psychoanalytical Library, The Hogarth Press). Six important books of Freud are included in the one volume: *Basic Writings of Sigmund Freud;* it contains: "Interpretation of Dreams"; "Psychopathology of Everyday Life"; "Three Contributions to the Theory of Sex"; "Relation of Wit to the Unconscious"; "Totem and Taboo"; and "The History of the Psychoanalytic Movement."

A complete edition of Freud's works in 25 volumes is announced: the *Freud Memorial Edition*. It will, however, take years to complete this edition, which will be sold in sets only.

(*b*) GENERAL BIBLIOGRAPHY

There is no space to mention here the works by Freud's chief followers. For a full bibliography of these writers and of psychoanalysts in general we refer to bibliographical lists already in existence, particularly:

RICKMAN, J., *Index Psychoanalyticus*, 1893–1926 (London, Hogarth Press, 1928). This bibliography includes the titles of nearly 4,000 books, and may be regarded as a more or less complete index to the literature of psychoanalysis up to 1926.

Moreover, the International Universities Press announces the publication of:

GRINSTEIN, ALEXANDER, *The Psychoanalytic Index*. A complete listing of the entire psychoanalytical literature in all languages, with English translations and a topical cross-index.

There is a good selection of books published on psychoanalysis up to 1932 in:

DE LA VAISSIÈRE, J., *La théorie psychanalytique de Freud*, Archives de Philosophie, Vol. VIII, cahier 1. New edition, 1932, pp. 104-127.

It is essential for anyone wishing to understand psychoanalysis not to be content merely with the work of Freud and his immediate followers. Besides the works already mentioned it is necessary to study current literature in the many psychoanalytical journals. Amongst the best known of the older ones are:

Internationale Zeitschrift für Psychoanalyse. Offizielles Organ der Internationalen Psychoanalytischen Vereinigung. Vienna. (Founded in 1913 and published under the direction of Freud himself.) Volumes I-V have appeared under the title *Internationale Zeitschrift für ärztliche Psychoanalyse und Psychotherapie.* Publication terminated in 1941 with Vol. XXVI.

Imago. Zeitschrift für Anwendung der Psychoanalyse auf die Natur- und Geisteswissenschaften. Vienna. (Founded in 1912 and also published under the direction of Freud.) Publication terminated in 1941 with Vol. XXVI. Volumes XXIV-XXVI were published in cooperation with the *Internationale Zeitschrift;* this journal was continued in the American *Imago*, edited by Hans Sachs (Vol. I, 1939).

There is also the oldest publication of the Freudian school, *Jahrbuch für Psychoanalyse*, founded by Freud in 1909 in Vienna. This was published annually, and six volumes appeared (1909-1914); the first five under the title: *Jahrbuch für psychoanalytische und psychopathologische Forschungen* (1909-1913).

The many magazines appearing at present include, in America:

Psychoanalytic Review (founded in 1913).
Psychoanalytic Quarterly (founded in 1932). This magazine is more progressive in tendency.

In England:

International Journal of Psycho-analysis, Ed. E. Jones.
The British Journal of Medical Psychology. (Though not explicitly

psychoanalytical, this magazine includes a great number of articles by members of the psychoanalytical school.)

In France:

Revue française de Psychanalyse. (Presses Universitaires de France.) *Psyché* (*Revue internationale des Sciences de l'Homme et de Psychanalyse*), Paris. Published under the direction of Mme. Maryse Choisy.

In Germany:

Zeitschrift für Psychoanalyse (edited by C. Müller-Braunschweig).

At the moment psychoanalysis is most active in the United States of America. A great many European psychoanalysts are in fact at present working in English-speaking countries. A selection of the most important articles that appear in magazines written in English is made yearly in:

The Yearbook of Psychoanalysis, which has been appearing since 1945 under the direction of SANDOR LORAND (New York, International Universities Press). Vol. VII was published in 1952.

The Psychoanalytic Reader (An Anthology of Essential Papers With Critical Introductions), under the direction of ROBERT FLIESS, proposes to publish regularly in English the more important psychoanalytical articles not previously translated into English and appearing in books not easily obtained. The first volume has already appeared. It contained articles dating from the beginning of the psychoanalytical movement, besides more recent ones. (New York, International Universities Press, 1948.) The second volume is in preparation (1953).

The reader will also find a good selection of recent articles on psychoanalysis (both theoretical and practical) in the symposium edited by LORAND, S., *Psychoanalysis Today* (New York, International Universities Press, 2nd edition, 1944).

An important specialized field of psychoanalysis is that of *Child Analysis*, with which Freud's daughter, Anna Freud, has been specially concerned. See: FREUD, ANNA, *The Psychoanalytical Treatment of Children* (London, 1946). *The Psychoanalytic Study of the Child.* An annual publication edited by Anna Freud, E. Glover, etc. The first volume appeared in 1945 and the sixth in 1952. It contains articles both theoretical and clinical. (New York, International Universities Press.)

FREUD, ANNA, *Psychoanalysis for Teachers and Parents* (first published under the title, Introduction to Psychoanalysis for Teachers. London, Allen & Unwin, 1931).

KLEIN, MELANIE, *The Psychoanalysis of Children* (London, Hogarth Press, 1932).

Interesting, too, in this connection, is the movement known as *pedagogic psychoanalysis,* in which the Swiss pastor, Oskar Pfister, is active. See, amongst others, PFISTER, O., *Die Psychoanalyse im Dienste der Erziehung* (Leipzig, Klinkhardt, 3rd edition 1929). Earlier editions of this book appeared under the title *Was Bietet die Psychoanalyse dem Erzieher* (1917). The same author has applied psychoanalysis to problems of spiritual direction. See, amongst others:

PFISTER, O., *Analytische Seelsorge. Einführung in der practische Psychoanalyse fur Pfarrer und Laien* (Göttingen, Vandenhoeck und Ruprecht, 1927).

In this field should be mentioned the magazine:

Zeitschrift für Psychoanalytische Pädagogik, Vienna (founded in 1926).

In the same connection it might be interesting to consult books on the psychoanalysis of the family, and especially:

FLUEGEL, J. C., *The Psychoanalytic Study of the Family* (London, Hogarth Press, 1948).

There is an account of *female psychology,* according to psychoanalytical ideas, in:

DEUTSCH, HELENE, *The Psychology of Women: A Psycho-analytical Interpretation.* I. Girlhood. II. Motherhood. (London, Research Books, 1946.)

On problems of delinquency:

FRIEDLANDER, KATE, *The Psychoanalytic Approach to Juvenile Delinquency* (New York, International Universities Press).

For the psychoanalytical interpretation of certain traits of character, consult, amongst others:

FREUD, S., *Charakter und Analerotik. Gesammelte Werke,* VII.

ABRAHAM, KARL, *Psychoanalytische Studien zur Charakterbildung* (Internationale Psychoanalytische Bibliothek, No. 16, 1925).

REICH, WILHELM, *Character Analysis* (New York, Orgone Institute, 1949³). Only Parts *one* and *two* of this book are important.

For psychoanalysis applied to organic complaints—psychosomatics—consult especially:

ALEXANDER, F. and FRENCH, T. M., Eds., *Studies in Psychosomatic Medicine: An Approach to the Cause and Treatment of Vegetative Disturbances* (New York, The Ronald Press, 1948). This work contains a series of medical articles by a large number of specialists on the psychic factors that enter into several categories of organic complaints.

A general introduction to psychosomatics will be found in another book by:

ALEXANDER, F., *Psychosomatic Medicine: Its Principles and Applications* (New York, 1949).

For the connection between experiment and certain psychoanalytical ideas and theories the best account will be found in:

SEARS, R. R., *Survey of Objective Studies of Psychoanalytic Concepts* (Social Science Research Council, Bulletin 51, New York, 1943).

(*c*) HANDBOOKS AND CRITICAL STUDIES

Many readers may prefer not to get lost in the enormous mass of psychoanalytical literature, and use instead a handbook or critical study on the subject. Amongst critical studies we specially recommend:

DALBIEZ, R., *La Méthode psychanalytique et la doctrine freudienne* (2 vols.): I. Exposé; II. Discussion. (Paris, Desclée de Brouwer et Co., 1936.) This is one of the best critical studies of psychoanalysis that has appeared, both from the scientific and the philosophical point of view. Its systematization of Freudian teaching is possibly somewhat overrationalized.

Highly interesting, too, is:

HORNEY, KAREN, *New Ways in Psychoanalysis* (London: Kegan Paul, French, Trubner & Co., Ltd., 1939; New York, Norton, 1939). This is a typical example of the progressive movement in psychoanalysis, emphasizing cultural and social rather than purely instinctive and genetic factors.

As regards textbooks, we suggest:

FENICHEL, O., *The Psychoanalytic Theory of Neurosis* (London, Kegan Paul; New York, Norton, 1945).

Good introductory textbooks are:

ALEXANDER, F., *Fundamentals of Psychoanalysis* (New York, Norton, 1948).
GLOVER, E., *Psychoanalysis* (London, Staples Press, 1949).

A work of great interest for the ego-psychology in psychoanalysis is:

FREUD, ANNA, *The Ego and the Mechanisms of Defence* (London, Hogarth Press, 1937).

The following book gives a good idea of the mental processes of which psychoanalysis generally makes use:

SYMONDS, P., *Dynamic Psychology* (New York, Appleton-Century, 1949).

On the Unconscious in general and the multiple significations of this notion, see:

MILLER, J. G., *Unconsciousness* (London, Chapman & Hall, 1942).

11. Adler's Individual Psychology

Of Adler's own works, should be read:

ALDER, A., *Über den nervösen Charakter* (1912). (München, Bergmann, 1928⁴.)

The best systematic account of individual psychology will be found in:

WEXBERG, E., *Individualpsychologie. Eine systematische Darstellung.* (Leipzig, S. Hirzel, 1928¹; 1931².) In translation: *Individual Psychology.*

See also:

ADLER, A., *Praxis und Theorie der Individualpsychologie. Vorträge zur Einführung in die Psychotherapie für Ärzte, Psychologen und Lehrer.* (München, Bergmann, 1927³.) In translation: *The*

Practice and Theory of Individual Psychology (New York, Harcourt, Brace, 1924).

ADLER, A. and FURTMÜLLER, C., *Heilen und Bilden. Grundlagen der Erziehungskunst für Ärzte und Pädagogen. Zweite Auflage redigiert von Dr. Erwin Wexberg.* (München, Bergmann, 1922.)

ADLER, A., *Menschenkenntnis* (Leipzig, S. Hirzel, 1926²).

A good account of Adlerian psychology was published by:

DREIKURS, R., *Fundamentals of Adlerian Psychology* (New York, Greenberg, 1950).

In 1914 there was founded an *Internationale Zeitschrift für Individualpsychologie. Arbeiten aus dem Gebiete der Psychotherapie, Psychologie und Pädagogik.* (The first volume appeared under the title *Zeitschrift für Individualpsychologie.*) This was suspended from 1916 to 1923. The third volume contains, amongst other things, special numbers on social psychology, the psychology of women and "*Schulkinderpsychologie.*" This journal is published now again (Vol. XX in 1951).

In English there was published, from 1935 to 1937: *International Journal of Individual Psychology* (Vols. I–III). At the moment there is *The Individual Psychology Bulletin.*

A complete bibliography of books and articles on Individual Psychology published in English appeared in the Alfred Adler Memorial Issue of *The Individual Psychology Bulletin*, 1947, VI.

III. Jung's Analytical Psychology

Jung's extensive work, though confused, is important. A good introduction is:

JACOBI, J., *Die Psychologie von C. G. Jung. Eine Einführung in das Gesamtwerk* (Zürich, Rascher, 1940 [2nd ed., rev., 1945]).

The English reader can study Jung in translation in:

JUNG, C. G., *Psychology of the Unconscious*, trs. B. M. Hinkle (London, Kegan Paul, 1921; 2nd. ed.: New York, Dodd, Mead, 1927).

—— *Psychological Types, or The Psychology of Individuation*, trs. H. G. Baynes (London, Kegan Paul, 1923).

—— *Modern Man in Search of a Soul*, trs. C. F. Baynes (London, Kegan Paul, 1933).

—— *Psychological Factors Determining Human Behavior.* Lectures at the Harvard Tercentenary Conference, 1936. (Cambridge, Harvard University Press, 1936.)

—— *Psychology and Religion.* The Terry Lectures. (New Haven, Yale University Press, 1938.)

—— *The Integration of the Personality*, trs. S. M. Dell (New York, Farrar & Rinehart, 1939).

iv. Psychotherapy, Clinical and Pathological Psychology[1]

To the books on depth-psychology already mentioned we must add a few works of more general interest in the field of clinical psychology. First, a few sketches of current tendencies in this field: "Current Trends in Clinical Psychology" (by several authors), published in the *Annals of the New York Academy of Sciences*, 1948, XLIX, pp. 867–928.

SNYDER, W. W., "The Present Status of Psychotherapeutic Counseling," *Psychological Bulletin*, 1947, XLIV, pp. 297–386.

For a general history of psychotherapy, see ZILBOORG, G. and HENRY, G. W., *A History of Medical Psychology* (New York, Norton, 1941). This book begins with the ancient Greeks and is excellent as a history of ideas about neurosis.

In the domain of psychopathology, remember that there is always a great deal to be gained from that great psychologist Pierre Janet. Several works of Janet have been translated into English.

Amongst more recent books by French writers, it is advisable to read:

HESNARD, A., *L'univers morbide de la faute* (Paris, Presses Universitaires, 1949). Also, *La Vie et la mort des instincts chez l'homme* (La culture moderne). (Paris, Stock.)

BARUK, H., *Psychiatrie. Morale expérimentale, individuelle et sociale. Haines et reactions de culpabilité* (Paris, Presses Universitaires, 1945). Baruk's big work, *Psychiatrie médicale, physiologique et expérimentale* (Paris, Masson, 1938) is more technical, but important.

DELAY, J., *Les déréglements de l'humeur* (Paris, Presses Universitaires, 1946). *Les dissolutions de la mémoire* (*Ibid.*, 1942).

BOUTONIER, JULIETTE, *L'Angoisse* (Paris, Presses Universitaires, 1945).

[1] This does not include the field of psychiatry proper.

ALLENDY, R., *Le problème de la destinée. Étude sur la fatalité intérieure.* (Paris, Gallimard, 1927.) *L'amour.* (Paris, Denoël, 1942.)

Sane and useful ideas for the treatment of many ordinary cases will be found in:

STOCKER, A., *Le traitement moral des nerveux* (Paris, Beauchesne, 1948).

From amongst the many works by Swiss authors we single out:

MAEDER, A., *Die Richtung im Seelenleben* (Zürich, Rascher, 1928). *Selbsterhaltung und Selbstheilung (Ibid., 1949).* More directly practical in nature is: *Wege zur seelischen Heilung. Kurze Psychotherapie aus der Praxis eines Nervenarztes. (Ibid., 1945.)*

REY, A., *Études des insuffisances psychologiques (enfants et adolescents)* I. *Méthodes et problèmes.* II. *Le diagnostique psychologique.* (Neuchâtel et Paris, Delachaux et Niestlé, 1947.)

ODIER, C., *L'Angoisse et la pensée magique* (Neuchâtel, Delachaux et Niestlé, 1948). As the sub-title of this interesting book indicates, the author gives a psychogenetic analysis of phobias and the neurosis of abandon. He emphasizes a point to which we too have drawn attention in the present work, namely, the connection between misery and the feeling of insecurity.

In the field of psychotherapy by suggestion there is:

BAUDOUIN, C., *Suggestion et auto-suggestion* (Neuchâtel et Paris, Delachaux et Niestlé, 1938[5]).

A German book of general interest, by a well-known follower of Adler, is:

ALLERS, RUDOLF, *Heilerziehung bei Abwegigheit des Charakters. Einführung, Grundlagen, Probleme und Methoden.* (Köhn, Verlagsanstalt Benziger, s.d.)

Still important is:

JASPERS, K., *Allgemeine Psychopathologie* (Berlin und Heidelberg, Springer, 5th edition 1948 [no change from the 4th edition of 1942]).

The importance of this book lies in its connection with the phenomenological orientation of psychopathology and the use of the comprehensive method (*Verstehende Methode*).

American literature has been particularly fruitful in publications on clinical psychology. From the many important works we pick out:

CAMERON, N., *The Psychology of Behaviour Disorders: A Biosocial Interpretation* (Boston, Houghton Mifflin, 1947). This book emphasizes the social aspect of personality and its deviations. From the same author: *Behaviour Pathology.*

WHITE, R. W., *The Abnormal Personality* (New York, The Ronald Press, 1948).

MASLOW, A. H. and MITTELMANN, B., *Principles of Abnormal Psychology* (New York, Harper, 1941).

MOORE, T. V. (O.S.B.), *The Nature and Treatment of Mental Disorders* (New York, Grune and Stratton, 1943). *Personal Mental Hygiene* (*Ibid.*, 1944).

PENNINGTON, L. A. and BERG, I. A., Eds., *An Introduction to Clinical Psychology* (New York, The Ronald Press, 1948).

A wide variety of recent articles on psychopathology will be found in:

TOMKINS, S. S., Ed., *Contemporary Psychopathology* (Cambridge, Harvard University Press, 1943). This book contains 45 articles, discussing experimental psychopathology, psychosomatic medicine, child psychiatry, etc.

On client-centred therapy:

ROGERS, C. R., *Counseling and Psychotherapy* (Boston, Houghton Mifflin, 1942); and *Client-centered Therapy* (*Ibidem*, 1951).

SNYDER, W. U., *Casebook of Non-directive Counseling* (*Ibid.*, 1947).

ALLEN, F. H., *Psychotherapy with Children* (New York, Norton, 1942).

AXLINE, V. M., *Play Therapy: The Inner Dynamics of Childhood* (Boston, Houghton Mifflin, 1947).

CURRAN, CHARLES A., *Counseling in Catholic Life and Education* (New York, Macmillan, 1952).

On group therapy:

KLAPMAN, J. W., *Group Psychotherapy: Theory and Practice* (London, W. Heinemann [Medical Books], 1946).

SLAVSON, S. R., *An Introduction to Group Therapy* (New York, Commonwealth Fund, 1943).

An up-to-date account of hypnosis will be found in:

ESTABROOKS, G. H., *Hypnotism* (New York, Dutton, 1943).

And for hypnotherapy, see:

BRENMAN, MARGARET and GILL, M. M., *Hypnotherapy* (New York, Josiah Macy, Jr., Found., 1944, II, No. 3). (See also on this subject the work of Maslow and Mittelmann cited above.)

v. Sexuality

Oswald Schwarz, former *Privat-dozent* in Vienna, has done most to bring out the connections between pathological sexuality and man's total personality:

SCHWARZ, O., *Sexualpathologie. Wesen und Formen der abnormen Geschlechtlichkeit.* (Wien, Verlag für Medizin, Weidman and Co., 1935.)

BOSS, M., *Sinn und Gehalt der sexuellen Perversionen* (Bern, H. Huber, 1947).

For normal sexuality see:

SCHWARZ, O., *The Psychology of Sex* (Harmondsworth-Middlesex, Penguin Books, 1949).

We specially recommend also:

ALLERS, R., *Psychologie des Geschlechtslebens*, in the 3rd volume of *Handbuch der vergleichenden Psychologie*, edited by Gustav Kafka. (München, Verlag von Ernst Reinhardt, 1922, pp. 331–506.)

Also well-known is:

HESNARD, A., *Traité de sexologie normale et pathologique* (Paris, Payot, 1933). This book gives an account of sexology from the pathological and biological point of view (with facts of animal and vegetable sexuality).

Finally we remind readers of the well-known works by Krafft-Ebing, Magnus Hirschfeld and Wilhelm Stekel.

The work of Havelock Ellis is already dated in several respects, and the method by which the facts were obtained is open to question.

Personality

Our aim here is to give a list of recent works that can help towards a deeper psychological study of human nature. We shall mention the most important American works, which have brought to light a great number of ascertained facts about the psychological, socio-cultural and biological study of personality. The theoretical outlook, however, is rather insufficient.

Previously, the study of personality was chiefly guided by typological methods which aimed at classifications according to structure; today the interest lies rather in the *development* of the individual personality and the various factors which influence it. Research is made into the factors of the individual's life-history—the social, cultural and biological factors which govern the growth of the personality and which account for the particularities in the concrete dynamic structure of any given individual. Recent American writing on personality usually follows this line.

We shall then mention some French and German works whose interest tends to be more philosophical but which are nevertheless indispensable for a deeper and more accurate conception of human psychology.

An excellent general account of the fundamentals of the whole study of personality will be found in:

ALLPORT, G. W., *Personality: A Psychological Interpretation* (New York, H. Holt & Co., 1937). The author has been in close touch with European trends in psychology. In this book he presents his well-known theories of the traits of personality and the functional autonomy of "motives." The latter theory, though in our opinion pushed too far, is of first-rate importance.

An excellent account of the dynamic, cognitive and social factors which affect human behaviour will be found in:

KRECH, D. and CRUTCHFIELD, R., *Theory and Problems of Social Psychology* (New York, McGraw-Hill, 1948).

MURRAY, H. A., *Explorations in Personality: A Clinical and Experimental Study of Fifty Men of College Age* (New York, O.U.P., 1938). This book contains the results of an inquiry into personality conducted for three years on fifty young men with the help of a great variety of psychological techniques. In tendency it is psychoanalytical in the wider sense of the word. Part of the book is devoted to theory and this is excellent.

An excellent synthesis which has been compiled on the study of personality from the experimental point of view is:

MURPHY, G., *Personality: A Biosocial Approach to Origins and Structure* (New York, Harper, 1947). This is an enormous book of over a thousand pages, and it assumes a profound knowledge of the general and experimental psychology of behaviour.

We also recommend:

DOLLARD, J. and MILLER, N. E., *Personality and Psychotherapy: An Analysis in Terms of Learning, Thinking, and Culture* (New York, McGraw-Hill, 1950).

The social, cultural and biological determinants of personality are well brought out in:

KLUCKHOHN, C. and MURRAY, H. A., Eds., *Personality in Nature, Society and Culture* (New York, Knopf, 1948). This book contains two introductory chapters by the editors themselves on the idea and development of the personality. The rest of the book is made up of an interesting series of essays by forty specialists in widely different spheres, which have previously been published in magazines but are not easily obtainable.

The following book contains the richest supply of *clinical and experimental* facts on all aspects of the normal and pathological personality:

HUNT, J. MCV., Ed., *Personality and the Behavior Disorders*, 2 vols. (New York, The Ronald Press, 1944). This important book has forty contributors and full bibliographies.

The statistical and factor-analytical approach is best represented by:

CATTELL, R. B., *Description and Measurement of Personality* (New York, World Book Co., 1946).

EYSENCK, H. J., *Dimensions of Personality* (London, Kegan Paul, Trench, Trubner & Co., 1947).

A final line of development of the utmost importance as regards both theory and experimental research is that deriving from Kurt Lewin (professor first in Berlin, then in the U.S.A.). A synthetic study of the main ideas and the results of the work of this school will be found in:

LEWIN, K., *A Dynamic Theory of Personality: Selected Papers*. (New York and London, McGraw-Hill, 1935.)

Finally, a work uniting the traditional spiritual ideas about human dynamic life with clinical and psychiatric data is that of the well-known American doctor and psychiatrist, and Benedictine monk:

MOORE, T. V., *The Driving Forces of Human Nature and Their Adjustment*. An introduction to the psychology and psychopathology of emotional behaviour and volitional control. (New York, Grune & Stratton, 1948.) This book is worth close study.

Recent French and German writing has thrown light on the problem of personality from quite a different angle from that adopted by American psychology. For this reason the works already mentioned remain insufficient, especially from the theoretical point of view. It is essential, to arrive at a deeper understanding of human personality, to study some of the following works.

There is in the first place the phenomenological point of view and the ideas resulting from it. The human person has been studied as "situated in" and "open to" the "world"; hence the increased attention to man's relationships with his fellow-men.

The most important ideas are those of Martin Heidegger and Max Scheler. Heidegger's work is difficult and is best approached through the excellent study by:

DE WAELHENS, A., *La Philosophie de Martin Heidegger* (Louvain, Éditions de l'Institut supérieur de Philosophie, 1942[1], 1948[2]).

SCHELER, M., *Wesen und Formen der Sympathie—Phänomenologie und Theorie der Sympathiegefühle* (1912). (Frankfurt-Main, G. Schulte-Bulmke, 1948[5].) The three main parts discuss "*Das Mitgefühl*," "*Liebe und Hass*," "*Vom fremden Ich*."

Read also this author's small book: *Die Stellung des Menschen im Kosmos* (1927). (München, Nymphenburger Verlagshandlung, 1947; new edition published by Marie Scheler.)

Following the same line of thought is:

BINSWANGER, L., *Grundformen und Erkenntnis Menschlichen Daseins* (Zürich, Max Niehaus, 1942). This book treats particularly of the different forms of "*Miteinandersein*" and "*Zu-sich-selbst-sein*" and also the problem of "*Liebe und Sorge*."

BUBER, M., *I and Thou*.

An important work, based on a more positive attitude in its facts and theories and having much in common with psychoanalytical thought (though it goes beyond it), is:

DE GREEFF, E., *Les Instincts de défense et de sympathie* (Paris, Presses Universitaires, 1947).

The psychological current deriving from Wilhelm Dilthey, which studies man by the so-called "comprehensive" method (*verstehende Psychologie*) is well represented by:

SPRANGER, E., *Lebensformen. Geisteswissenschaftliche Psychologie und Ethik der Persönlichkeit.* (Halle [Saale], Max Niemeyer Verlag, 1930[7].)

More philosophical, though also stemming from the "*verstehende Psychologie*" is the second volume of Karl Jaspers's *Philosophy*, entitled:

JASPERS, K., *Existenzerhellung* (Berlin, J. Springer, 1932). He discusses: "*Ich selbst in Kommunikation und Geschichtlichkeit*"; "*Selbstsein als Freiheit*"; "*Existenz als Unbedingtheit in Situation, Bewusstsein und Handlung*"; "*Existenz in Subjektivität und Objektivität.*"

For characterology, see the basic work of German characterology:

KLAGES, L., *Die Grundlagen der Charakterkunde* (Zürich, Hirzel Verlag, 1948[9]). The first edition appeared in 1910 under the title: *Prinzipien der Charakterologie.* The first edition under the new title appeared in 1926.

ROBACK, A. A., *The Psychology of Character* (London, Kegan Paul, 1927 [2nd edition, 1928]).

For the constitutional and typological study of personality, see especially the works of E. Kretschmer and more recently of Sheldon:

KRETSCHMER, E., *Körperbau und Charakter* (Berlin, Springer, 1921, 1941).

SHELDON, W. H. and STEVENS, S. S., *The Varieties of Temperament* (New York, Harper, 1942).

Also important are:

ALLERS, R., *Das Werden der sittlichen Person. Wesen und Erziehung des Charakters* (1929). (Freiburg im Bresgau, Herder & Co., 1935[4].) In translation: *The Psychology of Character*, trs. E. B. Strauss (Sheed and Ward, 1931).

GUARDINI, R., *Welt und Person* (Würzburg, Werkbund Verlag, 1940).

BRUNNER, A., *La personne incarnée. Étude sur la phénoménologie et la philosophie existentialiste* (Paris, Beauchesne, 1947).

In the field of general psychology there is an impressive idea of human personality in its productions and achievements in the work of Pradines, especially the second part, on *human genius*:

PRADINES, M., *Traité de psychologie générale*. 3 vols. (Paris, Presses Universitaires, 1943–6.)

NAME INDEX

SUBJECT INDEX

Needs, Fundamental (*Cont.*)
  –at psycho-social level, 218–
    219
  –at spiritual level, 226–229
  influence of individual and
    cultural evolution, 228
  two forms of this need, 221–
    226
Need for Self-Assertion
  –and critical spirit, 274
  –and cultural environment, 167–
    168
  –and human dynamic structure,
    209–210
  –and motivation of conduct, 130
  Adlerian system, 259–275
Negation, cf. *Judgment*
Neurosis
  Adlerian conception, 270–274
  Horney's conception, 84
  pre-Freudian conception, 4
  Freudian conception, 13–14
    cf. also *Libido, Oedipus com-
      plex, Repression, Sexuality,
      Unconscious*
  influence of sexual conflicts, 14
  influence of cultural factors, 84–
    85
  intentional character of symp-
    toms, 82–83
  –experimental, 109
  meaning of symptoms (Breuer),
    60
    (Freud), 14, 28
  –obsessional, cf. *Religion, Ther-
    apy*
Non-Directive Therapy, cf. *Therapy, non-directive*
Normal
  Freudian conception of, 169–170
  –and abnormal: psychopathologi-
    cal conception, 162
  difference, 115
  explanation of normal by ab-
    normal, 67–68
  identity of powers and mechan-
    isms, 27–28
  interference in processes of
    normal and abnormal devel-
    opment, 201–204

Obsession
  with evil and guilt, 100
    cf. also *Frustration, Neurosis,
      Religion*
Organism
  equilibrium of–and need, 210–
    217
Others
  –as limit of the ego, 223–226
  openness to–220–221, 223
    cf. *Self-giving*

Pansexualism
  criticism, 70–71
  Freud's protest, 69
Pathological
  emphasis on–169–170
  point of view to study of person-
    ality, 163–170
Personality
  (a) *Conception* of
    Adlerian conception, 262
    complementary nature of tra-
      ditional and Freudian con-
      ceptions, 140
    duality of scientist's concep-
      tion, 116–117
    Freudian conception, 41–60,
      69–71
      cf. also *Ego, Super-ego*
    importance of sexuality, 112
    importance for therapy, 112,
      113
    influence of clinical psychol-
      ogy, 251
    influence of depth-psychology
      on the ordinary concep-
      tion of personality, 115–
      116
    irrational aspect of the, 122–
      123
    need for synthesis of tradi-
      tional and psychoanalyti-
      cal conceptions, 253–254
    need for adequate conception
      of personality as a whole,
      112
    partial nature of psychoana-
      lytical conception, 253–
      254